Stolen Art

VICTOR PERRY

gefen גפן
publishing house בית הוצאה לאור
JERUSALEM ♦ NEW YORK

Typesetting: Marzel A.S. – Jerusalem
Cover Design: Studio Paz, Jerusalem

1 3 5 7 9 8 6 4 2

Gefen Publishing House
POB 36004, Jerusalem 91360, Israel
972-2-538-0247 • isragefe@netvision.net.il

Gefen Books
12 New Street Hewlett, NY 11557, USA
516-295-2805 • gefenbooks@compuserve.com

www.israelbooks.com

Printed in Israel

Send for our free catalogue

ISBN: 965-229-187-0

Library of Congress Cataloging-in-Publication Data

Perry, Victor, 1923-1992
Stolen Art

1. Slomovich, Erich – Art Collections. 2. Art – Collectors and Collecting – Yugoslavia – Biography. 3. Art – Collectors and Collecting – France – Biography. 4. Art Thefts – Yugoslavia – History – 20th Century. 5. World War, 1939-1945 – Art and the War. 6. Holocaust, Jewish (1939-1945) – Reparations. 7. Restitution and Indemnification Claims (1933-....) – Yugoslavia. 8. Restitution and Indemnification Claims (1933-....) – France. 9. Art – Private Collections – Belgrade – Serbia. 10. Narodni Muzej – Beograd. I. Title.

N5280.Y82 S586 1999 • 709'.2 – dc21 • [B] 99-047218 CIP

CONTENTS

FOREWARD

The issue of stolen art and other items which have now become subject to restitution lawsuits are elements that confirm some of the unique aspects of the Holocaust. For, in addition to the murder of six million Jews, Nazi Germany and its allies confiscated hundreds of thousands of art objects — paintings, sculptures, jewels, unique printed materials and other items. That such objects were looted was nothing new. However, the Holocaust, as Zygmunt Baumann has noted, was a modern event. This looting took place in a time when there were land deeds on properties, provenances on art objects, contracts, bills of lading and insurance policies. In short, there was a big paper trail, even though the victims had become ashes.

Victor Perry's journalistic account deals with the story of the collection of Erich Chlomovitch. Perry, who unfortunately did not live to complete his own account, nevertheless pursued this strange story of confiscated art like a detective. The story is interesting and adds to our knowledge of the monstrous pilfering that went on, especially against Jewish property.

Should a casual reader think that looting was something only the Nazis were involved in, that is not the case. Jews and looting go very well together. The Arch of Titus in Rome, built in 81AD, depicts in a bas-relief the loot from the Second Jewish Temple in Jerusalem being carried to Rome. Those items disappeared.

More recently, every war has seen looting. In the Napoleonic period, many art works were brought to Paris, then returned in 1815 after the French defeat. Napoleon had plans for making Paris the greatest center of art. He looted some of the most famous works of art from all over Europe. According to G rardand Isabey it was only the Republic of France, "thanks to her power and the superiority of her artists and educational system", where these works of art could be properly and definitely protected. The French certainly realized the legal aspect of their activity. Therefore, even simple pillaging often assumed the appearances of legality by including legal title to looted works as compensation in peace treaties.

International treaties, developed since the mid-19th century, have tried to protect art from being a hostage of war and being used as reparations. While intentions may be uplifting, the results have been unclear, as art works are still being held hostage by governments and art museums.

However, the issue of looted art has been in the news during since 1997. The most forceful case involved the alleged ownership of two paintings by Austrian painter Egon Schiele that were in a Museum of Modern Art (MOMA) exhibition in New York. This placed Ronald Lauder, President of the MOMA and also chairman of the World Jewish Restitution Organization (WJRO) Committee on Art restitution in a difficult situation. These paintings have been claimed by the Bondi family, who had left the works on loan when they fled from Vienna to London in 1937. An initial report indicated that 16,000 such paintings were in France alone.

During the period of Nazi Germany's domination of Europe, there were several levels of looting and destruction. The heaviest destruction was in the Soviet Union. Less destruction of buildings and art works occurred in the west because of the short duration of the war against France.

During the occupation of France, the German government established the ERR *Einsatstab Reichleiter Rosenberg,* under Alfred Rosenberg. In 1940, a secret document known as the Kummel Report, written by Otto Kummel, director of Reich's Museums, outlines works for looting. There were three categories: (a) works of special historical significance; (b) works of lesser importance; (c) works of local interest.

Kummel's directive sought to ascertain which works had once been in German ownership, and were hence *Aryan,* to be returned to Germany. Kummel tried to establish provenance of art back to the Napoleonic period. The report even requested return of items from the Metropolitan Museum of Art in New York and the Hermitage in Leningrad, now St. Petersburg.

An interesting "logic" of seizure of collections was developed by the Germans. First, art belonging to Jewish collections could be seized and looted. Thus, Vermeer's, *The Astronomer,* probably the most famous individual piece of looted art, moved from the Rothschild collection to Hitler's personal inventory.

However, because of ideological guidelines linked to Nazi attitudes toward "degenerate art," such items, usually abstract or expressionist items, could not go into German collections. Nevertheless, such items were seized, then sold abroad, usually via dealers in Switzerland, often winding up in private collections. Bogus galleries were sometimes set up in Switzerland to fence paintings. After the war, Switzerland made reacquisition difficult as it had a five year statute of limitations, beginning when the painting or art work was acquired.

After taking what was believed to lootable, meaning Jewish owned art, the Nazis attempted to and succeeded in purchasing large collections for themselves as individuals. Hitler, Goebbels and Goering were some of the strongest buyers. Collections were often purchased at undervalued prices. This led the allies to declare that all sales of art in the Reich after 1933 were "null and void."

On the Soviet side, where there was massive carnage to both people and civilization, Nikolai Shvernik was appointed in 1942 head of Extraordinary State Commission to investigate Nazi crimes on Soviet territory. In Spring, 1943, Professor Bogdanov and Igor Grabar from Moscow wrote a memo suggesting Soviets should receive artworks as compensation for damage done to Soviet collections. There was a great difficulty in figuring out financial equivalents for value of lost work because of advent of Communism and unfamiliarity of Soviets with western art markets and prices. Part of the emerging plan envisioned creating a supermuseum in Moscow of art that would be taken from the west.

Soviet trophy brigades were formed in early 1945 under the auspices of the Special Committee on Germany. All decisions about the removal of art from Germany were done personally by Stalin. As the Soviets captured Berlin, many artifacts fell into their hands from the salt mines at Grasleben, near Helmstadt (on future border of Soviet and British zones of occupation), the Schonebeck salt mines near Magdeburg, the treasures of Dresden were discovered in mine in Gross Cotta, near Pirna and were shipped to Moscow, while there was significant pillaging from art stored in Berlin's Zoo Flakturm and the Friedrichshain Tower.

The loot received by the Pushkin Fine Arts Museum in Moscow, which became a repository for Soviet trophy squads, was significant. In 1945 the

Pushkin received fifty-two crates containing coins and medals, arms, paintings and furniture. This included the personal collection of Otto Krebs, a German industrialist. Among the items were two Manets, ten Renoirs, four by Van Gogh, four Gauguins, five Cezannes, and other works by Signac, Matisse, Picasso. Many were sent to the Hermitage in Leningrad and were exhibited only in February,1995-96 (a 63 paintings exhibition) as "Hidden Treasures."

During 1955 and 1956, State Committee on Culture decided to return damaged art works to Germany, and objects from public institutions to the GDR. However, items from private collections were not included. By January 1959, 1.6 million objects were returned. But from 1964 until the present, the issues surrounding the trophy art were never talked about — top secrecy imposed by a declining Soviet regime. Some lists of objects were revealed, and a few concessions were made to private collectors, such as one Degas painting returned to Walter and Dieder Scharf, grandson of German collector Otto Gerstenberg.

Americans were also looters, and the trophies are still being sold, now via the world wide web on sites like EBAY. Individuals GIs often used the mails to get looted works back to USA. The smallest items were Nazi flags and papers, or an occasional nondescript painting on the wall of a house. The most famous case, however, involved Joe Meador, an American officer who stole the Quedlinburg treasures. These were found in 1990 in Whitewright, Texas and Germans paid $3 million ransom to get them back.

Perry's manuscript documents the search for art and its owners through another geographic area of the world, Yugoslavia. To whom did this collection belong? Erich Chlomovitch the heirs of Ambroise Vollard, or the Yugoslav government? The story is complex. It is about more than art, as it also involves the destruction of the Jews of Bacina, including the Slomovic family. And the answers to this mystery case, suggest the absence of both justice and equity that often accompanies long judicial processes.

Prof. Stephen C. Feinstein
Center for Holocaust and Genocide Studies
University of Minnesota, Minneapolis

PART 1

ERICH

Chapter I

40 YEARS IN A BANK VAULT

IMPRESSIONIST SALES FEATURE MYSTERY COLLECTION

Four columns in the March 1, 1981, issue of the Paris *Herald Tribune* announced the auction of an art treasure which has lain unclaimed for forty years in the vaults of the Société Général Bank in France.

Who owned the collection?

How was it acquired?

The catalog for the auction raises more questions than it answers. The sale is scheduled to take place at the Espace Drûout, Paris, on March 19 and 20. The catalog lists 190 items. Its title:

> "Collection Erich Chlomovitch. Provenance Ambroise Vollard."
> *(Collection of Erich Chlomovitch, origin Ambroise Vollard.)*

The collection is amazing. Marvelous. Valuable works by Cézanne, Matisse, and Dérain. Rare art albums and manuscripts, many of them autographed. There are numerous autographed engravings by the world's leading Impressionist and Post-Impressionist painters. Included is a real treasure trove of some two hundred photographs from the Parisian art world of the late 1930s. In the pictures, among the faces of famous artists such as Chagall, Maillol, Matisse, Bonnard, and Léger, an unfamiliar face appears. It is the face of Erich Chlomovitch, owner of this collection.

Who is he?

Erich Chlomovitch
(Photo taken in Paris in late 30's)

A young man, dressed immaculately in a dark suit and polka dot tie. He exudes the serious but self-conscious air of a man in the presence of his betters. His face is handsome and is framed by a shock of thick black hair combed back and unparted. His mouth is half hidden by a close-cropped but generous mustache, an effect that adds maturity to an otherwise youthful face.

I, myself, am a journalist. Many years in the field have left me with a somewhat jaded perspective, and as I look at these pictures, I think: This man certainly knew how to promote himself. He must have deliberately made sure that a photographer was present whenever he visited his artist friends.

The catalog describes him as a young, enigmatic Yugoslav of Jewish origin. An adventurer... personable... unassuming... a lover of paintings... possessing a rare flair and fine taste in art. At the same time, the reputable director of a Yugoslav museum is quoted as saying that Chlomovitch was "intelligent, but without any outstanding qualities."

The editors of the catalog believe that the major part of the collection originated with the collection of Ambroise Vollard, one of the leading art merchants and art publishers of this century.

The art works to be auctioned off in 1981 are part of a larger collection, one that has lain unclaimed in a Paris bank safe since the beginning of World War II.

Among the items found in the bank safe were thirteen rare art albums published by Vollard, many of them autographed by him, with paternalistic remarks addressed to Erich Chlomovitch. The collection included fifty-two sketches, some of which were autographed. Others bore handwritten dedications to Chlomovitch. There are gouaches and aquarelles by Cocteau, Jean Forain, Fernand Léger, Pablo Picasso, Odilon Redon, Pierre Auguste Renoir, George Rouault, Maurice Utrillo, and the renowned architect Le Corbusier.

One of the sketches is a portrait of a faun, done in China ink and colored crayon by Jean Cocteau. It reads: "Souvenir of a cruel world to Erich Chlomovitch, his friend Jean Cocteau, September, 1939."

No less than 106 original engravings, some of them in color, are included: Pierre Bonnard, Mary Cassat, Paul Cézanne, Edgar Degas, Maurice Denis, Raoul Dufy, Paul Gauguin, Aristide Maillol, Henri Matisse, Pablo Picasso, Camille Pissaro, Odilon Redon, and last (only because the listing is alphabetical), Pierre August Renoir. As their foremost patron, Vollard must have been a favorite

Picasso's portrait of Ambroise Vollard

subject in the early years of this century, for there are several engravings of him. One of them, by Picasso, was chosen by Vollard to illustrate the cover of his autobiography *Recollections of a Picture Dealer*.

In a few well-defined lines, Picasso manages to achieve what one reviewer described as "a sublime simplification of the technique of dry point engraving. Renouncing any pictorial accessories, Picasso evokes before our eyes the whole complex personality of Vollard... seizing not only the creative passion but also the loneliness of the old fighter, his impulsive lucidity, his weariness, his resignation" and, he might have added, his pugnacity.

Chlomovitch's eclectic collection provides rare insights into the personal interactions, the friendly banter that must have taken place between Vollard and the famous artists who surrounded him. The editors of the catalog claim that Vollard had been pestering Renoir for some time to sketch or paint him in an unusual costume. Renoir is quoted to have exclaimed: "Do not insist any more, Vollard. You can fucking well dress yourself up as a toreador and I'll do your mug." In a rare Renoir self-portrait, done in charcoal and dated 1915, a dedication in pen in the lower left-hand corner reads: "To Vollard, my sympathetic pest!"

This is quintessentially a Fauvist painting, Fauvism being the name that was given to the works of a handful of painters who burst briefly upon the art scene at the turn of the century. The painting, indeed, marks a major crossroads in the history of art. The Fauvists themselves (literally "wild beasts") achieved a liberating break from the Impressionists who had dominated the art world during the late 1800s. Instead of the artists depicting their impressions of reality, they were now encouraged to give free vent to their innermost feelings. Fauvism opened the way for Expressionism and a host of other new "isms" in art like cubism, surrealism, and dadaism, as well as to abstract and nouveau art.

Derain once described the new style: "Fauvism for us has been baptism by fire. The colors became bullets of dynamite. They were to shoot light."

Henri Matisse, the leading Fauvist artist, is represented in the Chlomovitch collection by his *Standing Guitar Player*. It was drawn in 1903, shortly before the Fauvist period.

Renoir's portrait of Ambroise Vollard

Vollard orchestrated Matisse's first one-man show in 1904. It was there that the *Guitar Player* was first exhibited. Vollard mounted Cézanne's first solo exhibit in 1895; Picasso's in 1901; Maillol's in 1902; Matisse's in 1904.

The French Ministry of Culture decreed that the Derain and Matisse paintings in this collection are national treasures and must not leave the borders of France.

What was the purpose of the 1981 art auction? Why auction off only a part of the Chlomovitch collection? Why then?

The collection had lain unclaimed and unpaid for in the bank's coffers for forty years.

The bank had sued the missing Mr. Chlomovitch for rental fees amounting to some 31,000 francs (about $6,000 at that time).

The court had ordered the bank to be paid from the proceeds of the auction.

The auctioneering firm of Jacques Lenormand and Patrick Dayen prepared the sale. Six months of extensive research, and the catalog appeared — detailed and in full color. The auction was set for March 18-19, 1981. The collection was estimated at 3,382,950 French francs ($626,000 at that time) — a modest sum when we consider the subsequent skyrocketing of art prices in the late 1980s. The collection ultimately increased in value more than 25-fold to an estimated $16 million or more. The Derain painting alone was later priced at some $6 million.

The auction stirred up publicity. Publicity engendered interest. The result: the first to show up for the upcoming auction were heirs, not buyers.

Paris. Mrs. Assunta Bertozzi Jonas, heiress of Ambroise Vollard, claimed that the treasure rightfully belonged to her. She charged that Chlomovitch had obtained it from Vollard on loan or by subterfuge.

Yugoslavia. The Foreign Ministry instructed its consul general in Paris to intervene on behalf of five former Yugoslav citizens who claimed succession as relatives of Chlomovitch. One of them resided in Yugoslavia. Four others, identified as the Herzler family, aunts and cousins of Erich Chlomovitch on his mother's side, lived in Israel.

Israel. The Israeli branch of the family did not want to be represented by the Yugoslav government. They filed suit independently.

Hollywood, Florida. Two years later, Zdenka Chlomovitch, another relative, this time on the father's side of the family, joined the chorus of plaintiffs.

The appearance of the first two plaintiffs was sufficient: the Paris court suspended the auction two days before it was scheduled to open. *Le Monde*'s headline, March 20, 1981: *La Vente Chlomovitch est Annulée: L'affair Chlomovitch Commence* (Chlomovitch Sale Annulled; Chlomovitch Affair Begins).

But they were wrong. The Chlomovitch affair had begun long before, in the Serbian town of Djakovo where Erich Šlomovič (Yugoslav spelling) was born on March 15, 1915; in Paris where he resided in the late 1930s; and in wartime Yugoslavia where he was murdered by the Germans.

Chapter II

THE ŠLOMOVIČ SAGA

I first heard of Erich Šlomovič in Israel in the early 1960s. I was living in an area called Shikun Shanghai (Shanghai neighborhood), named after Jewish immigrants who had fled the Chinese metropolis in 1949 on the heels of Mao Tse-Tung's victory.

Next to my home was a synagogue built with reparations from Communist China. The refugees from Shanghai had wanted to use the money to build a community center. But the Chinese communists insisted that it go for a synagogue, since the funds represented compensation for the original Shanghai synagogue which the regime had confiscated.

Although this quirk of history is no more than a footnote to my story, it does illustrate the polyglot nature of Israel. In fact, I was sandwiched between two other neighborhoods, Shikun Bulgarim (Bulgarian neighborhood) and Shikun Yugoslavim (Yugoslavian neighborhood). It was my proximity to the neighborhood of Yugoslav immigrants that drew me to the Šlomovič saga. It formed the prelude to a journalistic odyssey that has endured for more than thirty years.

Early one very ordinary Monday morning, my wife bumped into Dvora Goldfinger, an old Jerusalem school friend, at the local store. Her children and ours, it seemed, knew one another from school. Several days later Dvora's husband, Reuven, phoned me. He was a Yugoslav by origin, and he wanted to seek my advice. I invited him to come to my home. Of medium stature, with deep-set eyes, Reuven wore his hair unparted and combed backward, much like his cousin Erich's. For this Reuven Goldfinger, it transpired, was a first cousin of Erich Šlomovič.

Reuven looked concerned. "You're a newsman," he opened. "You know a lot of people. You must have ideas. Perhaps you can give me some suggestions, some contacts." He paused, took a deep breath, and continued, "I've got a problem." Before long, his story had unfolded into a gripping tale, even by my journalistic yardstick.

"I had a cousin in Yugoslavia by the name of Erich Šlomovič," he began. "His mother and my mother were sisters. Before the war he amassed a valuable art collection in Paris. Erich fled Paris just one month before the Germans invaded France. He returned to Yugoslavia, only to be killed there, not long after, by the Nazis. My sister and I had immigrated to Israel before the war reached Yugoslavia. Other family members, those who survived, came to Israel after the war. For several years now we've been involved in a drawn-out legal battle with Yugoslavia. We're trying either to recover the art collection or be compensated for it. The communist government has blocked us at every turn and we're getting nowhere. Do you have any contacts? Ideas?"

Reuven's story took but a few moments to tell. In the years since that evening, it has unfolded into a complex tale of talent, ambition, failure, tragedy, idealism, and greed. It is an adventure story. Like a peeled artichoke, the most meaty part is found only at its core. Here is the gist of the story as Reuven told it to me that night.

Erich was crazy about art. For him, art was an addiction, and he had studied it in France when he was a young man. In 1936 or 1937, he went to Paris to learn more. There he made friends with the famous art promoter and dealer Ambroise Vollard, and became part of the art world. Vollard opened many doors for him, and over a period of several years Erich managed, partly through Vollard and partly by his own initiative, to amass a valuable collection of Impressionist and Post-Impressionist art.

In 1939, Vollard was killed in a car accident. The war was closing in on France, and two months later the Germans invaded the country. The following spring, using all the by-now familiar tricks of survival, and with the help of some influential Yugoslav diplomats, Erich managed to spirit his collection across several hostile borders, to Yugoslavia.

(When Reuven Goldfinger was telling me this story in Israel, neither he nor his family knew that Erich had left a sizable part of his collection behind in Paris.

The Paris part of the collection was discovered only in 1981, when the bank opened the abandoned safe.)

The collection which Erich took with him to Yugoslavia consisted of 429 items. Among them were 51 works by Rouault, 48 by Renoir, 29 by Vlaminck, and six by Maillol. The collection also included more than twenty rare illustrated books and albums by France's most famous authors, including Honoré de Balzac, Guy de Maupassant, Paul Verlaine, François Villon, Octave Mirabeau, and two hundred original engravings by leading artists of the day: Pierre Bonnard, Paul Cézanne, Edgar Degas, Pablo Picasso, Pierre August Renoir, and George Rouault.

Toward the end of 1940, Erich issued a catalog and exhibited his collection in Zagreb. The event created a major stir. It was given a great deal of publicity in the local press, for it was, at the time, one of the world's greatest private collections of French Impressionist and Post-Impressionist art.

In the spring of 1941, Erich moved back to Belgrade to be with his parents and his brother. On April 6 of that year, German aircraft bombed Belgrade. Within three days the city was razed to the ground, and a week later Yugoslavia was overrun by Nazi troops.

The Šlomovičs — Erich, his brother Egon, and their parents, Bernard and Roza — escaped to the countryside, together with many other war refugees. They chose Bacina, a small village some 160 kilometers (100 miles) southeast of Belgrade. There they found refuge in a local home.

The family was soon joined by Mara Herzler and her two small boys. Mara was a Serbian Gentile who had converted to Judaism when she had married Freddy Herzler, Erich's first cousin. By the time the family escaped to Bacina in the early fall of 1941, Mara's husband was a prisoner-of-war; he was later murdered by the Nazis.

Erich brought his art collection with him to the village. He had packed it in four metal containers and one round cylinder. The villagers must have been among the Righteous Gentiles, because not only did they take the Jews into their houses, they also seem to have helped Erich hide his treasure. With the help of the villagers, Erich removed the paintings from their frames and hid them between the wall of one of the homes and another wall which they erected alongside the first especially for that purpose.

But in the early months of 1942, someone in the village denounced the Šlomovič men. They were seized and taken to the Sajmište Fairgrounds in Belgrade. The Nazi gas chambers had not yet been "perfected" and, grotesquely, the fairgrounds had been converted into a makeshift concentration camp. Erich, his father Bernard, and his brother Egon were gassed to death in sealed trucks at the fairgrounds. One cannot help wondering how many summers these men had played at the booths and merry-go-rounds of Sajmište. Egon was twenty-five years old when he was murdered, Erich was twenty-seven.

Roza, Mara, and Mara's two children were forgotten by the Germans. They lived out the war in Bacina.

Fall 1944. The area of Yugoslavia in which the Šlomovič women are hiding is liberated. Tito and the Partisans have emerged victorious from the war. Dr. Ivan Ribar, an old friend of the family and hero of the partisans, is nominated president of the National Assembly by the newly constituted government. Roza travels to Belgrade to meet him.

Ribar is a native of Djakovo, Erich's home town. Before the war he had practiced law and was considered a liberal (noncommunist) political leader.

Roza tells Ribar of her personal tragedy. She tells him that the surviving members of the family have no means of support. She says that she is willing to turn over her son's collection to the State, provided that she and any other surviving member of her family will receive compensation.

Ribar agrees. He makes arrangements for a special railway carriage to convey her, Mara, and Mara's two children, as well as the art collection, to Belgrade. Once again assisted by the local villagers, the two women pull Erich's metal containers from the double wall and load them onto the train at the nearby town of Varvarin. Then, together with Mara and her two boys, Roza proceeds to Belgrade.

It is December 31, 1944. Fate intervenes. At a railway crossing halfway to Belgrade, near the town of Mala Plana, an opposing train collides with theirs. Roza and Mara's two small boys are crushed to death. They are buried in a local cemetery, close to the scene of the train crash.

Mara herself is badly injured. It takes her several months to recover. While still convalescing, Mara recruits outside help and recovers the iron containers from the railroad authorities. They are still intact.

While Mara was recovering, a certain Dr. Izak Albahari came to visit her. He had been a doctor in the Yugoslav army, was captured by the invading Germans, and for the duration of the war was held in a German prisoner-of-war camp. There, despite being Jewish, he was treated according to the rules of the Geneva Convention, just like other Yugoslav army captives. Thus he got to share care packages which Mara used to send to imprisoned Yugoslav soldiers.

As with Mara, tragedy had befallen Dr. Albahari: his wife and two children had been killed in the war. Before long, Albahari and Mara decided to rebuild their lives together. They were married in October 1945. Before moving away with her new husband, Mara turned over the art treasure to a friend in Belgrade for safekeeping. She hoped that some members of the family had survived and might come someday to reclaim it.

But the Yugoslav Secret Police knew of the valuable art collection. It did not take long for them to come looking for it. Eventually they tracked Mara down, and within days the family treasure, in its various iron containers, was handed over to the Yugoslav authorities.

After many twists and turns, the collection found its way to the National Museum in Belgrade, where it has remained to this day.

Nobody knows how many works of art, if any, were distributed among the friends of the Secret Police before the collection reached its final destination, but the number of paintings in the National Museum of Belgrade was smaller than the number originally listed by its owner, Erich Šlomovič.

Moise Pijade was among those who first urged the Secret Police to search for the art collection, and who later followed it from its hiding place to the museum. Pilade was a Jew, a noted artist, a writer, and a communist who had sat in prison with Tito. He was one of Tito's closest deputies in the Partisan struggle and in the postwar government that emerged from it.

Back in 1940, Pijade had seen Erich's exhibit in Zagreb. Now that the war was over, he was eager to recover it for the benefit of the new Yugoslav state.

But what of Erich himself? What was he like? How had he managed to acquire such an extraordinary collection single-handedly, and at such a young age?

Reuven (my Israeli neighbor) was born in 1923 and was eight years Erich's junior. He remembers him as pleasant, though "a generally taciturn young man, always dressed to a T." He was pedantic, Reuven reported. "He would hold a book in his hand like a piece of rare china and turn each page with infinite care.

"From the age of sixteen he was obsessed by art. I remember that already at a young age he had written to Ambroise Vollard in Paris. His mother, Roza, was very ambitious for him and at one time sent him to a special boarding school in Cannes. I didn't see him much after he left home to live in France, mostly at the Passover Seders [ceremonial meal on the eve of the holiday]. The Seders were held in Djakovo, near the Croatian border, at the home of our grandfather, Joseph Herzler. Most of the family was born there. Our grandfather, Joseph Herzler, was the father of Erich's mother, Roza. He was a sort of combination beadle, cantor, and all-round supervisor at the local synagogue. We usually had about thirty-six people at these Seders. Half of them were first cousins."

No wonder. Erich's mother had four sisters and two brothers (see family tree on opposite page). One of Roza's sisters, Hilda Fleischmann, had escaped to Switzerland during the war together with a niece, Judith Herzler, daughter of one of Roza's brothers. Both immigrated to Israel shortly after the war. Reuven and his sister Ruth, whose mother was Roza's sister, had immigrated before the war. These four Israelis, together with Mara Albahari, eventually became plaintiffs for the inheritance in both the Yugoslav and the French courts.

Erich's father had one sister and one brother. The brother's daughter, Zdenka Šlomovič, presently residing in Hollywood, Florida, is the other claimant in the French court. These five heirs, all told, are the only survivors. At the outbreak of the war there had been over forty family members. Most were killed by the Croatian Ustashi, fascist collaborators of the Germans, who were notorious for their fanaticism and cruelty.

"I remember Erich once announcing his engagement to a French girl, not Jewish," Reuven told me. "His mother and father went off to Paris for the wedding, but it was canceled at the last minute. I don't know why.

"I remember also the day when I was packing to go to Palestine. It was in February 1941. I was eighteen years old at the time. I had gone with my mother to Belgrade, to Aunt Roza's home at 35 Dobracina Street, to get ready for the trip. Erich's father, by the way, had a shoe store, part of the Salamander chain, on Prince Michael Street, not far from there. Erich entered the room and suggested I take some of his paintings with me to Palestine and deposit them there in a bank. I remember his mentioning the Anglo-Palestine Bank. I can even remember one of the paintings. It was one of those pink-colored portraits of a girl's face, by Renoir."

Reuven points to one of the Renoir paintings in the Belgrade museum catalog. On closer inspection, it turns out to be one of Renoir's young son, Claude, with the long, soft hair of a girl.

"Just as Erich was helping me shove the rolled-up paintings among the clothes in my suitcase, my mother walked into the room. She... asked to see what I was hiding, but when she saw the paintings she said: 'Nothing doing. We've waited long enough for a transit visa through Bulgaria, and I won't let you take a chance on being turned back at the border because of illegal or suspicious items in your luggage.'

"Erich argued with her, but she was adamant."

Reuven was taking the Orient Express, often featured in murder mysteries and adventure films, to Istanbul. From there he was to proceed by boat to Palestine. Like his sister before him, he had received an immigration certificate through the Youth Aliyah organization, which brought young people to Palestine and looked after them there until their parents could join them. As was the case with the families of many Youth Aliyah wards in those days, Reuven's parents never made it; they were killed in the Holocaust.

"Mother's caution was unnecessary. The train left Belgrade at midnight on February 17. When I arrived at the Bulgarian border, an inspector came through the train and asked where my luggage was. I pointed to the rack above me. He looked up at it briefly, nodded, and moved on. I hesitate to think what the four paintings I left behind would be worth today!"

This encounter between Reuven and Erich occurred shortly after the latter's art exhibition in Zagreb, which ran for fifty-six days, from November 24, 1940, to January 19, 1941.

Reuven never saw his cousin again.

Chapter III

A COMMUNIST DISINHERITANCE

That was the story, brief and unembellished, as told to me in the early 1960s. It proved to be the tip of a very large, jagged, and sometimes polluted iceberg. The family's court case in Yugoslavia was the jagged edge. The Machiavellian machinations by the communist court system and its apparatchiks constituted, so to speak, the invisible, soiled part beneath the water line.

Few in Yugoslavia had heard of the story, since news coverage of the proceedings had been largely suppressed. The time had come to expose the details.

In 1956, Erich's four surviving heirs in Israel, together with Mara in Yugoslavia, instituted legal proceedings against the State of Yugoslavia in the lower court of Zagreb. Their aim was either to recover the collection or to receive compensation. Only after having battled with the courts for six or seven years without any results did Reuven Goldfinger approach me with his story.

I gave him some names and phone numbers and advised him to persuade the Israeli government and the Israel Museum in Jerusalem to fight the case on his family's behalf. The State of Israel vs. The State of Yugoslavia, I felt, would be more effective than the Herzler family vs. The State of Yugoslavia. (How powerless, indeed, Jews were before they had a country of their own.)

Reuven met with officials in Jerusalem on several occasions, but nothing came of it. Neither they nor his attorney were eager to spoil diplomatic relations with Yugoslavia at that time. Reuven recalls receiving word from the Israeli Legation in Yugoslavia that it did not feel the collection, then being held in the Belgrade National Museum, was sufficiently important to fuss over!

The Israeli officials might be excused for their oversight, since at that time and for many years afterwards the Belgrade National Museum kept the collection under wraps. On the rare occasions when some of the items were shown publicly, Erich's name was never mentioned. Indeed, the museum had good reason to conceal the identity of this particular collector.

Ever since 1949, when the collection was turned over to the museum, the directors had felt uneasy about it. On the one hand, it had belonged to a private individual who was killed in the war; on the other, the public knew of its existence from the much-publicized exhibition in Zagreb in 1940. To make matters worse for them, some of the family might still be around to claim it. Better to lie low.

This feeling was reinforced in 1956 when the heirs and Mara Albahari instituted their suit in the Zagreb Lower Court. In 1955, a new inheritance law had been passed in Yugoslavia declaring that, in the absence of a spouse or ascendants, siblings or the descendants of a deceased would become the legal heirs.

In filing their suit, the remaining relatives engaged an Israeli lawyer, Dr. Rozenberger, a former native of Zagreb whom the family had known before the war. Rozenberger had been a lawyer in Yugoslavia, also a well-known Zionist and editor of the weekly Zionist magazine *Zhidov*. He emigrated to Palestine in February 1941, two months before the German invasion of Yugoslavia. After the establishment of the state of Israel in 1948, Rozenberger became active in assisting *aliyah* (immigration to Israel) from Yugoslavia.

Moise Pijade was extremely helpful in facilitating aliyah. Rozenberger recalls that "his Jewish heart may have overcome his communist ideology. I remember when someone suggested to him that he conceal his Jewishness by changing his name. 'I am Jewish. That's my name,' he replied, 'I am quite satisfied with it. If anyone doesn't like it, it's his problem.'"

Rozenberger had met Pijade in 1951 to discuss the problems of aliyah and to thank him for his assistance. At that time he knew nothing of the latter's connection with the Šlomovič case. But he did know about the collection itself, since he, too, had seen Erich's much-publicized exhibition in Zagreb in 1940. It was shortly thereafter that he had left Yugoslavia for Israel.

Thus, in 1956, when the Israeli heirs engaged him, Rozenberger was the most suitable person in Israel to handle their case in the Yugoslav courts.

Rozenberger, a slight, short man with a gentle mien, belied in his appearance an underlying vein of determination and intellectual toughness. In 1992, already bent by his eighty-four years, he was reluctant to talk about his thirteen-year struggle with the labyrinthine communist court system, a struggle, moreover, for which he had never been compensated. It was only after I uncovered documents and information pertaining to the case which he had not been privy to that he opened up.

Rozenberger's first step in Yugoslavia was to establish the date of Erich's death. The family, having no other proof or documents, believed that Erich, his father, and his brother had been killed in Auschwitz. In December 1956, for lack of further evidence, the court set the date of their death as May 16, 1946. Such arbitrary legal procedures were common practice in Yugoslavia at the time, for there were many war victims whose date and place of death were unknown. If it served no other purpose, the procedure at least allowed widowed spouses to remarry.

But Rozenberger obtained new testimony: according to the 1947 Yugoslav War Crimes Commission, the three Šlomovič men had been killed during the first half of 1942 in the temporary death camp that had been set up at the Sajmište fairgrounds in Belgrade.

The first evidence that the men were killed in Sajmište came from Mara Albahari, who had been hiding in the town of Bacina with the Šlomovič family when the men were arrested. She submitted the following deposition to the court:

> I, Mara Albahari, was born January 23, 1912, at Globovica, in the district of Derventa. Father Ilia and mother Savica, born Knezevič, a Serbian citizen of the Federal Republic of Yugoslavia, married, mother of two children, residing in Semun, 10 Karadjordjev Square.
>
> I knew the late Erich Šlomovič and his family — father, mother and brother — living in the village of Bacina, where they had arrived before me from Belgrade. As I recall, Erich was arrested together with his father and brother by the Nebic Ljotic group in the

first days of January 1942, and taken away to Cuprija, where he was handed over to the Germans in the prison there. I cannot give the exact date, but I believe that Erich was there with his father and brother until the beginning of March 1942, at which time they were taken together with other Jews to the Sajmište camp.

While they were in Cuprija, his mother and I brought packages to them. When he was transferred to Sajmište, the link between us was severed. Despite all my endeavors to establish contact with him and bring more packages, I did not succeed. According to what I learned, Erich, together with his father and brother, perished in the gas chambers in Sajmište during the mass liquidation of Jews there toward the end of 1942.[1]

I lived in Bacina with Erich's mother Roza until the liberation when, in December 1944, she was killed in a railroad disaster.

Sometime in 1943, Slobodin Jelic [obviously an acquaintance of Mara's, unknown to the author of this book] returned from Germany because of illness. As a refugee from Nis, he lived in Varvarin and was later killed.... He told me that he had seen Erich and his people when they were taken to the camp in Sajmište, but unfortunately all traces were lost at the end of 1942 during the Nazi liquidation of Jews there.

This is all I have to say. I have read the statement and signed it.

The court also examined the minutes of the Yugoslav War Crimes Commission, headed by Dr. Albert Weiss, a well-known lawyer and one of the leaders of the Yugoslav Jewish community. One of the witnesses to appear before the commission was Hedvide Schoenhein, a Gentile woman from Belgrade who had been imprisoned in Sajmište together with her husband. Her husband was a Jewish physician, also killed at the Sajmište fairgrounds. A separate block had been set up at the camp for Jews, most of whom were women, children, old people, and internees from other camps, some six thousand in number. All of them were asphyxiated with poison gas in specially sealed trucks.

1. As mentioned, at the Sajmište fairgrounds victims were gassed in trucks. The gas chambers had not been developed at that time.

Of the six people who survived, all were women and all were Gentiles; Hedvide was among them. By the beginning of 1943, the camp was dismantled.

Further testimony came from one Natalia Putnik, whose brother had been in hiding in Bacina and was arrested together with the Šlomovičs. Natalia related how the men had been transferred from Cuprija to Sajmište and how she had gone to Sajmište to inquire about them. "In searching for them there," she said, "I learned that Bernard and Egon, as well as Erich, had been killed together with my brother."

Today the fairgrounds are almost deserted. A memorial plaque commemorates the slayings. It gives the total number murdered there by the Germans and their Ustashi collaborators as forty thousand.[1]

As a result of these testimonies, and since the precise date in 1942 was not known, on February 22, 1957, the Zagreb Court of Appeal readjusted the date of death to January 1, 1943.

This determination was vital to the plaintiffs, for it established that Roza had survived her sons and her husband and, as such, was the legitimate heir of the art collection. It also confirmed that after her death in the train crash, her sister, her two nieces, and her nephew in Israel, as well as Mara Albahari in Yugoslavia, all became legitimate heirs. They would not have been eligible for inheritance had Roza's husband and two sons died on May 15, 1946 (after her own death), the date that had been originally and quite arbitrarily set by the court. Apart from any other consideration, the 1946 date would have set Erich's (and his father's and brother's) date of death at one year after the end of the war!

On July 18, 1958, Rozenberger succeeded in getting the Belgrade museum to confirm for the Zagreb court that they had the Šlomovič collection in their possession. He then got the court to order the museum to relinquish the collection to the family.

All was going well; justice would be served. But the museum was not about to give up such a treasure without a fight. It turned to the federal prosecutor (or

1. Of Belgrade's 11,000 prewar Jews and another 1,500 from Serbia, only 1,500 survived the war. Of Yugoslavia's total prewar Jewish population of 73,000, only 14,000 survived. Some 5,000 fought with the Partisans, of whom 1,500 were killed. Eleven received Yugoslavia's highest award for bravery and fourteen became generals in the Yugoslav army after the war.

public defender, as he was called) in Belgrade, Erich's hometown. In his eagerness to save the collection for the State, the public defender pulled a stunt that had been invented by the communist regime, and was called "the protection of legality." It was little more than a legal trick that could overrule any court decision which the authorities felt overstepped the court's power, violated the public good, or negated the underlying principles of the regime.

There then followed four years of a seesaw battle during which the Zagreb court, unintimidated by the manipulation of the public defender, reconfirmed its decision. The victims' date of death, the court insisted, was still January 1, 1943.

By 1962, the federal authorities succeeded in transferring the case to Belgrade, to the First Municipal Court of the capital city. Rozenberger asked Prvislav Vasiljevič, the head of the National Bar Association, to represent him. Vasiljevič studied the case and accepted, saying: "Your clients are in the right. I don't doubt that their legitimate claim will be recognized in accordance with the law."

Several months later Vasiljevič was appointed minister of commerce and had to resign from the case. Rozenberger engaged another firm of Belgrade lawyers.

One of the first moves taken by the public defender was to obtain a letter written by Dr. Ivan Ribar on February 16, 1962. Ribar, as mentioned, was president of the National Assembly at the time of Yugoslavia's liberation, and the man to whom Roza had traveled before her fatal accident. Ribar quotes Roza as having said:

> "I have no more next of kin, having lost all those whom I had. As for the paintings, the collections, they bind me to my Erich, and as long as I live I will look at them and try not to be separated from them. After my death, the National Museum of Belgrade may inherit them, noting that they are a gift from Erich Šlomovič, because he also wanted this. Only if the collection remains complete and in its entirety, first with me and then in the museum, will it perpetuate his memory."

But Rozenberger had another letter from Ribar written nine years earlier, on December 10, 1953, and addressed to him in Israel:

Dear Sir,

I received both your letters. To the first one, of 16/10/53, I did not reply because I was absent from Zagreb for over a month.

I knew Erich Šlomovič and saw him for the last time in Bosnia on the day all of Yugoslavia collapsed. I knew well his family who lived in Belgrade before the war. Erich Šlomovič brought from Paris a very beautiful collection of well-known French painters.

After the war, Mrs. Šlomovič, the daughter of the later Mr. Herzler from Djakovo, visited me and informed me that all of her people had been killed by the Germans, the husband and both sons, and that she happened to survive. She wished that the paintings belonging to her son, which she had succeeded in preserving in a village in Serbia, be donated to a gallery in Belgrade, but for a *just compensation* [emphasis added], because she possessed no other means except for this collection.

However, a few days later she was killed in a railroad disaster.

I related all this to my comrade Moise Pijade, presently Vice-President of the Federal Executive Council in Belgrade. As far as I know, he personally took care of the paintings. What happened afterwards, I do not know....

Respectfully yours,

I. Ribar

To this day, no one has been able to obtain a copy of the letter that was allegedly addressed to the court in 1962, and that had not, allegedly, mentioned Roza's request for compensation. As for the letter of December 10, 1953, Rozenberger was not permitted to submit it to the court. The rules of evidence require a direct, authenticated communication to the court, not to a third party. They also demand the sworn testimony of the person communicating it.

It seems obvious from the evidence that Roza wanted to create a state-sponsored museum in Erich's name, not to donate the collection outright to the National Museum, where it would lose its identity.

Neither Rozenberger nor the public defender called Ribar to the stand, Rozenberger being afraid that Ribar might not confirm Roza's request for compensation, and the public defender fearing that he would. Besides, it was apparently not customary under the communist regime to call top government officials to testify in court.

There then followed three more years of delaying tactics in which judges and government attorneys were periodically replaced, hearings delayed, and bureaucratic paperwork accumulated. At one point the government's deputy public defender, Branko Niskovič, turned to the Herzlers' attorney and yelled at him: "Those paintings... you'll never get them!"

In the course of the proceedings, Rozenberger had produced Roza's death certificate of December 31, 1944, describing her as a "widow." With this and the latest court decisions, the public defender could hardly claim that the men had died after her. Thus, on October 28, 1965, the public defender, in summarizing the State's arguments, in fact corroborated and accepted the previous rulings of the court that the three Šlomovič men had died by January 1, 1943.

A few months later (March 12, 1966), the Federal Court in Belgrade reconfirmed that Roza had been Erich's only heir, basing its judgment on the title "widow." This opened the way once more for Mara Albahari and Erich's Israeli heirs to promote their claims. Again the public defender saw that the wind was blowing against him. Hence, he changed course 180 degrees: once more he questioned the validity of the evidence that the three men had been killed in Sajmište in 1942.

As Rozenberger described it: "The public defender came into contradiction with himself." For his part, Rozenberger acquiesced in the government's request that the case be transferred to the Belgrade Municipal Court to resolve these new contentions.

Needless to say, this took another two years.

During that period, the Israeli attorney got the court to have the National Museum in Belgrade submit an inventory of the *corpus delicti*. The request was sent on May 16, 1966; the reply did not come until March 15, 1968! In it, the museum's director Dr. Lazar Trifunovič states, among other things:

> There is no special collection of paintings in this museum registered under the title "Inheritance of Erich Šlomovič." Among art objects entrusted to this museum by government bodies after the war, there are also some paintings from the collection of the late Šlomovič. Registration of these works of art is done by artistic style and time periods. It is more than a year now that work on the extension and adaptation of the building has been completed. During that period all art objects were put into trunks and into the safe-vault for protection.[1]

After completion of these adaptation activities, the museum undertook to finally classify the art objects, and this work is still under way.

> Considering the classification work still to be completed, we envision concluding this work by the end of this year at the earliest. For these reasons, the museum is not able to satisfy the request of the court before the end of this year.

The museum never got around to "satisfy the request of the court." The woman judge who had made the request was transferred to another bench.

"I apologized to her for being the cause," Rozenberger recalls. "I remember her once giving me a wry smile and saying, 'Mr. Rozenberger, your situation is a very difficult one."

The museum was telling only half a lie when it wrote that it had no collection "under the title 'Inheritance of Erich Šlomovič.'" After all, the collection was kept under wraps and anonymous for over twenty years, at least until the early seventies, after the family had lost its court case and the coast was clear.

1. The building had formerly belonged to a major bank.

On one occasion, however, the museum did allow part of the collection to be publicly identified with Erich Šlomovič. This occurred in 1966 when Denis Rouart, a French art historian of some repute, came to Belgrade to produce an album on the forty-eight Renoir and twenty-nine Degas works in the collection. He called it *Le Degas et Renoir Inconnu* (The Unknown Degas and Renoir).

The album was printed in French and English and contained an extensive introduction, including a biographical review of Erich Šlomovič. Many questions about him and his collection were left unanswered, however, especially the question of how one so young had managed to accumulate such an astounding collection. Over the years the album was forgotten, and when in 1981 the second part of the collection was discovered in the Paris safe, few journalists recalled that the "mysterious Mr. Chlomovitch" had in fact been discovered by a Frenchman fifteen years earlier.

The museum's delaying tactics, in response to the court request to produce an inventory, did not help the government's case. The Belgrade Municipal Court, like the previous courts, did not buy the public defender's arguments, and on May 5, 1968, once more confirmed that the men had died by January 1,1943.

A new gimmick was needed.

It was at this point that the then-chief public defender, one Milan Antonič, took charge and, as he subsequently boasted, "saved the collection for the State." Antonič was a large, forceful man with a shock of blond hair and a long record as a practicing attorney. At one point he had served as chief legal officer for the Yugoslav army.

Antonič had a brainstorm.

Shortly after the May 1968 ratification of the January 1, 1943, date of death, Antonič secretly requested — more aptly instructed — the court in the town of Varvarin to review the case and to determine whether the Law on Property Abandoned in the War might apply to it. Varvarin, located just a few kilometers from Bacina, where the Šlomovič family had hidden during the war, was a sort of country seat which had legal jurisdiction over Bacina.

The Law on Property Abandoned in the War, promulgated in 1946 by the new communist government of Yugoslavia, declared that property abandoned because of the war, and not claimed within one year of the law's enactment, would revert to the State.

In a secret "extrajudicial hearing," of which the Herzler family attorneys were not informed and to which they were not invited, the Varvarin court ruled on July 12, 1968, that since the Šlomovič family had not filed a claim within one year, the law applied and the art collection reverted to the State.

Antonič took his decision back to the Belgrade court. The court accepted it, and on March 17, 1969, it suspended all proceedings *sine die*, declaring that since the property had reverted to the State, there was no property to inherit!

Antonič had more tricks up his sleeve. He invoked the infamous "protection of legality" clause, and appealed to the Supreme Court of Serbia to reverse the previous court rulings regarding the date of death. Once more he rehashed the lack of concrete proof regarding the date and place of death of Erich and his male kin.

Since Roza's death certificate attested that she had died in the train accident on December 31, 1944, she was the only one whose date of death could not be manipulated. But the State needed to show that she was the first to die.

The Supreme Court of Serbia again accommodated Antonič. Another hearing was convened. Again the Herzlers' lawyers were excluded. This occurred on July 8, 1969, four months after the Superior Court of Belgrade had already suspended the case on the basis of the Varvarin decision.

In this manner the wheels of communist justice turned. Slowly but surely they provided Antonič with insurance which he, in fact, no longer needed.

Incongruously, the Supreme Court split the dates of death, ruling that Erich had died on January 1,1943, while his father and brother had died on May 15, 1946. The court conveniently ignored the fact that Roza's death certificate described her as a widow, and that, therefore, her husband must have died before her.

But why did they need to split the dates of death?

This was the cleverest of all their tricks! Rozenberger and the previous courts were insisting that Erich had died by the above date. Fine, claimed Antonič and his cronies. Let them have their little victory. They didn't mind. They would simply nullify its value by declaring the death of Erich's father and brother to have occurred after that of Erich. This way, only the descendants of

Erich's father would be eligible to inherit. With one brilliant stroke, Antonič had excluded Mara and the Herzler/Israel contingent forever from the race.

The court case had lasted thirteen years.

Was this the end? Not quite.

Chapter IV

APPEALING TO TITO

Antonič's efforts on behalf of the State did not go unrecognized. On October 24, 1969, two months after the final decision of the Supreme Court of Serbia, the National Museum, at a special session of its board of directors, expressed its gratitude to him for "conscientious, reliable and skillful work on behalf of the community, in ending the legal proceedings."

Three years later, the government awarded Antonič the Order of Merit, bearing Belgrade's Coat of Arms in bronze, silver, and gold; the Order of the Republic, bearing a cross of honor with a silver palm for "services to the nation"; and... bonus of 250,000 dinars ($17,000), an amount equivalent, at that time, to five annual salaries of any top civil servant!

These latter awards were granted only after the Herzlers had made one more gasping but abortive appeal. The maneuver almost saved them, until Milan Antonič and the Belgrade Municipal Council administered the *coup de grâce*.

The last act began with what Rozenberger now felt was his only resort, a personal appeal to Tito, omnipotent president of the Republic. It took two years for Rozenberger to muster the courage for such an appeal, but on September 24, 1971, he transmitted to Tito's bureau a twenty-page, closely typed memorandum describing the "Via Dolorosa" of his case. He started with a rather naive appeal for justice:

> Mr. President,
>
> At the very beginning of this report which I submit to you, please believe that I am taking this action after much deliberation and

> hesitation, the reason being that I did not want to find myself in contradiction with a principle I have always advocated, namely to maintain a sense of evenhandedness and fairness. The thought of appealing to you ripened only a year or so ago, as the only means of aiding the legitimate interests of five people, the only survivors of a large family which was massacred and gassed by the Nazis and the Ustashi.
>
> I therefore take the liberty of requesting that you consider the matter out of humanitarian reasons and compassion for "the little man" whose rights have been trampled, and that you help restore justice and rectify the errors committed by certain branches of the court system with regard to the inheritance of the late Erich Šlomovič, comprising the art collection in his name held in the National Museum in Belgrade.

The memo then revealed details of the aftermath of the train accident that had never before been reported.

Roza had kept the keys to the containers in her purse, together with documents that had belonged to Erich. These fell out of the purse and were lost in the accident. When Mara was able to leave the hospital, she found a room in Belgrade, on Jevremova Street. All the containers were brought there (four heavy metal containers and a metal cylinder). Shortly after the war Judith Herzler (a niece of Roza's) returned from abroad where she had found refuge. Of all the relatives that she had left behind, Mara was the only one still alive in Belgrade — and she had decided to move to Kosmet. Together the two women placed the containers in the warehouse of a trusted friend by the name of Veljko Petrovič. They were to be kept there until such time as other surviving relatives might be found. If none appeared, they would seek advice from attorneys within their community.

Neither Mara nor Judith ever touched the collection.... This is what happened next:

The Security Services discovered Mara's address (by that time she was married to Dr. Albahari) and visited her in Kosmet. She was not able to give them the lost keys, but she gave them the whereabouts of the collection and transferred to them the only copy of the original catalog from the Zagreb exhibit (on which Erich had noted in his own hand what had been sold and to whom).

From that time on, the collection has been at the National Museum in Belgrade.

[In] 1965 I was received by the now deceased Dr. Ivan Ribar in his office at the Socialist Workers Council in Zagreb. We spoke about the collection. Dr. Ribar recalled his letter, of which I showed him a photocopy. He confirmed its contents, namely that the late Roza had told him that she would donate the collection, but against just compensation.

Rozenberger then noted that he had the Israeli family's written agreement that, in case Mara Albahari's claim was not recognized, she would receive from them whatever they recovered, in proportion to what her two children would have received had they remained alive. He then stressed that the family was aware of the collection's importance to Yugoslavia's cultural life and was ready to receive compensation in lieu of the paintings.

Next, taking up the cudgel against the public defender, Rozenberger noted:

> The Public Defender should have known that [Roza's alleged] donation had never taken place. There was only talk of such an intention. As lawyers, they knew that according to the law there is no donation without an actual handing over of the gift by the donor to the recipient. In the present case there is another factor, namely that Roza Šlomovič, in one of her declarations about the intended donation, as confirmed in her conversation with Dr. Ribar, mentioned that she is ready to donate the paintings, "but against fair compensation."
>
> [If the Public Defender was] of the opinion that the [1962] declaration by Roza [which he produced in evidence] had legal force, then certainly the other side of this declaration about fair compensation should also have legal force.

The Herzler attorney then pointed out that the public defender had been unable to produce evidence of an actual donation. "This," he wrote, "caused him to deny all the evidence he had officially presented to the court during the past several years."

Rozenberger then described the duplicity of the public defender's fight to get a ruling that the Šlomovič men had died after the mother. He told how the public defender had gone behind the Herzlers' back to the District Court in Varvarin to convince the court that Erich's collection fell within the purview of the 1946 Law on Abandoned Property. He wrote how the court had found that, since the property was not claimed within one year, as required by law, the collection had reverted to the State, and that, consequently, there was nothing to inherit.

But Rozenberger argued that this law could not possibly be applied to this case, since the property was never abandoned. It had remained in the family's possession from the time it was hidden in the double wall in Bacina, to the train accident and beyond, to the moment that Mara had given it to her friend for safekeeping.

The public defender, wrote Rozenberger, was not using the abandoned-property theses, because he understood all of the above. Instead, he now claimed that Roza was not the last heir. How, asked the lawyer, could the public defender suddenly switch directions in this manner? How could he deny the argument he had been proposing for the last eight years?

Yet he had done so by means of the "Varvarin maneuver." Here Rozenberger told Tito how the Lower Court in Zagreb, on its own initiative, had decided that Varvarin should have jurisdiction and even sent the court records there. The representatives of the heirs objected to this, pointing out that Erich Šlomovič never resided in Varvarin, and that it had only been a refuge and a shelter for him and his family during the war. The court accepted this argument. This decision was also accepted by the public defender, and the records were duly returned from the court in Varvarin to the court in Zagreb, only to be transferred still later to the Municipal Court in Belgrade.

Accordingly, there exists a court decision that the Municipal Court of Varvarin does not have jurisdiction over the inheritance of Erich Šlomovič. This decision was known by the Public Defender and all other legal authorities dealing with the case.... He nevertheless requested the Municipal Court in Varvarin on March 6, 1968, to rule, in an out-of-court procedure, that the inheritance be transferred to the State in accordance with the Law on Abandoned Property.

This... was kept secret from the litigants and from the court where the inheritance proceedings were being heard, and in which [the public defender] was an active participant.

The above request was eventually discovered by the court and by the litigants in the following manner: At a hearing in the Municipal Court in Belgrade on November 1, 1968, Branco Neskovič, who represented the Public Defender, stated that there was a decision by a court, he doesn't know exactly which, stating that Erich's inheritance was owned by the State. He could not say when this decision was taken, but created the impression that the Public Defender himself had only learned of it at the last moment.

The court ruled that within ten days the Public Defender must submit to the court a copy of such a decision. He did [so].... Only then did [the litigants] discover the secret contents of the original request to Varvarin and the following decision by the Varvarin court:

> "It is hereby established that the entire inheritance of Erich Šlomovič, formerly of Bacina, consisting of paintings and other valuable works of art, became the property of the State according to Article 7, Statute 3, of the law dealing with property which its owners had to abandon during the occupation, or which was taken by the occupying forces or their helpers."

The Israeli attorney concluded his memo with studied understatement:

> It is hard to believe that all of the above escaped the memory of the Public Defender. Because of his omission to inform the parties to the case of this request to the Municipality of Varvarin, the heirs could not be a party to such a request. And because they were not parties in the procedure, they had no right to appeal the Varvarin court's decision. This was in addition to the fact that their basic rights were jeopardized by this procedure. Their only legal remedy for questioning the legality of such a procedure was an appeal to the Public Prosecutor in Belgrade.

The representative of the heirs appealed accordingly, but the Public Defender decided that the proceedings had been legal and refused their request.

Based on the decision of the Varvarin court, and in accordance with the request by the Public Defender, the First Municipal Court in Belgrade decided that the proceedings should be suspended, since there was no inheritance to distribute. The appeal against this decision, submitted by the heirs, was rejected by the District Court in Belgrade, in consideration of the decision of the Municipal Court in Varvarin.

In his appeal, Dejan Zivkovič, Rozenberger's attorney in Belgrade, tried to present to the court a document signed by Dr. Ivan Ribar as president of the National Assembly. Ribar's document clarified the Law on Abandoned Property, under the heading: "Obligatory Interpretation to Article 7, Part 3" (of this law). The document stated that the heirs of such owners "are entitled to start proceedings for inheritance within a time limit of one year after this law was passed, or one year from the day the decision establishing the death of the [owner] went into legal effect."

The Belgrade court ignored this plea.

Rozenberger concludes his memo to Tito:

> What does all this lead to? I am not alone in my appeal. Many important legal personalities in and outside Yugoslavia agree with me, namely that this decision cannot and should not be the last word in the Erich Šlomovič inheritance dispute.
>
> After my great disappointment, I am now appearing before you, Mr. President, on behalf of five surviving members of a large Jewish family — taking into account their honest desire and readiness for a compromise resolution of the problem — with the request that you take the necessary steps to resolve the problem in the best way possible.
>
> Yours respectfully,
>
> Joel Rozenberger

Although Rozenberger and his Yugoslav attorney, Dejan Zivkovič, did not know it at the time, the memo did have its desired effect. More, in fact, than they had hoped for. In a letter dated March 14, 1972, addressed to the Belgrade Municipal Council, Tito's Chief of Bureau, Marko Vrhunec, writes:

> From: Bureau, President of the Republic
> To: Milan Vukos, Vice-President, Belgrade City Council
>
> ...we have examined the attached request [of Dr. Rozenberger], as well as all the accompanying material, and we believe it is important that you address yourself to it for examination and decision. We feel it would be correct and equitable if the municipality, without taking into account the negative judicial decision, decided to indemnify the heirs of the late Erich Šlomovič. In our view, the decision that there are no heirs is untenable. Meanwhile, from the legal point of view, it would be impossible to reopen the inheritance process of this affair, which was terminated in spite of the fact that we do not share the opinion of the court that there are no legal successors or heirs.
>
> We cannot reproach the court for deciding that such valuable and important works of art, which comprise Erich Šlomovič's inheritance, should not leave the country. Nevertheless, it is all to the advantage of Yugoslavia's and the city of Belgrade's reputation that the Šlomovič heirs should obtain compensation. All of Šlomovič's inheritance, comprising paintings by the masters, are to be found in the National Museum in Belgrade.
>
> Having undertaken to proceed with such a complex affair, and in order that in the end a decision by the municipality is reached to give equitable and optimal compensation, we request you, Comrade Vukos, to kindly designate some professional people to examine the entire matter and give their opinion.
>
> We also request that, while dealing with this matter, your experts confer with the advocates, Dejan Zivkovič, 37 Kralja Milutina, Tel: 333-185, Milovan Jovanovič, and Dragoslav Trniniè, who are representing Dr. Joel Rozenberger.

We would also appreciate your informing the President's Bureau as to the resolution of this affair and the decision of the municipality concerning fair compensation for the heirs, in response to the author of this request.

Marko Vrhunec s.a.

Chief of Bureau of the
President of the Republic

12 enclosures.

Untenable decision? Yugoslavia's and Belgrade's reputation? The heirs should obtain equitable and fair compensation? President Tito was indeed being helpful!

The Belgrade municipality turned the letter over to Antonič, the public defender, for a response. In a thirty-page reply dated May 23,1972, Antonič reviewed the case's legal odyssey "without" — as he later told me — "expressing any opinion."

Eighteen years passed before this "confidential" memo surfaced. Only then did Fernand Cohen, then prosecutor of the Herzler case in Paris, receive a copy from Antonič. "Antonič couldn't resist the pleasure of giving me a copy of the memo," Cohen notes, "since it stressed his personal merits as he saw them."

And so it was not until eighteen years later that Cohen laid his arguments before the French court. Cohen chose to quote only one passage from the memo: Antonič's explanation for the sudden turnabout in tactics, so bitterly condemned by Rozenberger.

It is true that in the beginning the Public Defender of Serbia, and after that even his colleagues, accepted as being true the report of Comrade Erin Kos, assistant to the director of the National Museum of Belgrade, wherein he stated that the collection belongs to the State because it had been given as a gift by the late Roza Šlomovič.

In order to prove the authenticity of this statement, Erin Kos referred to Dr. Ribar. Later, however, after the report had been checked, it appeared that the legal situation, as described in the report, was not totally in keeping with the truth. When the gift was made, there were certain formal legal shortcomings. Because of this, the validity of the gift would be questioned, and this is what the litigants counted on.

When the factual situation had clarified, the conclusion adopted was that the applicable law for the inheritance of the late Erich Šlomovič was the law concerning the treatment of possessions which their owners had to abandon during the occupation.

The Paris attorney's comment on this passage: "This couldn't have been stated more aptly, namely that after one maneuver had failed, efforts were made to try another." (I had the good fortune to interview Antonič in 1992. He made some rather startling admissions to me; but more on that later.)

June 2, 1972: the Belgrade municipality, basing itself on Antonič's memo, informed Tito's Bureau that, since there was no legal recourse left to change the decision, the case was closed. The chief of Tito's Bureau so informed Rozenberger verbally, ten days later.

Thus the balloon, which Rozenberger had inflated, and to which Tito's Chief of Bureau had given a brief buoyancy, was brought sadly to ground.

Chapter V

THE PARIS CHAPTER

The 1972 response to Tito's Bureau struck the final nail in the coffin of the Herzlers' case in Yugoslavia.

Nine years elapsed. Then, in 1981, a thunderclap from Paris announced the auction sale of the 190 items that had been left by Erich in the local bank vault.

The Herzlers were the third party to sue for the vault's contents, and the suspension of the auction. The first to act in France was the Yugoslav consul general. The second — one Mrs. Assunta Bertozzi Jonas — was an heiress, two generations removed, not of Erich but of the former art merchant, Ambroise Vollard.

Mrs. Jonas claimed that Erich Šlomovič had obtained the collection from Vollard under dubious circumstances and that it was thus not rightfully his. The Yugoslav diplomatic representative intervened to protect the interests of five former Yugoslav citizens: Mara Albahari and the four Herzlers then residing in Israel.

Two days before the auction was to take place, the Lower Court in Paris (Juge de Referes) rejected Mrs. Jonas's claim, ruling that it "prejudged the proprietary rights of a person who had already been named or identified"; in other words, possession is nine-tenths of the law.

Moreover, the court accepted the Yugoslav intervention and canceled the auction *sine die*. It then appointed a Mr. Gondre as temporary administrator of the collection and ordered it to be moved to a safe at the Société Général Bank at 16 Boulevard des Italiens.

In February 1982, almost a year later, Mrs. Jonas reinstated her suit on appeal, claiming all the items which had appeared in the Lenormand-Dayen

Paris catalog except for "personal photographs of Erich Šlomovič and various documents, autographs, sketches, gouaches and aquarelles dedicated personally to the said person."

Mrs. Jonas also demanded one million francs in damages from the bank for its negligence in having failed to inform the Vollard heirs of the existence of the safe's contents.

Toward the end of 1982, the Herzlers formally entered the proceedings.

On July 6, 1983, Zdenka Šlomovič intervened in the proceedings, contending that the Herzlers' claim should be dismissed, since she herself was the only legitimate heir on the father's side. She maintained that she would make an independent settlement with the other claimants. Zdenka was a first cousin of Erich, being the daughter of one of the two brothers of Erich's father. Her only brother had been killed in the war.

Zdenka's claim was based on the fact that the father, according to the Yugoslav court, was presumed to have died on May 16, 1946 (a year after the end of the war), together with his other son, Egon. Since his death would have occurred after his wife had been killed in the train crash, he and his descendants, including Zdenka, should be the sole heirs.

Zdenka had been cut off from the Israeli branch of the family for many years. She had left Yugoslavia in 1954 and, after three marriages, had settled in Hollywood, Florida, from where she filed suit in the Paris court. The family that had been so large and so united in life, that had such joyous memories of Passover celebrations and family reunions, had been reduced by the Holocaust to a handful of survivors. Even worse, the one possession that they shared now turned them into a house divided against itself.

By the time the main contestants had lined up in the Paris ring, expenses were soaring out of control, and Mr. Gondre, the court administrator, was authorized to auction off certain lithographs by Cezanne and Renoir, as well as eleven watercolors by Picasso. The art market had not yet shot sky-high, and the sale netted a paltry $13,000.

The Herzlers, as we have noted, were now being represented by Fernand Cohen, a Paris attorney of some repute. A native of Morocco, Cohen had studied law in the same class as Prince (later King) Hassan. He completed his studies in Paris with degrees in law, philosophy, and political science, and set up practice in

France in 1952. This was followed by a three-year interlude of legal practice back in Casablanca, and a two-year hiatus in the French army.

In 1989, after twenty-three years of successful practice in Paris, Cohen became a senior partner in one of the city's prominent law firms. Located on the Champs Elysées, his office was headed by Count René de Chambrun, a direct descendant of the Marquis de Lafayette. Chambrun was an adviser to the U.S. Army after World War II, and for many years served as president of one of France's oldest industrial firms, Baccarat Crystal.

Cohen was engaged not by the Herzlers but by Sotheby's, reputedly the world's largest auction house. The Israelis, being of modest means, had come to an agreement with Sotheby's whereby the latter would be entitled to auction off whatever would be won in the Paris court case; for its part, Sotheby's was responsible to hire and pay a lawyer on the Herzlers' behalf. (Rozenberger also worked on a contingency basis; he never received a penny for his efforts, nor even for his out-of-pocket expenses.)

"I took the case," Cohen affirmed, "because it is on the subject of art, in which I am very interested, and it concerns Jewish victims of the Holocaust and Israel — after all, I am Jewish. Also," he added, "the tradition of an *avocat* in France is to 'advocate' a just cause, even if it offers no compensation."

By placing art ahead of his Jewish identity, Cohen unwittingly expressed his assimilation into French society. As if to stress this point, he added: "I would have also taken the case had it concerned Arabs."

Whatever the conflicting motives or financial interests of the various parties involved, Cohen performed a yeoman's service for his clients. One need only look at his massive files, meticulously documented and authenticated, logically divided and carefully arranged, the result of ten years of intensive efforts. During this time he made two trips to Yugoslavia, where he uncovered crucial documents which no one had produced or known about before.

Let us therefore follow the tortuous road of "*L'affaire Chlomovitch*" (French spelling) as it unfolded in the French courts. In the process, a virtual *tour d'horizon* of the life and death of the enigmatic young Yugoslavian was exposed to view, demystifying part but not all of the drama.

The main preoccupation of the French court boiled down to one basic question: how did Erich acquire his treasure?

Did it constitute a loan to be returned, as Mrs. Jonas claimed? Or was it the result of years of laborious and sophisticated wheeling and dealing, as the Herzlers averred?

Here there were no extralegal acrobatics as had occurred in Yugoslavia. This was France, part of the democratic West, where law, it is hoped, took precedence over ideology, and individual justice over state prerogatives.

Paris, November 7, 1984. A major decision is reached by the First Tribunal of Appeal: the contents of the safe are awarded to the Herzlers. Zdenka's claim is dismissed for having been filed too late; Mrs. Jonas's claim is rejected for failing to prove her contentions, and she is ordered to pay 40,894 francs ($3,560) to the bank for forty years of storage fees.

French law, like that of most Western countries, presumes that the possessor is the legal owner. The Herzlers did not have to prove that Erich's possession was legal; Mrs. Jonas had to prove that it was illegal, or at least dubious.

Mrs. Jonas passed away shortly after the 1984 decision. Her case was taken over by her nephew and heir, Louis Sebastien.

On February 26, 1987, two and a half years later, Louis Sebastien and Zdenka appealed. The court made a complete about-face: it recognized both Sebastien and Zdenka as legitimate claimants, and appointed an art expert to help it determine which of the 190 items were acquired legitimately by Erich and which had, in fact, belonged to Ambroise Vollard's estate.

In explaining its rationale for appointing the expert, the court stated: "In coming to analyze the unusual character of the troubled times [when Erich deposited the items in the Paris bank], and in examining the origin of the disputed items, it is possible that Erich Šlomovič's keeping of the items, allegedly originating from Ambroise Vollard, did not constitute innocent possession and could have been of an equivocal and doubtful character."

The expert appointed to assess the situation, a man by the name of Fabrice Fare, was an art historian and researcher who specialized in 18th-century French painters. He was instructed to collect whatever information he could from Martin Fabiani, the administrator of Vollard's estate and the man who had managed the Vollard gallery during World War II. Fare was also requested to interview people such as Gilbert Patrides, an aging art merchant who had known both Vollard and Šlomovič, and Denis Rouart, who had in 1966 compiled the art album *Le Degas et Renoir inconnu* (The Unknown Degas and Renoir). The album contained reproductions of the works of those artists in the Šlomovič collection of the National Museum in Belgrade.

Fare was required to complete his report within eight months, and was allotted a modest 20,000 francs ($3,300) for his efforts. The assignment took him three years.

When he finally handed his report to the court on March 30, 1990, it contained three thick volumes and totaled 1,042 pages. Of these, half (524 pages) showed photocopies of various art albums in the collection and photostats of recent catalogs, one of them from the Belgrade museum (given to him by the Herzlers' attorney) and the other from the aborted Paris auction.

The report also included interviews with four people who had known Erich personally, an analysis of the items in the Paris catalog, especially those dedicated to Erich, as well as photostats of items of correspondence connected with the expert's work.

In his conclusions, Fare speculates about Erich and the life he led in Paris:

> his personality... is not easy to define... much is blocked. Out of curiosity I went to see the Hotel Ideal at 108 Blvd. Jourdan, where he was staying in September 1939, after some four years of living in Paris.[1] This hotel is located near the Port d'Orleans and is graded two stars.[2]

This odd fact further illustrates [his] complex and enigmatic nature.

Fare remarks that such a hotel was more suitable for an impecunious student than for an art collector of "passion and means." He then goes on to analyze the art milieu of Ambroise Vollard, in which Erich had moved in the late 1930s (Fare gives an incorrect address for Vollard).

Vollard, Fare points out, was much more than an art merchant; he was also a leading publisher of albums and a sponsor of major exhibitions. Erich's relationship with Vollard, he maintains, was more intellectual than commercial.

1. The building had formerly belonged to a major bank.
2. This is an error; it was near the Place de Gilgancourt, south of the Montparnasse.

There was no evidence that Erich ever acquired art objects from Vollard against payment.

On the other hand, Fare continues, there is evidence of independent activity by Erich, such as his "intention to write and publish works on the painters Georges Rouault and Pascin." Fare continues:

> To get a proper perspective on his complex personality, it would be necessary to study his collection as a whole, comprising both the French and Yugoslav parts, an exceptional collection indeed in 1939.

All agree that the bulk of the collection originated with Ambroise Vollard, except, of course, for such dedicated sketches as the one by Cocteau, as well as personal correspondence, documents, photos and perhaps the works of Utrillo... and others offered to him by Chagall, Bonnard and Lucien Vollard [Ambroise's brother and principal heir].

Most of these dedicated and personal items, Fare notes, are dated in the third quarter of 1939, after Vollard's death, which occurred on July 22 of that year. They are of lesser value and importance than the other works in the collection.

The expert dwells especially on seventy-nine photographs of the works of Odile Redon which, he says, are of great importance to art historians. The numbering of these photos indicates that some are missing. "Their removal could not have been intentional. Where are they?"

Fare than poses several rhetorical questions:

- Why would such a passionate collector be ready to relinquish valuable parts of his collection after having smuggled it across so many hostile borders during his flight from the encroaching Nazis?
- Why, in all the evidence gathered in Yugoslavia, was there no indication that Erich had left part of his collection behind in Paris?

And, the most obvious questions of all: how did Erich, who stayed in two-star hotels, support himself? How did he acquire such a collection?

Fare concludes: "A different personality might have provided us with more reassurance as to the origin... of such a large collection of art."

For his part, Fernand Cohen, the attorney for Sotheby's, treats Fare's report with disdain. He notes, for example, that it contains:

- Ten pages devoted to an investigation of the bank "which did not contain any new revelations."
- Four pages to Fare's fruitless search after Fabiani, the administrator of Vollard's estate.
- Two pages to his discovery that Denis Rouart, the author of the album on the Degas and Renoir works in the Belgrade museum, had died in 1984 during the course of his investigation.
- One page explaining how, despite his good connections, he was unable to establish contact with the Belgrade museum.

In his summary to the court, Cohen states:

> Without doubt, because [Fare] knows that he has done poorly, he abstained, before submitting his report, from claiming any addition to the very modest prepayment of 20,000 francs which was allocated to him by an order dated February 26, 1987, whereas Mr. Gondre, the court administrator, was awarded 190,000 francs for his silent participation in the expert's work.... It will be shown that, aside from various irregularities in his report, Mr. Fare has demonstrated in the execution of his mission a regrettable absence of competence and objectivity.

To overcome the shortcomings in the expert's report, Cohen traveled twice to Yugoslavia in 1990, to interview numerous people there familiar with the Šlomovič story and to gather crucial documents. Among the documents was an exhaustive catalog on the Šlomovič collection from the National Museum in Belgrade, which he gave to Fare, and which the latter promptly photostatted and included as a major part of his own report.

My own first exploratory trip to Yugoslavia came one month after Fernand Cohen's. The visit provided me, too, with a cornucopia of information that illuminated some of the darker passages of the Erich Šlomovič odyssey.

Chapter VI

GETTING TO THE SOURCE

Over the years, my interest in the Šlomovič story has waxed and waned. Every year or so I would call my former neighbors, Reuven and Dvora Goldfinger, to ask after the progress of the court case. "Still dragging on," was the invariable response.

By now the Goldfingers had moved to Rehovot, some fifteen miles south of Tel Aviv. Reuven continued to commute to his white-collar job in an electronics factory. But tragedy had caught up with them once again: their oldest son was killed in a traffic accident.

They had long given up hope of a victorious, i.e., remunerative, conclusion to their case. Instead, their endless court battles had turned into a frustrating mid-life struggle for vindication. By 1990 I decided to look into the story, with an eye to publishing it in book form. In May of that year my wife and I traveled to Yugoslavia to get a more personal sense of the Šlomovičs and their background.

A year earlier I had attended an international conference of Jewish journalists in Jerusalem. On a hunch, I had asked if there was any representative there from Yugoslavia.

"Yes, one from Belgrade," the organizer told me. "She's the editor of the *Jewish Bulletin* of the Yugoslav Jewish community. Her name is Lucy Petrovič. That's she, seated there in the auditorium."

I waited for the intermission to approach her. Lucy, a matronly woman of pleasant countenance and manner, was quick to answer my questions.

"Of course I know about the Šlomovič story," she said. "Mara and I are good friends."

"Mara Albahari? You mean she's alive?

"She's alive and well," Lucy told me, adding that Mara lived in Belgrade with her son David, a well-known author in Yugoslavia. She also had a daughter who lived not far from her. Mara's husband, Dr. Izak Albahari, had died only a short time before; he had suffered a stroke while on a visit to Jerusalem.

Lucy put me in touch with Mara's son David. The latter, in a most courteous and friendly letter, written in fluent English, said he would be glad to help me with my research. He doubted, however, that his mother would be ready to speak with me. "The subject is still too painful for her. But I know most of the story, anyway," he added.

My wife Carmela and I arrive in Yugoslavia in May 1990. We rent a car and drive through the mountains of Croatia where Tito's Partisans had saved several of my B-17 bomber crew comrades, shot down during the war. We take a ferry around the islands, which brings us within eyesight of the island Vis, Tito's headquarters during the last year of the war, and one of the places I had flown supplies to during those terrible days.

Belgrade: the Jewish Community offices are housed in a massive four-story building on a side street in one of the city's older quarters. Lucy Petrovič gives us a warm welcome. Her offices are on the fourth floor; we ride up in one of those turn-of-the-century glass-enclosed elevators, the brass, accordion-like door protesting loudly as it lets us in and belches us out.

Lucy briefs us, helps me make a few pertinent phone calls, and then directs us to the Jewish Museum two floors below. The museum is old and dimly lit. On its walls — a visual history of the ancient Jewish community of Yugoslavia from its early years of glory to its vale of tears in World War II. Among the pictures are photographs of Jewish men, women, and children being led through the streets of Belgrade to the two main death camps in the city. One of these is the Sajmište fairgrounds where Erich, his father, and his brother were gassed to death. Could the Šlomovič men be in these pictures. I peer closely at the faces on the wall, but they are blurred, as is the memory of those terrible events.

The following day David Albahari comes to our hotel room. We spend two hours talking. When he learns that my wife and I eat only kosher food, he invites us to his home. "Come meet my mother," he urges, "she will be ready to tell you her story."

My heart skips a beat.

The Albaharis live in Zemun, a suburb across the river Drava. As we drive over the bridge, we pass above Sajmište. There, on the riverbank, half-hidden within a glen of trees, we see the semi-abandoned structures of the old fairgrounds.

The countryside gives no hint of the horrors it had witnessed here.

David, his mother Mara, his wife Bojana, and their small son Natan live in one of the nondescript apartment buildings that clutter Belgrade's urban landscape.

The door opens as though of its own accord. Before us stands a peasant woman. She is of slight build, has a swarthy complexion and a face etched by her struggle against the hardships of life. Character, not beauty, has been her legacy. With a firm handshake and an unaffected smile, Mara ushers us into the living room. Her manner is simple, her speech direct, her mien stoic. I feel like a pearl diver who has just discovered a treasure. Only now have I come to the surface; my heart is racing, I am gulping for air.

A square antique table dominates the living room. We are invited to sit. Mara brings us the traditional sweets of the Sephardic, or Eastern, Jews. She talks. Her son and daughter-in-law translate.

I broach the subject of Erich gingerly, but Mara is prepared. She answers my questions in a steady, matter-of-fact voice. Once or twice a mournful expression flits across her weathered face. She shows me the album with photos of her two lost sons.

Mara was born in 1912 in what was, for the most part, a Moslem Bosnia. Her parents were Serbs. She had met Freddy Herzler, Erich Šlomovič's cousin, at a communal dance in the small Bosnian town of Dirvitia, and they were married in Croatia in 1931. She had converted to Judaism in 1937.

"The rabbi said I was crazy to do so," she recalls with a wry smile.

Their first son, Miroslav, was born in 1933, their second son, Aleksandar, in 1937. April 1941: the outbreak of war. Mara's husband serves briefly with the Yugoslav armed forces, is captured and disappears, one of the thousands of victims of the German-Ustashi murder network.

In August 1941, four months after the German blanket bombing of Belgrade, Mara and her two boys join the Šlomovič family in Belgrade. In December of the same year, they follow them into hiding in the village of Bacina.

"As a Serbian war refugee from Croatia, I was helped by the government. I also had documents which made traveling easier for me than for the Šlomovičs, who were Croatian by birth. In Bacina I lived near the Šlomovičs in a small apartment, with my two children... we supported ourselves by working for the farmers... we picked sugar beets and got food in return."

Mara would travel frequently by train to Belgrade to sell food products from the village or to trade them for other needed items. Thus she sustained the Šlomovič family. According to David, thousands of Jews were hidden in Serbia during the war, including one thousand in Belgrade. Ironically, in early 1942 the Germans had already declared that the "Jewish problem in Serbia was solved."

"There were two other Jewish refugees hiding in Bacina," Mara recalled, "the Pinto brothers. It is possible that one of them got drunk and blurted something out which eventually reached the Germans. The Šlomovič men were arrested sometime at the beginning of 1942. I didn't witness the arrest myself.[1]

"They didn't arrest Roza since, at the time, they were looking only for men. She was an older woman, and was soon forgotten by the Germans. I was protected by my documents, as a Serbian refugee from Bosnia."

Mara recounted how the men were first held in the temporary prison camp in the nearby town of Cuprija, where she and Roza would bring them fresh clothes and food every week.

"Around the third month we came and were told that the men had been taken elsewhere. Nobody could tell us where. Only later did I hear it was to Sajmište."

In September 1944 Bacina was liberated by advancing Soviet troops. Belgrade was liberated the following month. It was shortly after that Roza traveled to Belgrade to negotiate with Dr. Ribar regarding Erich's collection. Mara remembered that meeting and Roza's recounting of it.

"She told me that Dr. Ribar had promised to help the family get living quarters and a lifetime pension in return for the paintings." Roza and Mara had broken down the double wall. Then they had removed the metal cases holding Erich's collection. They gathered their belongings and, with the help of

1. The correct name was probably Putnik, not Pinto, as emerged from the testimony of their sister before the postwar Commission on War Crimes. The Putniks, like the Šlomovičs, were betrayed by a local collaborator, as I later discovered.

villagers, headed for Varvarin, six kilometers away, to load everything onto the special freight car that had been provided by Dr. Ribar. The train consisted mostly of freight cars, since there were no passenger carriages available in those early postwar days. The train was crowded with refugees who, like themselves, were making their way home to Belgrade.

At Velika Plana, halfway to Belgrade, their carriage was apparently torn loose from the rest of the train and was brought to a sharp stop. Mara got up to look out the window to see what had happened. As she did so, an oncoming train crashed into them. Because Mara was near the window, she was thrown clear to the ground. Her two boys, aged seven and eleven, and Roza were crushed to death — the only fatalities of the crash.

The train which crashed into them was carrying Bulgarian troops to the war front. Bulgaria, which had just been overrun by Soviet troops, had switched sides at the last moment and had sent troops through Yugoslavia to join Russian forces which were then (December 31, 1944) fighting in Hungary.[1]

"I suffered from internal injuries and shock and lay for three days in a hospital in a nearby town," Mara related. "It was there that Roza and my two children were buried. The railroad authorities recovered Erich's metal cases intact. I was helped by relatives to take them to Belgrade, where I got a room from the authorities. The keys to the metal cases and various documents which Roza was holding were lost."

While Mara was recovering, Judith Herzler, a cousin of Erich's, arrived in Belgrade from Switzerland where she had found refuge during the war. Judith was on her way to Palestine. The two consulted with friends and decided to give the cases for safekeeping to Veljko Petrovič, a merchant in Belgrade and a friend of Mara's.

"He had married a Jewish woman," Mara relates, "whose mother I had saved during the war. I smuggled her from Belgrade to Bacina on a train loaded with German soldiers."

Judith remarked to Mara that it was too bad she couldn't take the cases with her to Palestine.

1. Footnote p. 46 of manuscript

Mara was not aware of the value of the collection, nor did she care. About to remarry, she was eager to rebuild her life and put the past behind her. After her marriage to Dr. Albahari in October 1945, the couple moved to Pec in the province of Kosovo. Dr. Albahari was appointed chief of the gynecological department of the local hospital.

Around 9 p.m. one evening in December, Mara heard a loud knock on her door. Five plainclothes men from the Secret Service entered. For two years they had been searching for Erich's paintings. The search had been initiated by several artists who had known Erich and his collection before the war. Among them was Moise Pijade, one of the five most senior men in the Yugoslav government.

"I was pregnant then with my son David. My daughter, Belizia, had been born the pervious year. The police took my husband to the other room. The encounter was most unpleasant. I was interrogated by the leader of the group, Major Bora Neskovič. Right off, he accused me of absconding with the treasure. 'There,' he practically shouted at me. He was pointing to an unframed painting, leaning on a side table. It was a sketch by Degas that Erich had left with me. I also had Erich's original catalog from the Zagreb exhibition in 1940. He had made notations in it, indicating which paintings he had sold and to whom.

"I gave everything to Neskovič with a note to my friend, Veljko Petrovič, to hand over the iron cases. I couldn't give him the keys to the cases since they had been lost in the train crash. Neskovič kept pressing me about some offer to sell the collection to an American diplomat. I told him I knew nothing about it and that I was sure no one had opened the cases or touched the collection.

"I told him that Petrovič had nothing to do with the collection and that they should treat him fairly. Neskovič warned me that if anything was missing I would go to jail. The interrogation lasted until 2 a.m."

A few weeks later Mara received a phone call from Neskovič. Everything had been accounted for and she was in the clear.[1]

1. Footnote on document p. 48?

Chapter VII

ON PUBLIC VIEW FOR THE FIRST TIME

Nineteen eighty-nine. A spirit of liberalization engulfs Eastern Europe, sweeping away in its wake some of the communist cobwebs in Yugoslavia. The National Museum in Belgrade decides it is time to show Erich's collection to the public.

Until now the museum has put thirty items from the collection on permanent exhibition and kept the rest in storage. The displayed items were marked as belonging to the Erich Šlomovič collection, but they were interspersed among other works of the same period. Only after the Herzlers lost their case in the Yugoslav courts did the museum begin to identify the works. From time to time, they even took them out for special exhibitions in Yugoslavia and abroad. But only "safe" countries were chosen, usually venues that were behind the Iron Curtain, where the works could be safely identified as belonging to the Šlomovič collection. Only in 1988 did the museum allow the paintings to be shown in the West, in Stockholm and in Tokyo.

It is only toward the end of 1989 that the museum decides to mount a comprehensive exhibition. A total of 113 of the best works have been chosen and prepared for display as a unit, to be identified for the first time as the "Erich Šlomovič Collection." A comprehensive catalog is issued — another unprecedented event.

The exhibition is launched with a festive opening in Zagreb to mark the 50th anniversary of Erich's first and last showing there. (The date chosen, December 7, 1989, actually marks forty-nine years.) A few months later the exhibit is moved back to the museum in Belgrade. There it is launched with a similar festive opening, attended by the Minister of Culture and other VIPs.

Suddenly Mara Albahari is taken out of mothballs. Out of the blue, she is invited to Belgrade as an honored guest. She refuses to attend; her son David goes in her place.

My wife and I are fortunate to arrive in Belgrade in May 1990 while the exhibition is still in progress. With the help of the curator at the Jewish Museum, we are introduced to Irina Subotič, curator of fine arts at the National Museum and one of the organizers of the Šlomovič exhibition. Irina, who is attractive, trim, perky, with a close-cut crop of Slavic blond hair, is efficient and helpful — up to a point. On the more salient questions regarding the Yugoslavian court case, the inaccessibility of the collection for fifty years, and recent rumors of missing items, she is circumspect. She pleads ignorance. She refers me to her superiors.

Irina, together with her Belgrade and Zagreb colleagues, has issued a luxurious, full-color, 184-page catalog which not only identifies the exhibition as part of the "Šlomovič Collection," but also includes well-researched articles, photographs, and documents about Erich, ranging from his school days in Belgrade to his last days in hiding. In an appendix, there is a complete listing and description of all the Šlomovič items in the museum's possession.

The National Museum in Belgrade has no idea what a Pandora's box it has just opened.

The venue chosen for the inaugural exhibit in Zagreb is the Prostor Museum, formerly a Jesuit monastery, perched on a hill in the center of the city's old town. The organizers in Zagreb would have preferred to mount the collection in the Art Pavilion, where Erich had originally shown it in 1940. The Pavilion is an imposing building: circular white walls, majestic pillars. A place of serenity and reflection. It was designed by Ivan Mestrovič, Yugoslavia's preeminent artist and sculptor. But in 1989-1990, it is occupied by a permanent exhibition of the Partisan struggle during World War II.

The Prostor Museum is an eclectic institution which specializes in itinerant exhibits of every variety, from classical art to the history of the Yugoslav Jewish community. Unfortunately for the National Museum in Belgrade, it is directed by a staff of independent-minded people, original thinkers who are infused with a good dose of Croatian nationalism. For them, everything from Serbia is suspect.

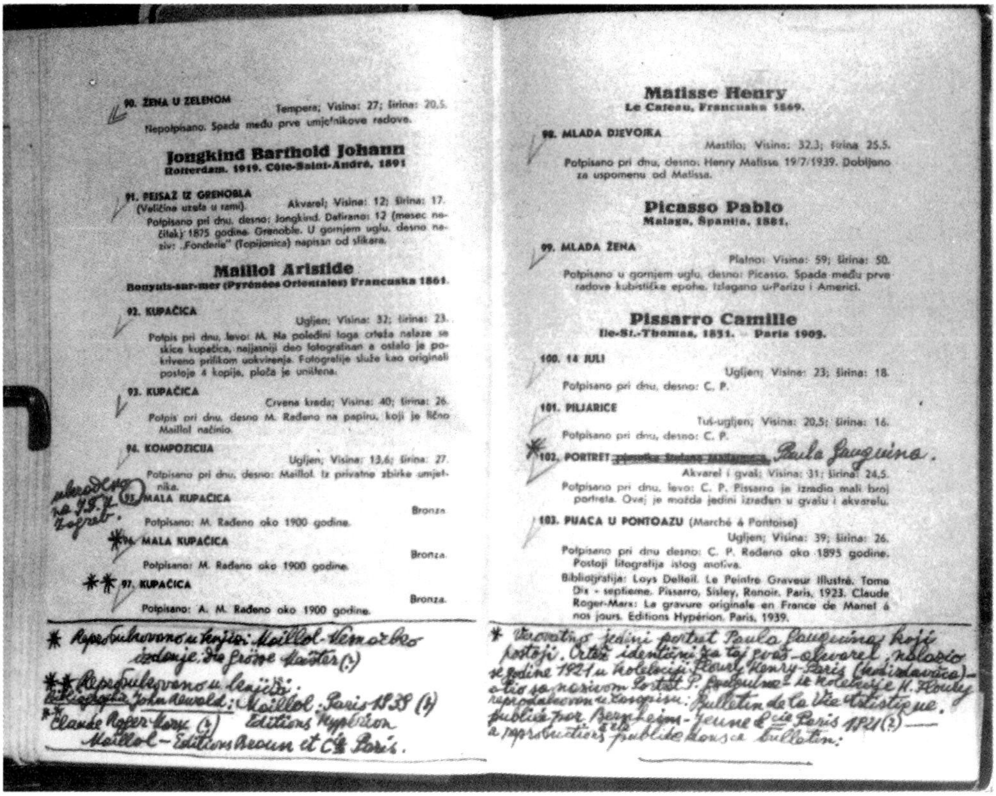

90. ŽENA U ZELENOM
Tempera; Visina: 27; širina: 20,5.
Nepotpisano. Spada među prve umjetnikove radove.

Jongkind Barthold Johann
Rotterdam, 1919. Côte-Saint-André, 1891

91. PEJSAŽ IZ GRENOBLA
(Veličine uzete u rami). Akvarel; Visina: 12; širina: 17.
Potpisano pri dnu, desno: Jongkind. Datirano: 12 (mesec nečitak) 1875 godine. Grenoble. U gornjem uglu, desno naziv: „Fonderie" (Topionica) napisan od slikara.

Maillol Aristide
Bonyuls-sur-mer (Pyrénées Orientales) Francuska 1861.

92. KUPAČICA
Ugljen; Visina: 32; širina: 23.
Potpis pri dnu, levo: M. Na poleđini toga crteža nalaze se skice kupačica, najjasniji deo fotografisan a ostalo je pokriveno prilikom uokvirenja. Fotografije služe kao originali postoje 4 kopija, ploča je uništena.

93. KUPAČICA
Crvena kreda; Visina: 40; širina: 26.
Potpis pri dnu, desno M. Rađeno na papiru, koji je lično Maillol načinio.

94. KOMPOZICIJA
Ugljen; Visina: 13,6; širina: 27.
Potpisano pri dnu, desno: Maillol. Iz privatne zbirke umjetnika.

95. MALA KUPAČICA
Bronza.
Potpisano: M. Rađeno oko 1900 godine.

96. MALA KUPAČICA
Bronza.
Potpisano: M. Rađeno oko 1900 godine.

97. KUPAČICA
Bronza.
Potpisano: A. M. Rađeno oko 1900 godine.

Matisse Henry
Le Cateau, Francuska 1869.

98. MLADA DJEVOJKA
Mastilo; Visina: 32,3; širina 25,5.
Potpisano pri dnu, desno: Henry Matisse 19/7/1939. Dobijeno za uspomenu od Matissa.

Picasso Pablo
Malaga, Španija, 1881.

99. MLADA ŽENA
Platno: Visina: 59; širina: 50.
Potpisano u gornjem uglu, desno: Picasso. Spada među prve radove kubističke epohe. Izlagano u Parizu i Americi.

Pissarro Camille
Ile-St.-Thomas, 1831. — Paris 1903.

100. 14 JULI
Ugljen; Visina: 23; širina: 18.
Potpisano pri dnu, desno: C. P.

101. PILJARICE
Tuš-ugljen; Visina: 20,5; širina: 16.
Potpisano pri dnu, desno: C. P.

102. PORTRET Paula Gauguina.
Akvarel i gvaš; Visina: 31; širina: 24,5.
Potpisano pri dnu, levo: C. P. Pissarro je izradio mali broj portreta. Ovaj je možda jedini izrađen u gvašu i akvarelu.

103. PIJACA U PONTOAZU (Marché à Pontoise)
Ugljen; Visina: 39; širina: 26.
Potpisano pri dnu desno: C. P. Rađeno oko 1895 godine. Postoji litografija istog motiva.
Bibliografija: Loys Delteil. Le Peintre Graveur Illustré. Tome Dix - septième. Pissarro, Sisley, Renoir. Paris, 1923. Claude Roger-Marx: La gravure originale en France de Manet à nos jours. Éditions Hypérion. Paris, 1939.

Mimeographed catalog on "cheap, greying paper" of missing items.

One of the organizers of the Zagreb exhibit is Vlado Buzancič, the stormy petrel of the art critics' fraternity in Yugoslavia. In his leading article in the catalog, he raises a specter.

He points out that of the 429 items exhibited by Erich in 1940, 19 were disposed of. Some were given away as gifts to artist friends who had helped Erich organize the Zagreb exhibit. Most were sold to rich collectors in Zagreb to help cover his expenses.[1]

This leaves 410 items, more or less. But the National Museum in Belgrade lists only 352 works in the present catalog.

Where, asks Buzancič, are the 58 missing works of art?

1. Footnote of document p. 49

"These works," he declares, "should be shown in a museum, not in private apartments, homes, or offices."

To reinforce this not-so-subtle accusation against the communist regime, Buzancič quotes passages from the booklet by Bora Neskovič, the Secret Service officer who had recovered the treasure from Mara in 1948. After having collected the four iron cases and one metal cylinder from Mara's friend in Belgrade, Neskovič ("partisan of the hour," as Buzancič describes him) had taken them to the offices of the Yugoslav Security Services. There, the paintings, wrapped in cloth, were carefully removed, photographed, cataloged, and compared with Erich's original catalog from the Zagreb exhibit.

Since the original catalog also contained Erich's handwritten notations, indicating which items had been sold or given away and to whom, it was possible to make an exact accounting. Moise Pijade had been called in at that time as an art expert and as one familiar with Erich and his collection.

Then, notes Buzancič, "the collection was removed and put in the hands of an official body, not named." The National Museum in Belgrade was thus the second, not the first institution to receive the works of art from the police. It was at this juncture, Buzancič implies, that some sixty or more works of art disappeared. The assumption is that they found their way into the hands of various communist and government officials and their cronies.

To add insult to injury, Buzancič and his colleagues mount a special display during the last two weeks of the exhibit in Zagreb, under the title: "Searching for the Truth about the Erich Šlomovič Collection." They hang fifty blank frames alongside the Šlomovič works, with the name of a painting in each blank space, accompanied by a large question mark and the query: "Where is this painting?"

To twist the knife a little further into the heart of the National Museum in Belgrade, the Zagreb organizers issue a special catalog to accompany their incendiary display. Simply mimeographed on cheap, greying paper, and interspersed with badly reproduced black-and-white photographs of the allegedly missing items, the catalog renders a precise accounting and description of these works. Among them are twenty works by Rodin, eleven by Degas, six by Bonnard, eight by Picasso, and eight by Yugoslav artists.

Buzancič notes further that, of the 352 items listed in the Belgrade catalog, 49 were not shown in Zagreb in 1940. Among them were works by such Post-

Impressionists as Leger and Braque, which Erich had mentioned to journalists as being in his possession.

In other words, Erich kept these works, and perhaps others, for himself and hid them later in the iron cases. This would make for a total of 459 items (i.e., the original 429, minus some 19 disposed of in 1940, plus the above 49). If one then subtracts the 352 listed in the 1989 Belgrade catalog from the 459 which should have been there, one arrives at 107 missing items.

Buzancič has a point, but he exaggerates.

On December 27, 1989, the National Museum received from the State Bureau for the Preservation of Cultural Treasures all or most of the twenty-four Vollard art albums listed in the original Zagreb catalog. They had been stored for forty years, gathering dust and moisture, and were in a partially deteriorated condition. Because of their late delivery they were not included in the catalog that accompanied the anniversary exhibitions in Zagreb and Belgrade and were thus erroneously listed by Buzancič as missing.

Their sudden appearance clarifies the issue raised by Buzancič about the whereabouts of the collection after it left the Security Services. It was the State Bureau for the Preservation of Cultural Treasures, and not the National Museum, which had received the collection from the Security Services. This is what Buzancič had claimed earlier when he wrote that the Security Service had passed the collection on to an "unnamed body." This same State Bureau had kept the collection for several months before turning it over in 1949 to the National Museum in Belgrade. But when it turned the collection over, the art albums were missing.

Why?

The official reason: the custodians at the Bureau could not decide whether the albums should go to the National Library or the National Museum.

Why has it taken forty years to decide?

No one can say for sure. The word "bureaucracy" is bantered about as a possible excuse. But Buzancič's list would not have to be reduced by the twenty-four art albums recently added to the collection in the National Museum. Deduct another eight missing ceramics, which were probably broken or lost in the train crash, and Buzancič's list will have to be whittled down further.

We still have seventy items or more unaccounted for.

The art albums contain hundreds of original sketches and engravings, art works of France's leading artists, commissioned by Vollard to illustrate his albums. But many of these illustrations — mostly original lithographs — are missing, perhaps removed from the albums by the time they arrived at the National Museum in 1989.

A thorough search revealed that many of the missing lithographs and sketches had somehow become a part of the museum's Šlomovič collection, and were listed accordingly in the 1989 catalog. It is thus difficult to come up with the precise numbers of missing works. Buzancič pointed out that some items had been listed singly in the 1940 catalog, whereas actually they were part of a series.

The best guess is that the missing items disappeared during their sojourn with the Security Services, and later with the Bureau for the Preservation of Cultural Treasures. There is evidence that someone had tampered with the art albums while they were in the custody of the Bureau.

Buzancič regarded Aleksandar (Marko) Rankovič, then minister of the interior, as responsible for the thefts. The Security Services, for whom Bora Noskovič worked, were under the authority of the Interior Ministry. Rankovič, who had been a senior member of the Partisan Supreme Command during World War II, held the rank of vice-premier as well as of interior minister. He was considered the number three man in the communist hierarchy after Tito.

Buzancič assumes that the Security Services, together with the Bureau for the Preservation of Cultural Treasures, "sold some of the items for much-needed foreign currency, and distributed the rest to communist cronies." The easiest items to dispose of, of course, were those additional works of art which Šlomovič never exhibited and which never reached the National Museum. But Buzancič, in his special catalog of the missing items, also lists dozens of works which were included in the 1940 Zagreb catalog, but not in the Belgrade Museum catalog of 1989.

Early 1992. I meet Buzancič at the richly furnished wood-lined artists' club in Zagreb. All the museums in town are closed as a continuing precaution against aerial bombing. In 1991, when civil war erupted following Croatia's declaration of independence, the city had been badly bombed.

Buzancič: a tall, blustering, fifty-three-year-old man with a typical Croatian mustache. He makes his points forcefully, waves his arms around a great deal, gesticulates from time to time at a pile of documents, and raises his decibels for emphasis.

Buzancič was one of the few journalists in Yugoslavia to raise his voice against the communist establishment, when it was not yet fashionable to do so. The fact that the establishment against which he railed was in Belgrade, the capital of Serbia, only served to strengthen his Croatian credentials.

"Once, for three months," he boasts, "I was under surveillance by the Secret Police." But he dismisses the incident with a twist of his wrist and a hearty guffaw.

Buzancič believes that sixty percent of Erich's collection originated with Vollard, twenty percent came as gifts from artists — as evidenced by the personal dedications — and twenty percent were purchased directly, with a lot of wheeling and dealing, by Erich himself.

"As Vollard aged, he became more generous and also more dependent on Erich, who had great energy and ambition. Vollard built him up with the artists and also gave him many albums with original art work, which Erich augmented from the artists themselves.

"Erich wanted to be somebody, a big collector, a rich merchant... he wanted to create a museum in Zagreb of French art, together with Yugoslav art, a sort of East-West institute of art and culture."

"Why Zagreb, why not the capital, Belgrade?"

"Because the museum was under the control of Prince Paul, who also had his personal collection there, and Prince Paul was playing cozy with the Germans. The Nazis had declared French art degenerate and decadent. There was general fear of Germany then, and also a general atmosphere of anti-Semitism. Prince Paul was probably jealous as well and did not want another exhibit of French art competing with his own collection of French art... also Erich may have been tactless in the way he went about it."

"But why Zagreb? In the war the Croatian Ustashi arrested and murdered more Jews and Serbs than the Nazis did!"

"True. But the Ustashi represented no more than five or ten percent of the population. The Germans put them in power and imposed them on Croatia.

They also murdered plenty of Croatians. Tito was a Croatian. Also, you've got to remember that Croatia was for many centuries part of the Austro-Hungarian empire, and was thus closer to the West than Serbia, which was under Turkish domination."

The reader might recall that Prince Paul Kargeorgevič was the regent in Yugoslavia before the outbreak of World War II. He favored a policy of appeasement toward Germany. On March 25, 1941, at a secret meeting in Vienna with von Ribbentrop and Count Ciano, the German and Italian foreign ministers, Yugoslavia acceded to the Three-Power Pact of the Axis powers.

Word of the agreement leaked out. Two days later, on March 27, popular demonstrations broke out in protest. These were followed by a *coup d'état* which toppled Prince Paul and his government. Prince Paul was arrested and deported by his own people. Hitler flew into a rage. April 6 Hitler's bombers began a three-day methodical destruction of Belgrade.

Next: German troops invaded Yugoslavia.

Historians agree that this diversion delayed Hitler's invasion of the Soviet Union from May to the end of June, thus bringing his troops to the gates of Moscow as winter set in. It was "General Winter" that stopped Hitler, as much as the Soviet resistance.

The Šlomovič family was in Belgrade during the bombing. A friend of Erich's recalls seeing him in the Red Cross air raid shelter, near his home in central Belgrade. She describes him, uncharitably, as sitting on a trunk "feverishly holding his wealth."[1]

In his article in the 1989 catalog, Buzancič writes:

> Erich was better known for the stories about him than for his worth as a human being... more was written about the mystery surrounding him than about the art itself. From 1948 to date, no space has been devoted to him in the National Museum in Belgrade, except for a number of items on permanent display, and others taken on tour from time to time.

---

1. Footnote on p. 54 of manuscript.

In the six or seven years of his career, Erich performed miracles and should be considered among Yugoslavia's artistic elite. No one like him has appeared in Yugoslavia before the war or until now. Who else living in Yugoslavia or abroad has ever brought to the country works of such world-famous masters?

Buzancič then goes on to speculate what Erich's attitude might have been toward a Yugoslavia turned communist: "One wonders whether Erich would have stayed in such a Yugoslavia or have preferred to return to Paris where he could have revived his contacts (without Vollard, it is true) .... Or would he have accepted life in Yugoslavia where private property had been abolished? Without money or possibilities to do business... he could always have chosen Israel ...."

And so the story comes full circle, to myself, a journalist in Israel. With the confidence that statehood bestows, I can afford to fight for the rights of a disenfranchised family, to be intrigued by the mystery of an entrepreneur, not much more than a youth, who made a killing in the art world at the outset of World War II. But the story is yet unfinished, for the art collection is still in the museums of Paris and Belgrade, and justice has not yet been served.

Chapter VIII

SECRET POLICE TRACK DOWN THE TREASURE

Bora Neskovič's version of his encounter with Mara Albahari paralleled hers, but with a number of inaccuracies and distortions.

In July 1969 he wrote a series of articles in *Borba*, Yugoslavia's leading daily newspaper, telling how he had tracked down the collection after the war and saved it for the Yugoslav state. Unfortunately for him, man landed on the moon around the same time and the public didn't pay much attention to his revelations.

In 1987, already thirty-five years retired from the Security Services, Neskovič published a booklet entitled *The Odyssey of the French Impressionists*, based on the articles in *Borba*. The booklet, which was written in the third person in a transparent attempt to conceal Neskovič's role, was followed in 1989 by an extensive article in Belgrade's leading newspaper *Politika*, this time in the first person, adding new information on the "odyssey." The article was timed to coincide with the opening of the anniversary exhibit of the Šlomovič collection in Zagreb, to which Bora Neskovič had been invited.

Neskovič began his professional career in 1935 as a copy editor for *Politika* and subsequently for *Avala* (later *Tanjug*), Yugoslavia's principal news agency. With the outbreak of war in 1941 he joined the Partisans, rising to the rank of major. After the war he was employed by the Bureau of National Security (UDB) and was involved in investigations connected with the trials of Draza Mihailovic and Andrija Hebrang (both later convicted of treason).

In 1947 Neskovič was assigned by the Security Services to locate the Šlomovič collection. The Secret Service had been eavesdropping on the American diplomatic mission in Belgrade and had come to the conclusion that some unknown persons in the city had offered to sell a large collection of art to a Mr. Clifford, the cultural attaché at the American embassy.

Neskovič consulted some of his former newspaper colleagues, including the noted cartoonist Pjer Krizanovič, who surmised that this could very well be the Šlomovič collection. Krizanovič had known Erich before the war and had once drawn a caricature of him that had become part of the collection. Erich was rumored to have had an affair with Krozanovič's wife Liza.

Neskovič next approached Moise Pijade and Dr. Ivan Ribar, at that time vice-president and president, respectively, of the National Assembly. Pijade recalled seeing Erich's exhibition in Zagreb after the war and making a portrait of Erich in oil at that time, but he knew nothing of his fate after that. Pijade, among the top five men in Tito's ruling circle and a leading artist and man of letters in his own right, asked to be kept informed of the investigation's results.

Ribar recalled his meeting with Erich's mother, Roza, and the fact that she had never shown up again after he had arranged the special train carriage for her. Perhaps, he speculated, she had changed her mind about giving the collection to the state. Ribar, under the pressure of state affairs, had not pursued the matter further.

In his booklet, Neskovič reconstructs the encounter between Roza and Dr. Ribar, using the strained hyperbole of a Secret Service operative turned author:

> Only 15 days had passed since the liberation of Belgrade after a long and cruel occupation. Military patrols guarded government institutions and offices. In the capital, life was getting back to normal. People working tirelessly day and night. A special atmosphere pervaded the former royal palace in which AVNOJ [the provisional parliament] was now located.

On a November day [in 1944], in an interval between two meetings, a dispute occurred in front of the cabinet of the president of AVNOJ.

"I must see Dr. Ribar," begged the little old lady with her eyes full of tears. She was pleading with the secretary of the cabinet, gesticulating with her hands, because she had been waiting there more than three hours for the meeting in the president's office to end.

The secretary was trying to reassure her: "I told you that the comrade president cannot see anyone today. Please come tomorrow in the morning."

The old lady opened her teary eyes: "Listen to me, to what I am telling you. I have come from the countryside. Dr. Ribar is a friend of mine."

She then took out a note from her purse and handed it to the secretary.

"Please give this to Dr. Ribar."

The secretary took the note — on which only two words were written, the first and last names of the old lady. The secretary didn't know what to do since the president had told her that after the lengthy meeting he wanted to be left in peace to review some documents. The secretary nevertheless entered his office and, apologizing, told him that he had a visitor from the interior.

"Is this possible?" said the president in an astonished tone as he read the name on the note. "Can it be that old Roza has survived this terrible war in which the Jews were destroyed without mercy?"

A few minutes later when the elderly and weary lady stepped into his office, Dr. Ribar rose to meet her and without a word took Roza Šlomovič by the hand and seated her next to him. Ribar was deeply moved since he had known Roza and her family for many years before the war. The old lady was sobbing. For a long time she couldn't say a word. Dr. Ribar collected himself and then asked her about her husband and two sons. She let out a deep sigh. For a few moments they looked at each other without words.

Then Roza, amid tears, told him the tragic story of herself and her family.... The tragedies of the two families had united the two parents in grief. [As will be recalled, Ribar had lost his two sons and wife in the war; Erich had gone to school with the sons.]

Neskovič proceeds to tell the Šlomovič saga in elaborate and often mistaken detail, interspersing it with his story of the search for the treasure. After a particularly flowery and imaginary description of the train accident, Major Ilič (as he calls himself) gives the text of the cable sent by the railroad authorities, at the scene of the accident, to their head office in Belgrade:

> Attention, attention all. This morning at 3 a.m. on the open railroad track, seven kms. Before Velike Plana, a special freight train with Bulgarian troops crashed at full speed into a mixed passenger and

> freight train. Several cars of the mixed train were destroyed. The last car completely crushed and thrown off the tracks. Three brakemen of the mixed train injured. In the crushed car two small children and an elderly woman killed. Younger woman suffered light concussion. Locomotive of special Bulgarian train also damaged. Investigation under way. According to testimony of personnel of mixed train, at the moment of the crash there was dense fog and visibility was poor. The engineer/driver of the special Bulgarian train only noticed the other train at the last moment so that braking did not help. Send workers with crane to clear the tracks.

After recounting how Mara recovered from the accident and left the paintings with her merchant friend in Belgrade, Neskovič returns to the story of his search for the treasure. It was at the horse races in the Belgrade hippodrome, he writes in his booklet, that "Major Ilič" got his first concrete lead on the treasure's whereabouts. The clue came from an acquaintance, Radoslav Panič, a former cavalry officer in the Yugoslav army, whom Ilič happened to meet at the horse races.

During the war Panič was wounded in the brief fight against the invading Germans and went into hiding in his native village of Mala Krusevioca. The village happened to be only some twelve miles from Bacina, where the Šlomovičs were hiding at the time, and Panič and his wife, who apparently had known them previously, had been in contact with them.

While recovering in his village he was mustered, reluctantly, into the pro-royalist, largely collaborationist, Cetnik forces and served with them as adjutant to one of their top commanders, General Dronja Trifumovič. Panič soon made contact with the Partisans and began feeding them intelligence on the Cetniks. When the Russian forces swept through his battlefront, toward the end of 1944, he joined them and helped them pursue and capture a number of Cetnik commanders. He also turned over vital Cetnik documents to the Partisans.

Under the influence of the xenophobic Soviet NKVD secret services, which became all-powerful in Yugoslavia after the war, the new Yugoslav government subsequently arrested Panič on charges of wartime collaboration with the

Cetniks and the Germans. In the ensuing investigation, in which Neskovič took part, Panič was cleared of all charges and released from prison. As Neskovič wrote in his booklet: "There was no proof that Panič participated in Cetnik war crimes. He had no blood on his hands."[1]

When Neskovič met him and his wife, by chance, at the races, Panič was chief instructor for a leading riding club in Belgrade and the holder of many trophies for riding competitions abroad and in Yugoslavia. In the ensuing conversation Neskovič mentioned that he was looking for the Šlomovič art treasure and Panič's wife, Eva, exclaimed: "Why, I knew the Šlomovičs during the war."

Was this the break Neskovič (alias Major Ilič) had been waiting for? He invited the couple aside to hear their story:

> When Erich, his father Bernard, mother Roza, and brother Egon escaped from Belgrade in 1941, they took shelter in Varvarin at the home of the lawyer Marinovič, Panič and his wife recounted. The lawyer, born in Croatia, was married to a woman from this region. Unfortunately, Marinovič was killed in 1943 by the Cetniks.

From a subsequent conversation with the Šlomovič family, Panič and his wife learned that Marinovič recommended them to friends in the village of Bacina and took them there, five kms. Away from Varvarin. Here Marinovič brought Šlomovič to the mayor, Ljupceta Pantič, who agreed to put them up in his own large house.

"I went several times to visit the Šlomovič family there," Eva Panič recalled. "In the fall of 1941 considerable German forces started foraging in the villages, spread out along the railroad track between Belgrade and Nis. I warned the Šlomovič family that they were not safe in Bacina.

"I suggested to them several times that one of their sons should come to our village of Mala Krusevica and the other son should be placed in another village, Karanovač. But it didn't help. To the father and mother I offered that they should

1. Neskovič did not reveal in his booklet that Panič was rearrested by the Tito government two years later, together with his wife, that Panič committed suicide in jail, and that his wife emigrated to Israel in 1966. More on that later.

come to Cernica. I mentioned that in these villages they would be safer because they would be further away from the main communication centers.

"The parents answered with silence.

"In the end I told the family that these mountain villages were safe and that in this region, already a very large (and well-known) family, Tajcatak, from Krusevica, was in hiding. The Tajcatak family, of Jewish origin, survived the war.

"The Šlomovičs replied that their safety was guaranteed by the mayor in whose house they were living. They were adamant about staying in their present residence in Bacina. They wouldn't accept our advice at all. Something tied them down to the house in Bacina as if it was their own."

And what was it that tied them so strongly, asked the investigator.

"We had no idea and we couldn't understand what it could have been," answered Panič's wife.

Was the Šlomovič family rich, and if so did they bring their wealth to the village?

"As far as I know," said Panič's wife, "we knew each other from Slovenia where I lived before the war...."

The investigator concluded that Panič and his wife had no idea that Erich Šlomovič could have brought his art collection to the village and hidden it there....

Meanwhile the elderly Šlomovič and his sons were taken by the Germans at the end of 1941, supposedly to use them as interpreters for the German punitive expedition sent to clear the nearby Juhora mountain region of the Partisans. They were never heard from again.

"Do you know what happened with the elderly mother?" the major asked Eva Panič.

"The elderly Šlomovič lady was still alive in the autumn of 1944 as far as I know. My husband and I visited her often. At that time in Bacina a distant woman relative [i.e., Mara] with two children lived with Roza Šlomovič and took care of her during the occupation. What happened to the two ladies and the two children I do not know."

In 1991 I managed to locate Eva Panič. She was living in Israel with her second husband at Kibbutz Sha'ar Ha'amakim near Haifa, where she had settled upon her arrival in the country in 1966. Her last name was now Nahir. A small, wiry lady, already seventy-three but radiating an elemental life-force, nurtured by self-confidence and determination, she confirmed the essence of Neskovič's tale but with some corrections and additions.

Her recollections were interspersed with bitter remarks on the Tito regime and on Neskovič himself, who she felt could have done more to help exonerate her husband when he was rearrested two years after the 1948 encounter with Neskovič at the racetrack. Eva was also arrested shortly afterward, but managed in 1953 to get out before her husband and made her way to Israel. Her husband, however, losing hope of being exonerated by the very people he had helped in the war, committed suicide in jail in 1951.

Eva's wartime visit to Bacina to warn the Šlomovičs to seek another hiding place occurred only once, not several times as in Neskovič's tale. She went alone, without her husband, hitching a ride for the twenty-kilometer journey in a farmer's buggy. It was toward the end of 1941.

"Many people in the village seemed to know that Jews were hiding there so I had no problem finding them. The people in the village were Serbs and wouldn't betray them. But I knew the area was controlled by the Cetniks.

"The Šlomovičs lived together in a spacious house of a well-to-do family. I found them all seated in the living room. Before me I saw a typical well-to-do, Jewish bourgeois family, well dressed, cultured, and unaware of what was going on in the world around them. I noticed Erich especially. He was very handsome and quiet; he seemed a bit bashful.

"These people were unlike my husband and me. We had both been active politically before the war in the socialist movement and were well aware of what was going on.

"I told them: 'You're crazy to stay here. Your village sits on a paved road frequented by the Germans. It's full of Cetniks and enemies of the Jews. They'll be jealous of your wealth and could easily betray you to the Germans.'

"I explained to them that my husband's village could be reached only by a dirt road which the Germans, even with their motorcycles, were too lazy to travel on. They nodded but said they felt quite secure in Bacina. The people there took good care of them. They were trustworthy and would not betray them. They even invited me to come and stay in their village.

"I tried to persuade them. I told them that with their money they could easily get a place to hide. But nothing helped. After an hour and a half I raised my hands and left. Later, I heard that the Šlomovič men were arrested a few days after my visit."

In his booklet, Neskovič fills in other details:

> The major left the hippodrome without waiting for the races to end. He could not sleep that night and at 0710 the next morning took a jeep from his headquarters and headed for Bacina. There he sought the wartime mayor, Ljupce.

At the mention of the name Šlomovič the mayor started up and recalled that the family was brought to him by a friend who said they were rich people and asked that they be taken into the mayor's house.

"I arranged with the family to send them a vehicle to Varvarin in order to collect their household goods and baggage, which were transferred on Varvarin's market day in one vehicle while the family came in another vehicle."

The arrival of the Šlomovič family in the village did not attract much attention since it was not unusual, the mayor pointed out. A great number of people came there after the bombardment of Belgrade (on April 6, 1941) to escape to the interior of Serbia to find refuge with family and friends....

"Meanwhile," the mayor continued, "I temporarily put the Šlomovič family into one of the larger rooms in my house. As mayor, one of my duties was to be in charge of settling refugees in the village. Since I found dwellings for them in the village homes it was only right that I also take someone into my own house.

"The Šlomovičs were rich people, and their son Erich emphasized this from the first day. Many times he said that he would pay well for everything, including lodging and food. They did pay honorably.

"After a few days, as we got used to each other and drew closer, Erich Šlomovič spoke to me eye to eye and told me that the metal boxes which he brought with him contained paintings and books which to him personally represented the greatest of treasures. He told me that he wished to keep them safe for the rest of the war and asked me where he could find a hiding place for them.

"Because my house was too small for both my folks and the Šlomovič family," continued Ljupce, "I suggested to Erich that he, his father, mother, and brother move to the house of Dusan Spasič, who had a large house next door to the municipality. His wife lived alone in the house because he was working in Jagovina as a policeman and only came home from time to time. As for the articles in the metal containers, I agreed with Erich to have them transferred in greatest secrecy to a third location in order to be sure that the Germans wouldn't find them if they should search my house or Spasič's. Erich agreed because I gave him my word that the house of Marisav Ristič, which I had selected, would be secure.

"As agreed so it was done. Sometime later I arranged for the Šlomovičs to be transferred to the house of Spasič, and Erich and I took the cases secretly to Ristič where they were put into a [double] wall so that neither the Ristič family nor the other people in the house knew anything about it."

How did they live in general? asked the major.

"Since they lived near the municipality we saw each other every day. They were, so to speak, under my constant protection. Every day I supplied Erich with newspapers and other news."

Further conversation with the former mayor revealed that the Šlomovičs never left the village. They even avoided the company of their neighbors. The villagers explained this behavior as the result of their misfortunes, like many refugees from Belgrade who had lost their homes in the bombardment.

"News from the papers often disturbed them," Ljupce related, "because they realized the war was spreading and the end could not be foreseen. The Šlomovičs had come to Bacina with a distant relative of theirs name Maca [Mara]. Her husband was killed in the war and she was left alone with two children. She and her children were placed in the house of Milan Soskič, my good friend whose house was across the street from the Spasičs. Maca was at the Šlomovičs' every day."

It was already well past midnight as the investigator listened silently to the mayor's story.

"The life of the Šlomovič family was peaceful and pleasant until the late fall of 1941 when the situation deteriorated. The Germans were coming into the villages more frequently to forage and search along the Morava River. They also came into our village, asking about Partisans, always in daytime.

"You know how it was. In the whole country the guns were firing, bridges and railroads were flying in the air. The Germans felt unsafe even in the cities. At the end of November and the beginning of December, the Germans started bringing in reinforcements. Winter was on the threshold and the Partisan movement in our region was felt more and more. One day big columns of Germans came along the road from Varvarin.

"The news went through the village that the Germans were starting an offensive against the Partisans. I was called into my office in the municipality. There, an officer asked me for guides and an interpreter. Somebody suggested that we call the Šlomovičs, assuming they knew German. The Germans ordered that all three Šlomovič men come immediately to the municipality.

"I went to the Spasič home where I found Erich and his family. They were very nervous. At that moment Erich turned to me and said: 'Ljupce, take this as a souvenir in case we don't return.' He removed from his left hand a golden Schafhausen wristwatch and handed it to me, saying that I should take care of his mother and his art collection." Ljupce opened his shirtsleeve and showed the watch, which he still possessed.

"The only thing left over from the Šlomovič family is a book and notes which Erich asked me to keep. He told me then, 'If anything happens to us and we do not survive the war, it will be known from these [documents] who the Šlomovičs were and what they had.'

"The Germans placed the Šlomovič men with their troops and together they headed toward the Juhora mountains.

"... As I said," continued Ljupce, "the Šlomovičs did not return after this German punitive search mission. The old lady Šlomovič was desperate. I can't describe her pain and suffering. Still, the poor woman kept hoping during the entire war to at least hear about her husband and children, but no voice was heard.

"During the entire occupation their relative, Maca, stayed near the old lady. She would inquire among the villagers and other people about who had been released from jails and concentration camps, whether they had heard anything of the missing men. In the village there was talk that Maca was trading in merchandise along the railroad track between Stalač and Lapovo."

What were the old lady and the two children living on?

"Roza Šlomovič had money. Perhaps she also had gold and other valuables which Maca converted into money, but I believe this was all of secondary importance. To Maca this served as an excuse to get out of the village and circulate in the area among the villages and to inquire about the fate of the Šlomovič men. She also returned with new information and this gave hope to old Roza and kept her from dying of pain and sorrow.

"Old Roza sometimes accompanied Maca to Cuprija, to where they took food packages which she gave to the administration of the detention camp there (the Šlomovič men were being held there temporarily). After a while the administration refused to accept the packages (since the men had been transferred to the Sajmište death camp), an event which hit Roza very hard. She began to lose hope that the men were still alive...."

When did the women leave the village and where to? Major Ilič asked the former mayor.

"Since this part of the country and Belgrade were already liberated (in November 1944), Roza and Maca traveled to Belgrade. They came back after two or three days and announced that a good friend of Roza's had made it possible for them to move to Belgrade."

Since their departure didn't you even hear anything of the Šlomovičs until now, nor about her companion... what do you know about Maca... where did she come from... what was her last name?

"She arrived in the village with her two children after the Šlomovičs. They knew her previously. Her husband was killed in the war... she was always traveling somewhere. Everybody knew her as Maca. People at that time did not register [with the authorities] because they already had papers of their own.

"I know that her former husband was Jewish and that he was killed. But Maca had her papers in her maiden name so she was not under suspicion. In time of war all this was normal and not unusual. There were a lot of refugees in the village and we accepted all of this calmly. All I knew was that she was a refugee."

...Ljupce shows the book and notes [he got from Erich] to the major.... On the book's front cover, already worn, is a painting of a ballerina under which was written "French Art from the Collection of Erich Chlomovitch." This was the catalog from Erich's 1940 exhibit in Zagreb... the mayor leafs through and sees the names of the famous artists... "there was no doubt that the art collection being offered to Clifford [of the U.S. embassy in Belgrade] must be from the Šlomovič collection."

In 1992 I visited Bacina and found several of the people still living, who had hidden the Šlomovič family and the art collection. Their story added some fascinating and ominous details to Neskovič's recollections. More on that later.

* * *

Neskovič returned to Belgrade stirred by what he had heard in Bacina. But none the wiser as to the treasure's whereabouts since no one there knew what had happened to it after the train accident.

He decided to follow up on the alleged offer of French art to the American cultural attaché, Clifford. In the process, the Secret Service operative gives some rare insights into the regime's methods of snooping on foreign legations, including planting secretaries in their offices. In the end, the trail leads to a dead end since both the seller and buyer got cold feet. As Neskovič put it, "Suddenly the investigation began to unravel."

Neskovič decided to try and trace the collection along the railway line where the accident occurred. He soon discovered a railroad worker who remembered Maca's (Mara's) frequent traveling along the line during the war.

"Yes," the railway worker recalled, "she told me that she was a refugee, that she had lost her husband and had to take care of her children now... she wouldn't say exactly what she was doing... but she was traveling a lot, selling and buying."

Did you see Maca after the war? The major asked.

"I met her once when she was in Kraljevo. We greeted each other and she told me that she had remarried after the war and that she lived with her husband in the area of Kosovo... her husband had been working in a hospital in Serbia before their marriage...."

The investigator proceeded to the region of Kosovo.... After checking at several hospitals he finally heard that an anesthesiologist, with a wife named Maca and two children, worked at a sanatorium in Pec.... Assisted by the local intelligence center... he checked at the sanatorium as to when he could find the doctor there.... He found that on that day he would be on night duty... that his wife was not working... she was shortly before giving birth and therefore she was at home... so he decided to go directly to her home.

In the room in which he found Maca, he was most astonished: on a desk resting against a lamp was the painting *Ballerina in Blue,* standing frameless, attached to a large piece of carton. The investigator looked at the painting and saw the name Degas written on the bottom. This told him everything. He looked at the woman and then at the ballerina.

He addressed the woman: "During the war you lived in the village of Bacina. You knew the Šlomovič family. The painting on the desk is from that collection, is that not so?" the major said calmly.

The woman replied silently, nodding her head.

Not wanting to tire her out at such a late hour and shortly before giving birth... [after various questions] Maca told how Roza had got help from Dr. Ribar... a special rail carriage... how she, Roza and the two children traveled on the train in the same car in which all the household goods and the art collection were stored... about the collision at Velika Plana with the Bulgarian military train in the middle of the night... she started crying and told how her children and Roza were killed....

The investigator... came to the point and asked her where the containers with the art works now were.

She replied that they were in Belgrade at the home of the former merchant Veljko Petrovič....

Are you sure they weren't already sold to someone?

The woman turned around, went to the closet and took out something wrapped in paper. Unwrapping it she revealed a set of keys. Handing them over to the investigator, Maca said: "These are the keys to the metal boxes. I guarantee that the paintings have not been sold."

He wanted her to come to Belgrade with him, but she said it was too difficult in her present condition and instead gave him a note addressed to Petrovič requesting that he give the investigator the collection. He asked Maca to wrap up the *Ballerina in Blue* and cautioned her that she would have to give an accounting of how she came to possess it. He also told her to keep everything secret and not tell anyone about what had transpired.

Major Ilič promptly proceeded to Mara's friend in Belgrade, Veljko Petrovič.... On the way to the warehouse where he had sequestered the iron containers, Petrovič said to the investigator: "I have no connection with the collection. I only consented to take it for safekeeping because it belonged to a family that perished in the war. I will hand it over to you the way I received it."

Neskovič continues with his story:

On reaching the warehouse Petrovič knocked on the door three times. From inside, movement could be heard. Only after Petrovič repeated his knock was the door opened. Two young men came forward as Petrovič entered with his escort. Petrovič ordered them to get the containers and hand them over to the man in uniform who accompanied him. The two frightened men turned around and quickly opened the door to a storage room, from which they removed three metal containers. The third was the largest. They were all fastened with large chain locks.

They then removed a fourth long metal container, which had a cover on one side fastened with a lock and chain.

"There are the containers I received for safekeeping," said Petrovič calmly.

The major asked the two men to help load the containers into the jeep and instructed the driver to take them to the conference room next to the chief investigator's officer and then to return and take Petrovič back home. When the driver left with the boxes, Major Ilič asked Petrovič to come out to the street and wait for the jeep to return.

While pacing in front of the shop, Petrovič said, "Believe me, I got involved in this matter in good faith. I took a very great responsibility upon myself."

You know that this type of matter involves certain legal responsibilities, said the major. We will talk about it at a later date. You'll be called upon or I'll come to you.

A day or two later a special commission was appointed to review and identify the paintings. It consisted of personages from artistic and literary circles, with the participation of the head of the Security Service in Belgrade,

Svobodan Penezič, and Major Ilič. Their work was made easier by the fact that in one of the metal boxes they found a catalog with a list of paintings which Erich Šlomovič had printed in Belgrade in 1940 for the exhibition of his collection in Zagreb.

It was thus relatively easy to identify the articles in the collection. After finishing their work, which took 10 days, the commission wrote a report and the collection was transferred to the responsible governmental office for safekeeping and subsequent disposition.[1]

Neskovič had made a complete inventory and photographed each item separately. In comparing the items with the original Zagreb catalog, he discovered that Erich's notations indicated that he had sold at least nine paintings and two ceramics to local collectors. Taking these into account, he notes that only one item was missing from the entire collection: a gouache of the Montmartre by Utrillo.

But this, too, was eventually found and returned to the museum. Erich had sold it to a wealthy industrialist from whom it had been confiscated after the latter was found guilty of collaborating with the enemy.

When Pijade heard that Erich's collection had been found, he gladly accepted the invitation to come and see it at the offices of the Security Services. He was deeply moved by what he saw, having heard before of the fate of the Šlomovič family. He remained at the offices well into the night, admiring painting after painting as they were taken out and inventoried. He was especially pleased to see two of his own works in the collection.

One was a self-portrait rendered by Pijade as a young man in 1910. It shows him bare from the waist up, exposing a thin, sinewy torso, topped by a lean face with a thick shock of black hair that drops over one brow, *pince-nez* glasses, and a closely trimmed mustache. He had apparently given the painting to Erich as a gift.

The other was a portrait in oil of Erich that Pijade had done in 1940 shortly after being released from prison, where he had served fourteen years of a twenty-year sentence for communist activities. Pijade had seen Erich's exhibition in Zagreb at that time and had been so impressed by the young man

1. This was the Commission for the Preservation of Cultural Treasures, which turned the collection over to the National Museum (minus the art albums) some six months later.

that he decided to do a portrait of him. Erich added this portrait to his collection and hid it in the iron cases together with the other works.

Another drawing of Erich, a caricature by his artist friend Pjer Krizanič, was also found in the collection.

After the catalog of the collection was completed, Neskovič went to see Dr. Ribar at the parliament. The following is his account of that encounter:

I came to inform you about the Šlomovič family.

"What are you saying," Dr. Ribar cried out, "what's with Roza? Is she alive and well? Why didn't I hear from her until now?"

Old Roza was killed in a train collision in 1944, Comrade President.

Dr. Ribar lowered his head and thought for a long moment. "Poor woman," he whispered. "Please tell me all you know about her."

...Major Ilič recounts the story... and Ribar recalls his conversation with Roza shortly after the war... "poor woman, she was still hoping then for some miracle."

Comrade President, Major Ilič declares, the collection has been found!

Recalling his last meeting with Roza... Dr. Ribar declared: "Poor Roza told me that she was going to gather the paintings and would donate them to the government in memory of her son.

The question as to whether and under what conditions Roza promised the collection to the Yugoslav government became a major issue in the subsequent court case instituted by Mara Albahari and Erich's heirs in Israel. Neskovič conveniently omitted Ribar's promise to compensate Roza and any surviving family members for the collection. Nor did he bother to clarify that Erich never offered his collection for sale and that the Degas drawing in Mara's possession had been given to her by Erich.

Chapter IX

DREAMS, PLANS, AND REALITY

As Neskovič indicated in his memoire, Erich's meteoric art career began not in Paris, but two years earlier in Belgrade with the launching of the *Kolektanea* project. He was in his third year of high school at the time, chafing to get into the art world. His mind was not on his studies; his high school report cards show a student with good deportment, barely average grades, and repeated failures in mathematics. Even in drawing and art, his favorite subjects, he got only "sufficient" grades. The only subject in which he excelled was French. At the end of his third year he was dropped from school for having failed a repeat examination in mathematics.

In 1933, when Erich was eighteen and still in school, he initiated his *Kolektanea* project, a compendium or anthology of Yugoslavia's leading men of arts and letters. This project was the first indication that Erich wanted to do more with art than merely accumulate it.

One of the first persons to contribute to it was Pavlé Vasič, a well-known art expert who, in 1992, at a spry eighty-five, recalled the occasion well.

"It was in 1933. I was a young aspiring artist, I had just taken an atelier in Belgrade when Erich Šlomovič came to visit me. I had not known him until then. He was a young man with a sallow complexion, courteous but rather taciturn. He told me about his *Kolektanea* project and asked if I could introduce him to some leading artists. He also asked if I could do a portrait of him for the frontispiece of the compendium.

"I did the portrait, and when he came to pick it up he looked at it carefully and said simply, 'You succeeded.' He didn't comment on whether it was good or bad, or whatnot, just, 'You succeeded.'

"I arranged introductions for him to various artists, including Pedra Milosavljevič.[1] I believe I launched Šlomovič on his art career."

Vasič later became an assistant curator under Milan Kasanin at the Prince Paul Museum (later the National Museum) in Belgrade.

"One day," he recalls, "Kasanin called me in to ask what I knew of Erich Šlomovič. He had received a gift from him, a Vollard art album, and also a letter requesting that the museum mount an exhibition of his collection. I neither praised nor criticized Šlomovič; I just told about our first encounter and the little else I knew about him. There was no mention of any intention by Šlomovič to sell his collection to the museum, just to exhibit it.

"I believe Kasanin refused Šlomovič's request because of German influence, especially after the defeat of France. It was no time to show French art. I don't believe anti-Semitism was involved. There was no anti-Semitism in Serbia."

Vasič was referring to Erich's first approach to Kasanin in October 1939, three months after Vollard's death. Erich, still in Paris at the time, gave his brother, Egon, a letter to take to Kasanin in Belgrade, together with two art albums which were to be given as gifts, one for the museum and the other for Kasanin personally. After trying to ingratiate himself with Kasanin by letting him know how much he enjoyed the latter's articles on art, Erich writes:

> I am sending you with my brother one of the first art books published in this century [*Parallelment*]. It was put out by Ambroise Vollard and includes engravings by George Rouault and some words by Vollard.
>
> My friendship with Vollard permits me, even after his death, to send you this book for your museum.
>
> Permit me, at the same time, to send you another book published by Vollard on Degas and Renoir, as a memento to you from a great man who very much valued your work.

Egon forwarded this letter and the two albums to Kasanin on October 16, 1939, the day after his arrival in Belgrade from Paris. He attached a covering letter

1. The man who, as cultural attaché of the Yugoslav embassy in Paris, helped Erich transport his collection to Yugoslavia in 1940.

written on his own stationery, headed with his name and underneath it the title "Chemist." In the letter he requests a meeting as well as permission for his brother to submit an article for a publication which Kasanin was preparing. The article would be on the sculptor Aristide Maillol, "with whom [Erich] had his picture taken."

Unimpressed and perhaps put off by this amateurish approach, Kasanin, on October 30, rejected the overture of the art albums; in a handwritten note at the bottom of Erich's letter, he scribbled: "refused as a result of the oral report by Pavlé Vasič."

Prof. Vasič remains puzzled as to how Kasanin could have come to such a conclusion from his very neutral remarks about Erich. The mystery, as will be seen, was solved many years later by the Herzlers' Paris attorney, in his presentation before the French court.

And what happened to the *Kolektanea*?

"I don't know," answered Vasič, "but I would like to see it, especially the portrait I did of Šlomovič for the anthology's title page.

One man in Yugoslavia knew the answer: Bora Naskovič.

In his booklet, Neskovič, who goes into great detail on Erich's ambitious *Kolektanea* project, points out that Erich gathered material not only on men of art and letters but also on leading politicians of the day. This took place in 1934 (after Erich had dropped out of high school), at a time when Yugoslavia was in political ferment under the dictatorship of King Alexander. Opponents of the regime, especially communists, were being thrown into jail by the thousands, tortured, and executed.[1]

The *Kolektanea's content, Neskovič concludes, indicated that "during this politically dark period Erich had progressive and far-sighted views on the development of the country's cultural and political life." Neskovič pays special attention to the political figures appearing in the Kolektanea.*

What he does not mention is that in 1948, when he apparently got his hands on the compendium, the Security Services of the new communist regime found it of special interest since it contained a treasure trove of information on their prewar friends and foes.

1. Tito was released from prison in 1934 after serving five years together with Moise Pijade. The latter, as noted, was released only in 1939, after fourteen years in prison.

Erich had planned to expand his project to include personalities from other parts of Yugoslavia, outside of Belgrade, but discontinued it after a year of intensive effort when, in 1935, he went to Paris to seek his fortune.

What finally happened to the *Kolektanea*?

According to Neskovič, Erich carried it with him to Paris and brought it back with him to Yugoslavia in 1940, together with his collection. Since he was close to the artist Vladimir Zedrinsky, who was then a contributor to the *Politika* newspaper in Belgrade, Šlomovič handed over the *Kolektanea* to him temporarily with the request that he make the emblem for the cover, to which Zedrinsky acceded.

Shortly afterward, the Germans attacked Yugoslavia and Erich fled inland with his family. The *Kolektanea*, Neskovič said, remained in Belgrade with Zedrinsky. During the war Erich wrote to the latter that in case he, Zedrinsky, should leave the country he should take the *Kolektanea* with him and sell it to a certain collector, because Erich would need the money to survive the war.

According to Neskovič's booklet, Zedrinsky sold it after the war to a Swiss antiquarian in Zurich. It remained there until 1961, when Vojislav Neskovič, Bora's brother, bought it. Vojislav was at that time trade and finance adviser to the Yugoslav embassy in Switzerland. He allegedly kept the *Kolektanea* for many years and then, when he died in the late 1980s, it passed by inheritance to his family, which included his brother Bora.

When I interviewed Neskovič in his Belgrade apartment in 1992, he gave an I-don't-know shrug whenever I tried to pin him down on various inconsistencies in his *Kolektanea* story. When I asked where the compendium was now, he contradicted his original story and said his brother had sold it to a Swiss art gallery before his death and that he did not know what had happened to it.

But when he came to my hotel on the day of my departure, to bring me photographs of himself as a young man, he admitted under persistent questioning that he had in his possession a full copy of the *Kolektanea*.

The convoluted story told by Neskovič in his booklet and orally to me was designed to cover his tracks as to how he really got his hands on the *Kolektanea*. The truth, most probably, is that Erich never parted with it and that the Security Services found it among his collection in the iron cases that Mara had recovered from the train accident. They decided to keep it to themselves because of its revelations about various political personalities, friends and foes of the communists before the war. As the chief investigator of the Šlomovič case, Neskovič had easy access to it.

Art historians in Yugoslavia, not to mention the Herzlers, would be only too happy to get their hands on it.

When I met Neskovič in 1992, he was eighty-one years old. He had a tired look in his round face, but his manner was pleasant and accommodating, belying his former reputation as an authoritarian Secret Service man.

He resided in one of those massively built, decoratively designed apartment buildings that dot Belgrade and were, by 1992, grimy with age. I entered his ground-floor apartment through a small hall with led into a moderate-size living room-dining room, dominated by a heavy table. Neskovič seated himself to my left while his wife, a biology teacher, sat to my right and acted as interpreter. The spacious walls of the high-ceilinged room were covered with paintings, most of them by Yugoslav artists. One of them was by Erich's friend the noted cartoonist Pjer Krisanič, with whose wife Erich was rumored to have had an affair.

Neskovič had retired from the Security Services in 1951 with the rank of colonel, and gone back to work as a copy editor for the Tanjug news agency where he remained until 1966. In recounting his involvement with the Šlomovič collection, he expressed resentment against the National Museum in Belgrade.

"For twenty years," he said, "they never revealed what they had and never showed it. They kept the collection under lock and key. And when they finally showed some items, from time to time, they never identified them as belonging to Erich Šlomovič."

Although the *Kolektanea* was Erich's largest art project outside of his Paris collection, it was not his only one. Several months after his return from Paris in March 1940, he began working on a new idea: an indigenous Yugoslav art magazine. To advance that project, Neskovič related, Erich traveled from Belgrade to Ljubliana, the capital of Slovenia, to discuss the matter with a noted man of letters, named Othon Zupancič. He also met with other well-known intellectuals to gain their support. He planned to publish the magazine in Ljubliana, then known for its excellent printing standards.

The new publication was to have editorial offices in Ljubliana, Zagreb, and Belgrade; editorial material would be gathered from the Belgrade office. The magazine would maintain editorial independence and would feature high-level articles and reproductions of works of art. It would be a quarterly with some 250 pages.

According to Neskovič, several leading personalities in Yugoslavia had promised their cooperation. Erich also enlisted leading lights from France, including André Gide who promised to contribute unpublished texts.

Erich also planned to open a gallery in Belgrade for modern art which, he said, would show "only painters who had rid themselves of foreign influences and were creating completely original works." During this period the ambitious art entrepreneur also began to seek a suitable location for his future museum. His personal notebook is full of notations regarding buildings and plots he had looked at and real estate agents he had contacted.

As recalled by his friend Oton Gliha, Erich had been making rough sketches of his "dream museum" and had also contacted the famed architect Le Corbusier about designing it. On March 29, 1941, two days after Prince Paul's regime was toppled, Erich acquired a building plot in Belgrade for which he reportedly paid cash.

Before and during his exhibition in Zagreb, which lasted from November 24, 1940, to January 19, 1941, he gave lectures and wrote a number of articles for local publications on artists he had known in Paris, including Rouault, Vuillard, and Matisse. He also submitted an article on Maillol to Kasanin.

Erich had built up a strong rapport with Rouault, whose somber style had intrigued him.

"Your art," he wrote Rouault, two months after Vollard's death, "is the cry of our suffering humanity." Rouault's art was a world apart. It fit no existing style, though it could merit the general description of Expressionist. Rouault used deep shadows and heavy black brush strokes to evoke the extremes of the human condition, from the abyss to evangelical fervor, confining himself to essentials in a rough outline form that succeeded on conveying his most deeply felt emotions. He once said: "Subjective artists are one-eyed; objective artists are blind."

Erich had planned to publish a series of books entitled "The Masters of the Occident," one of which would be devoted to Rouault's art and poetry. Toward this end he addressed a twenty-six-point questionnaire to the artist, who responded patiently on nine closely handwritten pages, dated October 1939. Rouault's answers deal with his tastes in painting, sculpture, literature, and music; with his life, recollections from his youth, his relations with Ambroise Vollard, his pictorial and literary work.

Among the Rouault memorabilia found in Erich's Paris safe were the following handwritten comments by the artist, under the headings "Introduction to the Spiritual Life of Pictorial Art" and "Confessions":

> I have registered much more through the eyes, the ears, more than the realists suppose.... I am not a partisan of theses and declarations of faith... I go so far as to say that I am outside the sentimentality of literature as it is generally understood, at its antipode.... My involuntary nonconformism has inclined me toward bad times.... It is through my most violent detractors that I have got to my present position.

Erich also managed to obtain from Rouault fourteen pages of various poems in the artist's hand, reflecting on his life, liberty, the human condition, art, the condition of the artist, the art critic, and politics. The latter category included repeated criticisms of Hitler and his Nazi philosophy. Some of this material appeared in Rouault's books, *Soliloquies, The Oasis,* and *Miserere*; some had never been published.

One of Rouault's poems, "The Circus of the Shooting Star," is elaborately hand-drawn and is dedicated to Erich with a small oil painting at the bottom of the page entitled *The Saintly Face,* signed with the initials G. R., and dated 1939.

> Everything could be a chimera,
> Dear vision, let me finally fix you
> With my poor means at this gray time.
> You will have disappeared in a moment.
> The spirit never ages, the adorable vacancy,
> The poet loves his dream more than his life —

Pictures — tragic all serene,
Lively, colored, bare, all legendary
To see and see you again since I was born in such a gloom.
In shadow or light, the heart in jubilation,
Come again to console me
Because in my last hour I shall rot and turn to dust.

At the top of the page, on the right-hand side, Rouault writes: "To Mr. Erich Chlomovitch and not for the Belgrade Museum."

The reference is to the abortive gift of a Rouault-illustrated book published by Vollard, which Erich had sent to Kasanin as director of the National Museum, and which the latter had rejected.

Among the Rouault works in Erich's Paris collection is a colored etching entitled *The Old Clown,* done in 1930 for a Vollard book called *The Circus* and written by André Suares.[1] Vollard never published it, because in it Suares had violently attacked America and Vollard did not want to antagonize his American clients. The etching is printed on Vollard's favorite paper, *Montval,* developed originally by the sculptor Maillol and adopted by Vollard with his own watermark for most of his art albums.

Erich tried to establish a rapport with Henri Matisse as well, but with less success than in the case of Rouault. His admiration for the artist was no less than for Rouault. In an article on Matisse which appeared in one of the Zagreb newspapers during his exhibition there, Erich writes, among other things:

I used to visit and discuss art with him... many times I had come at 6 a.m. because he started working early.... Many people think that to be a painter means creating works for exhibits, according to size and quality.... But being a painter means to work constantly in search of truth and beauty... we would sometimes go to Matisse's atelier, which was somewhere on the outskirts of Paris, and along the way Matisse would buy "still life" flowers.

Matisse's methods consist of resolving fauvistic coloring [i.e., bright and basic colors] within the framework of contemporary forms of classic painting.... Many people think, Matisse told me, that his paintings are more or less

1. Two days before his death Vollard had written to Suares, introducing Erich and asking Suares to help Erich in his project of "propagating French art in Yugoslavia."

schematic because of their simplicity of form. But they are wrong. The schematic form does not exist in modern paintings. These are experienced and then rendered only through the painter's personality.... "As for my own work," Matisse says, "it is not accidental. Every work I create is a result of long study and a difficult inner struggle. There is never an easy solution to problems, which my ability might allow me to utilize."

...Here Matisse shows me a whole group of studies, beginning with the realistic drawings which he simplifies in a linear way until they are reduced to their essential form, expressing what he wants to represent. "I am like that not only in my work," Matisse says, "but also in my life. I discarded all superfluous things from my surroundings, keeping only the most essential for my work.

"...and now no more talk. I want my head to be clear so that I will be calm. I believe that every painter working in his atelier should have the same feeling as if he were present in the church of his ideals, liberated of all care and worry."

In Matisse's paintings there is still a distant fauvist echo, though it is disappearing. In engravings, wherein intelligence and experience dominate and where everything is reduced to its most elementary form, Matisse is conservative. Thus, by drawing on his natural sensitivity he obtains the maximum from this elemental process.

Today, when we can view drawings by Rodin and Matisse on the same wall, we ask ourselves: didn't Rodin in his drawings prophesy the coming of Matisse?

As such, the works of Matisse confirm everything that Rodin wanted to prove in his drawings.

Like a single-minded but blinded mariner, raising his sails in the face of an approaching storm, Erich continued to pursue his artistic ambitions. He did so up to the last minute, when Belgrade was bursting with antigovernment manifestations and war was at its gates.

On March 17, 1941, ten days before the *coup d'état* in Belgrade, Erich wrote a long, repetitive and cumbersome letter to Matisse in Paris reminding him of Erich's project of publishing an album of Matisse's works, and repeating his previous requests that the latter send him forthwith samples of his work, photographs, and commentary; Erich's attitude of reverence and subservience, evident in his tone, is also evident from the photograph of his visit with the Master at his Paris studio. Matisse is seated at his worktable, which Erich, like a waiter in a fancy restaurant, bends over in deference, holding his notepad delicately like a tray in a gloved hand.

Dear Master,

You cannot imagine how much pleasure it gives me to be able to write to you. Since I have been here in Yugoslavia, I have created much publicity for French art and above all for your art, which is so close to me and of which I have become a fanatic.

Today I sent you clippings from some of the articles I have written about you. In one of the articles you will find the reproduction of your palette and the girl's head, which you were kind enough to do for me in July 1939 in your studio next to Place d'Alesia. For your 70th and your other birthdays I organized lectures and wrote articles in remembrance of my visit to your studio.

Although the reproduction of the palette (in the newspaper) is not bad, I regret not having the original here. I left it in Paris in a safe.[1]

My dear Master, if you need anything I beg you to let me know so as to enable me to have it sent to you.

At present, I am preparing a very important publication about your work but I would like it to be different from the other books about you that have been published up to now....

First of all, I think that I will have this monograph published in Serbo-Croat, and then in other languages immediately after the publication of the original. To prepare this monograph I would be *most happy to obtain your assistance.*

As to reproductions, I contemplate 300 reproductions of your paintings. They should be chosen by you, with each painting bearing the title you chose to give it. There would be reproductions of 150 drawings and 50 lithographs and engravings. As for the sculptures, I leave you free to choose them and determine their number.

1. This only known mention by Erich of the Paris safe became crucial evidence for the Herzlers' attorney in Paris.

The text would only consist of your biography (if possible written by yourself) and a few pages of commentary. There would be a bibliography about the books and studies published about you.

The monograph would start with the articles on art which you have already written.... It would be very well if these articles could be accompanied by *small drawings or photographs, in order to show the evolution of a particular painting* (from the first drawing to the canvas).

If you remember, dear master, I already discussed this idea with you in Paris and you approved. You promised to gather for me all the articles you have written on art and to give me a manuscript.... Also that you would make for me a few small drawings from the beginning to the end; all this would be photographed in order to simplify the evolution from the drawing to the finished painting.

[As of] today I have been able to assure a very significant sum of money which would allow me to publish perhaps one of the most important monographs about you until now.

As for the opening page, you can, dear master, do something that you have already done before with the only difference that your name would appear in large print and the name of the writer (Erich Chlomovitch) in small print.

I believe, dear master, that you will trust me to do this monograph because this is one of my *dreams*. As to the financial aspects, I already have everything that is necessary and the printer is waiting to be able to continue his work.

Dear master, I would like to ask you to write an introduction for this monograph, which you would forward to me in the form of a letter and which will give me the possibility of reproducing your manuscript as a facsimile.

Please send me all the reproductions with exact titles to be published in the monograph, as well as the introductory letter (which will be reproduced as a facsimile), a biographical note and unpublished information.

The first page will contain only your name and that of the writer, Erich Chlomovich.... As everything is ready and part of the text already printed, I am only waiting to obtain from you the items mentioned above...

My thanks in anticipation. I would be happy if you would answer me very soon. Kindly accept my most sincere regards.

Erich Chlomovitch

Dobracina Ulica 35
Belgrade (Beograd)

Please note that in French my name is written, Erich Chlomovitch, and in Yugoslav, Erich Šlomovič

In another P.S. Erich repeats his requests, summarizing them once more. To make doubly sure, the persistent publisher follows up the letter with an urgent telegram, pressing Matisse to expedite the matter.

Nowhere in the correspondence is there any mention of how Matisse would be compensated for his contribution to the album. Although the omission seems strange, it does not mean, of course, that such an agreement had not been made already or would not be made in the future.

With the German bombing of Belgrade three weeks later, Erich's dreams went up in smoke.

From the dust and destruction there arose the enigma of his collection, its origin, its legitimacy, and its ultimate destiny. When the National Museum in Belgrade decided in 1989 to give the Šlomovič collection its first major public showing, the French court was still seeking the answers.

Chapter X

THE DONATOR

Among literary and artistic figures in Yugoslavia who were struck by Erich was Veliko Bulajič, one of the country's leading film directors. He decided to produce a full-length feature film on the Šlomovič saga, called *The Donator,* that would premier at the opening of the art exhibition in Zagreb in 1989.

Bulajič studied film direction in Italy under such motion-picture greats as Vittoria De Sica and Luigi Stampa. He went on to produce a dozen full-length feature films in his native Yugoslavia, attracting wide audiences and winning many local and international awards. His epic *Battle on the Neretva*, about one of Tito's most crucial encounters with German forces in World War II, was nominated for an Oscar.

A tall, handsome man with heavy eyebrows, a full mane of blond hair combed back pompadour-style, and a casual but gracious bohemian air, Bulajič exuded stage presence and a natural charm.

"The story of Erich Šlomovič," he told me, "symbolizes the universal human tragedy of an idealist who lives for art and is ready to make any sacrifice for it, but at the worst of possible times."

In the film, which he coscripted with Ivan Bresič, Bulajič sought to show "the tragic... destiny of all those... connected with this collection and man's powerlessness to overcome fate."

The film succeeds, to a large extent, in conveying those themes. It also casts a powerful spotlight on some of the more dramatic moments in the career of the young art collector, providing in the process penetrating insights into his strengths and weaknesses.

(Erich enters, immaculately dressed in light blue suit, vest, and tie, carrying a coat over his left arm.)

Vollard: *(curious but cordial)* Good day.

Erich: Good day, sir.

Vollard: You say you have an invitation, but I don't remember having met you?

Erich: You wrote me ten years ago. *(Hands him the letter.)*

Vollard: *(quickly skimming over the letter)* Yes, it is I who wrote it. *(Turning to Bonnard)* Listen. My dear young friend, learn, educate yourself, and when you grow up I'll be glad to see you if you come to Paris... and my signature... *(turning to Erich)* only I don't remember the motive.

Erich: As a child I read your books on Renoir and Cezanne. I was thrilled. That's what I wrote you.

Vollard: Yes, I remember now. You said you wanted to be like me. What I liked especially about your letter, you didn't ask for anything. You've grown up. Let's see what you've learned. *(With a sly look at Erich)* Do you paint, perhaps?

Erich: No sir, I have no hand for painting. But I have a good eye... I believe.

Vollard: The eye... *(chuckles and turns to Bonnard)* What did Renoir say about the eye? Once, when gazing at the glistening white moon, he said: "Look, Degas, how much red is there..." ah, beautifully said.

(Vollard turns to the butler, whispers in his ear, then turns to Erich.)

Here's a chance to test your eye. If you were an art dealer like me, which of these paintings would you choose? *(Vollard points at the row of paintings on the floor. Erich steps to the end of the row, as the butler takes his coat from him; walks slowly and deliberately down the row, returns, pauses briefly, and points to one of the paintings.)*

Erich: Mr. Vollard, I would choose this one.

Vollard: And the others?

Erich: None.

Vollard: Why this particular one?

Erich: *(picks up the painting, a rough-hewn, half-length portrait of a ballet dancer in bright colors and heavy black lines)* Because it shows a restrained passion... as if it were about to explode... so full of fervor. That's art. These black strokes emerge to dominate.

Vollard: Bravo. Well done, bravo.

Bonnard: As if he had heard Renoir. He said it took him forty years to realize that the queen of colors was black.

Vollard: That's the latest Rouault. The rest is trifling (*picks up a painting propped up against his chair*) ... and this one?

Erich: But Mr. Vollard, that's an extraordinary Bonnard. I like him a lot.

Vollard: Bravo! (*Returning the painting to his side*) With a good sense of commerce you'll be a great art dealer.

Bonnard: (*rising from his chair*) I don't know, Ambroise... the time for talent scouts has passed. Men like you belong in museums.

(*The butler puts his coat on for him.*)

Thank you, Francoise. (*Turns to Erich*) I'm having an exhibition next month. I'll be glad to see you there. My name is Pierre Bonnard. (*Erich, taken aback, stands speechless as Bonnard walks out.*)

Vollard: (*chuckles*) You see... I discovered him, launched him, and he's ready to send me to a museum already.... Sit down, young man. (*Changes to a fatherly and gentle tone*) Tell me about yourself. You speak very good French.

Erich: Yes, but with an accent.

(*Vollard looks Erich over from head to foot. The scene fades and returns to the butler continuing with his recollections for Major Handke.*)

The movie, in a later scene, implies a homosexual relationship between Erich and Vollard. The notion that Erich had such a relationship with Vollard, and possibly with some artists as well, was rumored for years. It was meant to explain how such a young man could have gathered such an extraordinary collection from the likes of Vollard and from the many artists with whom Erich later developed close friendships. All the evidence, however, is to the contrary; namely, that Vollard was not homosexual and that Erich maintained normal relations with the opposite sex.

In real life, of course, Erich had written a letter to Vollard, as he later told his artist friend Oton Gliha, and as portrayed in the movie. Gliha, later a resident of Zagreb and one of Yugoslavia's leading painters, was a struggling artist in Paris when he first met Erich there. It was Gliha who in 1940 helped Erich organize his exhibition in Zagreb.

On the occasion of the opening of the anniversary exhibit in Zagreb in 1989, a singular and intimate look at Erich and his life in those days was given by Gliha in an extensive interview on Yugoslav TV:

"One day Erich told me that at the age of twelve [in 1927] he read Vollard's autobiography, *Recollections of an Art Merchant,* and also his books about Cezanne, Renoir, and Degas. The French usually gave the address of the author at the end of the book, so Erich was able to write to Vollard and tell him of the great pleasure he had in reading his books. Vollard, in his response, suggested that Erich contact him on his first visit to Paris.

"...It was in 1939 [Gliha recalls] that I first met Erich Šlomovič. I was studying art in Paris on a French scholarship. At the time there were many Yugoslav painters there — Lubarda, Milunovič, Peja (Predrag) Milosavljevič [a key figure in unraveling the mystery of the collection's origin], and many others. We had organized an exposition at the Bernheim gallery during that period.... I believe it was in the autumn of 1939 that I attended an exposition of the artist, Oton Friesz, at the Katya Granoff gallery on the Boulevard Raspail. I was speaking to a colleague when a young man approached me. I was also young then, about twenty-four or twenty-five. He said, 'Excuse me, but I heard you speaking my language.'

"'Are you a painter?' I asked.

"'No,' he said, 'I'm involved with art but not like you'."

"We then exchanged a few words and he told me that he had some paintings of Renoir, Picasso, Cezanne, Gauguin, and so on. He gave me his calling card and invited me to come and see them. He lived at the Hotel Ideal near the Porte de Clignancourt. This all seemed to me a bit bizarre... to hear a Yugoslav talk like that. I thought, what the hell, how could it be? In a way I was a bit fearful that he might not be quite normal.

"For a long time I didn't go there, until one day I found myself at the flea market near his hotel and I stopped by to ask for him. He came down to greet me. I remember well how his nose was running... he was hoarse and all muffled up. He invited me to come upstairs. I climbed with him up to the top and what do I see... a room full of paintings. I was stupefied. I looked at it all and said: 'My God, what's all this?"

"'There's more,' he said, 'in another room on the second floor. It's also full of paintings'."

"It was really funny. That's how we established a sort of rapport. Besides the fact that he was an art connoisseur, his intuition told him that I could be useful to him... and so we began to meet regularly.

"At that time he was trading paintings, sketches, and other works of art with the Petrides gallery. Petrides was a Greek Cypriot who had come to Paris in earlier years and worked as a tailor. Painters, who were still not well known then, used to have him make a suit or coat for them in exchange for their works.

"Eventually Petrides became a great collector. He married a Frenchwoman, Odette. His gallery became famous; it's located on the Rue Boetie. I believe it is still there today. Petrides, who died recently, had the rights to Utrillo and no work by him could be authenticated without Petrides' certification.[1]

"Utrillo's best works were done at the beginning of his career. Šlomovič had many works by Renoir and other artists and he would exchange one of them from time to time for an Utrillo. I used to whisper to him, in our language, to take an earlier Utrillo than the one Petrides would offer him. But that Greek, Petrides, knew our language a bit.

"I once told Erich: 'Demand that other painting there, instead of the one he's offering.' So he said: 'This one or nothing.' And Petrides gave in to him. I believe that it is thanks to me that certain works of Utrillo are in the Šlomovič collection today.

"Erich acquired a pile of works during that period. We would sometimes hire a taxi to transport ten or fifteen paintings at a time [to his hotel].

"It's curious that he had confidence in me. One day he said to me: 'You know, you're the only one among the Yugoslavs in Paris who never asks me how I acquired all this stuff. And that's why I'll tell you and I don't want you to tell the others.'

"That's the first question everyone asked him. But not me. I never asked him. I thought, O.K., this man is an art dealer. He's going to take his collection

---

1. This was incorrect. Petrides was still living in 1992, aged ninety-one, but under a dark cloud: in 1979 he had been sentenced to three years in prison for giving a false certificate of authentication for a Utrillo painting.

to Yugoslavia... it seemed out of place to interrogate him on this subject. And that's how he began to tell me his story.

"Šlomovič began to be interested in art very early. Already in Belgrade, when he was a young man, he would go to all the art events. He carried a large notebook which he took with him to the homes and studios of the painters so that they could write something in it for him. He had an innate sense of appreciation of art and one could see that he wanted to develop it.

"Vollard probably saw in Šlomovič someone like himself, a person with a good intuition. And here is where the mystery begins. Was he an advisor to Vollard? Later, one knows that he became something like a secretary to him.... Vollard was killed in a car accident in 1939 and everything Šlomovič received from him was through his will.... There are different theories and approaches [regarding the will]. As for me, I know absolutely nothing about it."[1]

Gliha then recalls the 1940 exhibit in Zagreb which he and another artist, Tartaglia, helped Erich to organize. Another "helper" was Jela Tadijanovič, secretary of the Art Pavilion in Zagreb where the exhibit was held. An attractive young woman, Jela was reportedly the object of much flirting by Erich and his artist colleagues.

Jela, who was eighty-one years old in 1992 when I visited Zagreb, was too ill to see me at that time but gave me some of her recollections over the phone.

"Erich was a very intelligent young man, very level, neither an introvert nor an extrovert. He was obsessed by art, a bit of an exhibitionist, with a sense of humor from time to time. Vollard gave him the collection as a gift and the two agreed to make a joint permanent exhibition in Yugoslavia. They preferred Zagreb, since it was more Western-oriented than Belgrade. Yes, I believe Erich had other paintings in his possession which he didn't exhibit. He would meet with the sculptor Ivan Mestrovič from time to time for advice. I heard he had a girlfriend in Paris but I don't think it was serious."

According to Gliha, Šlomovič returned from Paris with the idea of creating a museum of Western art which he would build in Zagreb or Belgrade.

"Šlomovič was more attracted to Zagreb," Gliha said, "because in Belgrade he encountered an awkward situation with Prince Paul. He offered to the latter a

1. In the court case in Paris, the Herzlers' attorney pointed to various contradictions in Gliha's story and disproved the supposition that Vollard had ever willed anything to Šlomovič.

large part of his collection... on condition that it be identified as the Šlomovič Collection. Prince Paul eventually responded, to the best of my knowledge, that Šlomovič could make his offer but that there was no question of mentioning his name.[1] This was offensive to Šlomovič, who wouldn't accept such a condition... so one day he said to me, 'Listen, let's go to Zagreb.' And that's how the exhibition was transferred to Zagreb.

"On that occasion I was in Belgrade and I met his family there. He had a brother, Egon, who was a photographer. He used to accompany him to Paris and in Yugoslavia, and everywhere he took pictures of historic interest, like those [of Erich] with Maillol, Chagall, and many more....

"I remember well how Šlomovič would make sketches of the future museum he dreamed about," Gliha continued. "He asked me to make some sketches too.... Later he established contact with [the famous architect] Le Corbusier and with others, which means that if this exceptional man had not disappeared we would have in Yugoslavia today something remarkable...."

Contrary to Gliha's testimony there is abundant evidence that, apart from the idea of creating his own museum, Erich tried to mount an exhibition of his own at the Prince Paul Museum in Belgrade and not to donate it in his name. It was only after he was refused (as we saw earlier) by the museum director, Milan Kasanin, that he decided to move the exhibition to Zagreb.

Why did Kasanin refuse him?

The film, *The Donator,* comes closest to the truth on this chapter. The story emerges in a scene showing the German officer, Major Handke, arriving at the museum in Belgrade to interview Kasanin as to the whereabouts of the Šlomovič collection. The time is at the peak of the war, around 1943-1944, two years after the German invasion of Yugoslavia.

Major Handke: How come you kept your post? Many left because they didn't want to serve the Germans.

Kasanin: I'm not serving anyone. Politics never interested me. But I obey the law.

Handke: Let's get to the point. You knew Erich Šlomovič well.

1. Prince Paul, after whom the Belgrade museum had been named, had studied art at Oxford in England and had acquired a sizable collection of his own which he had placed in the museum. The prince, as mentioned, was ousted as regent in the popular upheaval of March 1941.

Kasanin: Relatively well. I first met him when he came from Paris. He gave a valuable book to the museum (*Kasanin rises and takes a thick album out of a glass-enclosed bookcase behind him*) ... published by Ambroise Vollard.

Handke: (*leafs through it*) Wonderful... I need to know when Šlomovič returned to Belgrade. Did he bring the collection with him?

Kasanin: He wrote to me from Switzerland[1] asking me to organize an exhibition. I went to the station to meet him.

(*The scene shifts to the Belgrade railway station and an emotional encounter between Erich and his parents. Kasanin also greets him there and in response to Erich's question as to the chances for exhibiting his collection at the museum, Kasanin replies:*)

Certainly it would be a real cultural event.

(*He invites Erich to visit him at the museum. Erich carefully supervises the unloading of several large trunks from the train and turns to his mother:*)

Erich: What I've brought here has never been seen before. I want to build a museum of East and West. Le Corbusier himself made the design for it.

(*The scene shifts to the museum and a flashback of the encounter between Erich and Kasanin, as recalled by the latter for Major Handke's benefit.*)

Erich: I'm here for the fifth time already. I just want to know the result.

Kasanin: The government believes the timing is wrong. The political situation... relations with Germany... Berlin could take it as if we were parading with your name.... You should understand that.

Erich: What? ...that I am a Jew? ...so the exhibition is off.

Kasanin: For the present... maybe later.

Erich: Cursed be the day I came back. The best thing is to run away from here... far away from mediocrity.

Kasanin: I understand your anger, but measure your words.

Erich: Measure them? Just out of spite I'll have an exhibition in Zagreb. (*Storms out in a huff, then rushes back and confronts Kasanin.*)

Let me tell you one more thing. This is not a museum of art.... This is a government agency, collaborating with the Germans.

---

1. Evidence that Erich was in Switzerland on several occasions, including on his way back to Yugoslavia from Paris, has led many persons involved with the case to suspect that he may have left other valuable items in a numbered safe there. Secretive Swiss banking regulations have prevented any serious investigation about this possibility so far.

(Kasanin then recalls how Erich opened his exhibition in Zagreb on November 24, 1940.)

Kasanin: Five months later the government fell. I looked for him to offer him an exhibition in Belgrade but I couldn't find him.

This scene in the movie, according to Milo Grigorjevič, editor of the weekly magazine *Nin*, was at one point omitted in the Yugoslav screening of the film since "it was understood as an indirect accusation of anti-Semitism in the capital which, in fact, did not exist."[1]

Nikola Kusovič, who later became director of the History of Art Department at the National Museum in Belgrade, knew Kasanin well and spoke to him on several occasions about Erich Šlomovič.

"Kasanin denied that his refusal had anything to do with politics or anti-Semitism. He felt the collection was not important enough to merit a separate exhibition. Obviously, he misjudged it. He also told me that Šlomovič had offered to sell the collection to the museum and he didn't like this."

Despite this testimony, the overwhelming evidence, later reinforced in the French court, supports the film version — namely, that Erich wanted to exhibit his collection, not to sell it.

The film gives several illuminating scenes of Erich bargaining with Petrides, who, since he was still living at the time, was given a different name in the film. Some rather sharp bargaining takes place in which Erich manages to augment his collection.

In another scene, when he and Juana are already living together, we see Erich, in a rather seedy Paris apartment, bargaining with an elderly lady who is offering a heavily framed painting for sale.

Erich: 300 francs for this junk? The colors are cracked and it's so small.

Woman: 300 francs. That's the price.

Erich: How much do you want? Your last price?

Woman: 300 francs and that's final, young man.

(Erich steps to the other room and whispers to Juana, "A real Fragonard," then returns to the woman and says:)

Erich: My last offer... 150 francs.

1. The Serbs, in fact, were the least susceptible to anti-Semitism, having hidden thousands of Jews during the war, including one thousand in Belgrade alone.

Woman: The frame is worth more than that.

(Juana enters the room.)

Juana: Oh Erich, you'd give 150 francs for that? Don't do it. Please. (*She turns around and leaves the room.*)

Woman: Oh, well... 250.

Erich: Out of the question.

Woman: All right (*pushing the painting towards him.*) Take it and go to hell.

(*Erich peels off the money and follows her out the door where he takes another bill out of his pocket.*)

Erich: Here, for you — 20 francs.

Woman: Thanks.

Erich: But the painting, is it yours?

Woman: What do you take me for, a thief? That's a lot of nerve.

Erich: No, no... it was a pleasure to meet you.

(*He rushes back to the room, does a somersault, hugs Juana and exclaims:*)

Juana, you've been wonderful. My God, a Fragonard.

(*He then grabs the painting and, displaying it proudly, declares once more triumphantly:*)

A real Fragonard.

There is no work in Šlomovič's collection by Fragonard, a pre-Impressionist painter. But considering his known penchant for wheeling and dealing, similar scenes were probably enacted in real life many times over.

The above scene in the movie is witnessed by Vollard's chauffeur/butler (Marcel in real life), who happened to drop by as Erich began his bargaining. While Erich is overcome with joy at having acquired a "real Fragonard," Marcel is not amused.

Marcel: Mr. Šlomovič, you astound me. What you are doing is not worthy of you. Monsieur Vollard will not be happy about it... especially your living in such a place.

Erich: It's easier to find paintings in this area than at auctions. Here, look at these... I bought them all quite cheaply... Mary Cassatt, Gauguin, Utrillo, Picasso.

Marcel: (*unmollified*) A veritable Ali Baba's cave. Don't tell me you found them all at the flea market?

Erich: No, but fleas played a part in them.

Marcel: You have to hide these treasures. What if someone in this neighborhood hears about them?

Erich: (*changing the subject; pulls out a painting standing against the wall*) Look, this Gauguin is worth its weight in gold. I think I'll give it to Monsieur Vollard.

Marcel: Give it? Giving doesn't exist among art merchants. Make an exchange.

Erich: Right. Let him give me two Bonnards in exchange, though that would hardly be enough. He could add *The Woman Bathing* by Renoir.

Marcel: (*by this time more amused than chagrined*) A real devil.

Would Vollard have approved of his protégé's behavior?

Probably yes, notwithstanding Marcel's admonitions. Erich, no doubt, reminded Vollard of his own beginnings. Besides, the latter showed his appreciation of the young man by showering him with gifts of his art albums and reproductions from his collection, as witnessed in the Paris catalog. Many of the items were autographed by Vollard and dedicated to Erich with warm, fatherly remarks.

What sort of person was Vollard? What kind of friendship could have developed between this rough-and-tumble, aging curmudgeon and his aspiring young protégé? While Vollard's name appears abundantly in Erich's Paris collection, Erich is not mentioned in Vollard's files.

It behooves us, therefore, to take a closer look at Erich's benefactor and examine the common sea in which these two individualistic fish swam. Was Vollard a predatory shark or a benevolent dolphin? Whichever, he was a great if not the greatest art merchant of his time. But he was more than a merchant: he was a true patron who gave many of the world's famous artists their entrance to success.

As one art critic described him, he was an "impresario of the arts… a genius at discovering genius."

Who, then, was the real Ambroise Vollard?

Chapter XI

VOLLARD: ART CONNOISSEUR EXTRAORDINAIRE

Ambroise Vollard was born in 1867 on the island of Reunion, the remote French possession near Madagascar in the Indian Ocean. He was the oldest of ten children.

In 1890 he went to Paris to study law. Some say his move was more in pursuit of the love of his life, Madelaine de Galea, whom he had known in Reunion and who had moved to Paris shortly before him. Whichever, he soon tired of law, though never of de Galea.

He had been drawn to art after successfully selling some drawings and engravings which he had bought on an urge at the secondhand book stalls along the Seine. He decided to work as a salesman in an art gallery. His first job was for Alphonse Dumas, an aspiring but undistinguished painter who had opened a picture gallery which he called, with some presumption, the Union Artistique. Dumas had not opened it to make money, he told the young Vollard, but rather to balance the expenses of his own painting by the profits to be made out of selling other people's works.[1]

"It is not a shop," he stressed, "it's a salon."

But Dumas's artist-friends did not come to his "salon" to bring their paintings or to buy, but to gossip. Customers were few and far between. Vollard tells of one customer who came in one day to "buy pictures of animals since he

---

1. This quote and further citations are from Vollard's autobiography, *Recollections of an Art Merchant* and from *Ambroise Vollard, Editêr,* by Una Johnson, former curator of the Brooklyn Museum in New York.

was tired of seeing people in his office all day." Another wanted a picture in which one of the subjects would be a Zouave soldier, which the customer had once been; he didn't have time to pose for it himself.

On another occasion a gentleman came in to buy a painting showing a girl "warming a turtle dove on her dainty little breasts."

"Is it all right to give a picture like that to one's fiancée?" the customer asked timidly.

Vollard assured him that it was.

"Every day on my way to the office," the customer confessed, "I've been going out of my way to have a squint at that juicy little bit. It's nice, isn't it, giving presents that one can enjoy oneself?"

Vollard remarked to Dumas: "If that's his idea of a present he'll probably buy his wife a sporting rifle after he marries her." This incident reminded him of another customer who bought his wife a Meerschaum pipe for their wedding anniversary. When she expressed surprise, he pointed to the man's head which formed the bowl of the pipe and said, "It reminded me of your father."

During this period Vollard heard only criticism of the new Impressionist painters. So one day he removed from the display window a work by one of the more acceptable painters of the time, and put a work by the Impressionist, Sisley, in its place. Five minutes later it was sold.

Dumas did not approve and asked Vollard to tell the purchaser next time he found that the firm "does not deal in that sort of stuff, and that the painting had been on display only by chance."

One day Dumas told Vollard that he had three hundred thousand francs to invest and couldn't decide what to invest it in, "like the donkey before two bales of hay."

"If I were you," Vollard told him, "I would spend it buying Renoirs, Cezannes, and Degas." Dumas wouldn't listen to this or other advice, so Vollard decided to strike out on his own. The year was 1892.

"I had been reduced at that time to living on ship's biscuits, because they were cheaper than bread," Vollard recalls. He decided to try and sell one of the drawings he had bought out of his meager savings as a student. He had heard that a wine merchant in Bercy went in for "modern" drawings, so he decided to try him. Vollard lived at the time near Clichy, in the north of Paris. Bercy was at the southern end of town, the equivalent today of some twenty subway stops away. To save money, Vollard walked.

He took with him a drawing of Forain, later recognized as one of the leading Impressionists. He asked 120 francs for it.

Taking a wad of bills out of his pocket the wine merchant said, "Ill give you a hundred."

It was most tempting, but remembering a story told to him by a colleague about a customer who tried to knock down the price, Vollard replied: "You want to beat down my Forain? Very well. It's no longer 120. I'll take 150 for it."

"You've got some cheek, I must say," said the collector. "But I'll take it."

On another occasion a "brother-in-trade" told Vollard that a client of his was on the lookout for Forains, Guys, Rops, Steinlens, everything in fact that passed at that time for "advanced" art. "I know you have some of those," the business colleague said, "and if you care to get rid of the lot I'll take them."

Vollard replied evasively, figuring he'd be better off selling to the client directly — if he could only find him. So the next time he met his "brother-in-trade" he repeated to him exactly what he had told Vollard previously. "I have a client," Vollard said, "who buys Forains, Rops, Steinlens, all the modern school, in fact."

"I can guess who that is."

"I know you're as sharp as they make them," Vollard responded, "but how on earth, with such a vague hint as I have given you...?"

With that the man revealed the client's name.

"Well, really, how extraordinary," Vollard said. "I'm just writing a letter to him. Have you anything to say to him?"

"No. I don't think so."

Vollard borrowed a piece of paper from his friend and began writing a note. He then took an envelope and wrote down the name of the client. Turning to his friend, he said: "I shall have to go home. I have forgotten the address."

The friend, to show how well he could remember things by heart, wrote down the address on Vollard's envelope. Vollard sent the letter off and in a few days the client came to him and bought the whole collection for 1,000 francs in cash. The following week, Vollard noticed one of the paintings for sale in the gallery of a colleague. This taught him the importance of maintaining turnover, but also the value of "sleep on it" until prices rose.

After a few more such deals, financed by a pawnbroker with whom Vollard left valuables as security, the young entrepreneur felt ready to strike out on his own. He moved from his modest garret at the top of the Montmartre to its lower slopes. There, at 41 Rue Lafitte, he acquired a small shop with some back rooms where he set up his living quarters. A basement housed his kitchen and dining room, which soon became the camping ground for the great and about-to-become-great of Paris's artistic and literary world.

The year was 1893. By that time Rue Lafitte had become known as the "rue des tableaux" where a number of important art dealers had set up shop. Paris in those years enjoyed a renewed prosperity under the Third Republic, after recovering from the devastating siege of 1870 in the Franco-Prussian War. The Montmartre, topped by three windmills processing gypsum into plaster and the white dome of the church of the Sacré Coeur, had become the mecca of Paris's effervescent artistic community. (After World War I the artists shifted to the Montparnasse.)

Van Gogh had lived here with his brother, Theo, from 1886 to 1888. So did Renoir and Degas as well as Susan Valadon, Degas' model who later became an artist in her own right, until eclipsed by her son, Maurice Utrillo. A struggling twenty-year-old Picasso took lodgings at the foot of Montmartre in 1901, where he worked nights and slept days.

Vollard's shop was just a few blocks away. This newest of the district's art merchants soon showed the prophetic good taste, the aggressive and enterprising shrewdness which would bring him to the top. One day a client told him that a dealer, whose name he would not reveal, had discovered a rare collection of paintings by a recognized artist and intended to sell them to a relative of the artist.

Vollard, determined to discover this lode himself, concluded by a series of educated deductions and fortuitous hunches that the relative referred to was the noted artist Berthe Morisot, sister-in-law of Edouard Manet,[1] the father of the

1. Berthe Morisot was also the grandmother of Degas Rouault, the French art expert who in 1966 brought out the special album on *The Unknown Degas and Renoir* in the Šlomovič collection in Belgrade.

Impressionists. Manet had died ten years earlier in 1883. The hunch, however, did not tell him where the drawings could be found.

Eventually, he tracked down the dealer who had made the discovery and overheard him telling his client — who had revealed the story in the first place — that in short order he, the dealer, would conclude the business, but since it had to do with a woman he wanted to take his time.

Who could the woman be? Vollard thought. Why, Manet's widow of course. So he hurried to see her and discovered a hoard of drawings by the master. Many in the art world had known about them, but did not want them since they were "merely" sketches. Vollard bought the lot, arranged a special showing, and launched his career as a successful art merchant.

A short time later he returned to Madame Manet's and managed to buy from her another "unsalable" Manet work, the famous *Execution of Maximilien* (the French-installed ruler of Mexico). Actually, it was a variant of the original painting; the family, not wanting to put both up for sale at the same time, had kept it aside. Madame Manet's brother, to make it more salable, decided to "improve" the painting and create a second one by cutting out from it a sergeant loading his rifle for the execution. Unable to get the asking price of 6,000 francs for the larger work, he then sold the sergeant separately. Madame Manet rolled up what was left of it and stored it in the lumber room under a cupboard. When she unrolled it for Vollard to view, there was a cracked fold running across the bellies of the soldiers of the firing squad.

Not hesitating for a moment, Vollard bought it and took it for restoration. "But Messieur Vollard," said the restorer, Chapuis, "that's the same painting from which the sergeant was taken that I had stretched for Degas. He was told that the rest of the painting had been destroyed by accident."

When Vollard later showed the work to Degas, the latter insisted on buying it. But he asked Vollard to return to the family and try to recover the sergeant's legs which, for some unknown reason, had been cut off. When Vollard returned to the widow he found that her brother had cut off the legs because he considered them unsightly and had thrown the fragment into the fire.

The sequel to the story is that at the great auction of Degas' works after his death, from which Vollard benefited considerably, Manet's *Maximilien* was bought by the London National Gallery. The Gallery restored it better than before but decided to separate the sergeant, which Degas had pasted onto the canvas, and frame it separately.

By 1895 Vollard felt sufficiently established to take the biggest risk so far of his short career — an exhibit devoted to the barely recognized and much-maligned Paul Cezanne.

Vollard first became interested in Cezanne when he saw two men standing outside the window of Pere Tanguy's gallery commenting on a painting by the artist displayed there. One was a "gentleman"; the other a "workman."

"Isn't it shameful to murder nature like that," said the gentleman in the bowler hat. "Trees that can't stand up; a house that may topple at any moment; water the color of lead; and just look at the sky! If nature was like that no one would want to go outdoors."

"Well, it's the other way with me, sir," said the workman. "Every time I look at that picture I say to myself: 'There's a place I'd like to go and fish on a Sunday! Aren't the blokes lucky that they can treat themselves to a house like that! I know what I'm talking about. I'm a bricklayer'."

Vollard, "the genius at discovering genius," felt then and there that if he ever had the opportunity he would mount an exhibition of this unusual artist. But first he had to find him. Cezanne was a recluse who would seldom give his address to anyone. Vollard thought he had finally tracked him down only to find he had recently moved. But a neighbor recalled that one of the movers had said they were taking the furnishings to a street in Paris with the name of a saint and an animal.

Thus, Vollard finally found Paul Cezanne on the Rue des Lions-St. Paul. Cezanne's son, who many years later became the executor of Vollard's will, helped to convince his father to go ahead with the exhibit. He did not persuade him, however, to frame the one hundred or more paintings destined for it; Vollard had to arrange this himself. The exhibit was a moderate success and helped launch the careers of both Cezanne and Vollard.

As Vollard mentions in his autobiography, the exhibit attracted many young artists who, unlike the critics, were greatly impressed and began to fall under Cezanne's influence. Among the buyers at the exhibit was a blind man accompanied by his secretary. He was especially interested in Cezanne's advanced ideas, which he credited to the influence of his close friend Emile Zola.

Cezanne and Zola had grown up together in Aix le Chappelle and Cezanne had done several portraits of the young author, one of which found its way into Erich Šlomovič's Paris collection.

Cezanne was the first to break with the Impressionists, emphasizing structure and solidity as opposed to flimsy design and evanescent effects. He wanted to paint nature from the eye of the beholder, as the Impressionists had done, but to give it a greater sense of order and harmony.

"The outstanding lesson of Cezanne's life," Vollard remarked, "was his modesty and unremitting toil in the service of his art. He was a Don Quixote of painting."

He was also an exasperating perfectionist. Vollard relates how he survived more than a hundred sittings for Cezanne's portrait of him. The artist's only remark to him after the hundredth sitting was, "I haven't done so badly with the front of your shirt."

Cezanne had placed Vollard on an unstable platform so that if his subject should fall asleep while posing he wouldn't do so again. Once when Vollard dozed off and came crashing down to the floor, Cezanne rushed up to him: "You wretch. You've upset the pose. You should sit like an apple. Whoever saw an apple fidgeting?"

As Vollard remarked later, "Motionless as that fruit may be, Cezanne was sometimes obliged to leave a study of apples unfinished, because they rotted before he managed to finish the painting."

Vollard had an uncanny ability to sense every new trend in art at its inception. It was thus he was able, in the last decade of the 19th century, to spot Cezanne, the father of modern art. Then, in the first decade of the 20th, he discovered, in the persons of Matisse and Derain, the Fauvists and their wild Expressionist reaction to the Impressionists.[1]

Vollard was ready to back his hunches with his pocketbook. He gave Cezanne and Matisse their first solo exhibits in 1895 and 1901, respectively.

---

1. Both of these artists are amply represented in the Šlomovič collection. Derain's *Cork Oaks* is featured on the cover of the Paris catalog and at one time reached a peak value of some $6 million. It was many years after Vollard's death that the *Fauves* were recognized as marking a historic transition in the history of art, thus increasing their value astronomically. Erich had a number of Matisse paintings and kept in close touch with the master, as noted previously.

Also in 1901 he took a similar risk with the century's greatest artistic innovator, Pablo Picasso.

A few years after these pioneering exhibitions Vollard risked an exhibition with another unknown, this time posthumous artist, Vincent van Gogh. He showed sixty paintings from Van Gogh's Amsterdam studio, "without counting a lot of his watercolors and sketches." Vollard's comment on the exhibition: "The most important of the paintings, such as the famous *Poppy Field*, were not priced above 400 francs. But except for the young painters, the public showed little enthusiasm." Twenty-five years later (ca. 1928), *The Poppy Field* was worth 300,000 francs ($12,000). By the 1980s, Japanese moguls were paying $40 million and more for Van Gogh. Although Vollard does not follow up the story of Van Gogh in his autobiography, it is clear that this was one of the few instances where he failed to follow his hunches. No Van Goghs are believed to have been found in Vollard's massive collection, after his death.

Similarly, Vollard points out how Picasso's famous *Saltimbanques (The Frugal Repast)* was sold by the artist in 1908 for 1,000 francs, resold in 1931 for 11,500 francs, and in 1931 was bought at a sale in the United States for $1,000,000. There is a valuable lithograph, a trial proof, of this famous etching in Erich's Paris collection.

No wonder that at the age of twelve Erich, a precocious and artistically fine-tuned Yugoslav neophyte, was already impressed by Vollard, this "impresario of art," and dreamed only of absorbing his aura.

This aura was cultivated early in Vollard's career. At the turn of the century, his cellar at 41 Rue Lafitte became the mecca for all of the "who's who" in the art world. They came to partake of scintillating repartee and home-cooked chicken curry, the national dish of Vollard's native island of Reunion. In his autobiography, Vollard nonchalantly drops the names of his guests — Renoir, Degas, Forain, Cezanne, Redon, Rodin.

One evening a lady guest, who had just published a volume of verse, got up and, with little persuasion, began to declaim one of her poems. "This," Vollard recounts, "threatened to be followed by the whole volume, barring some unexpected intervention."

"While the poetess was pouring out her verses, my cat began showing signs of uneasiness. The poetess, having ceased for a moment, the cat, reassured, started licking its kitten. Alas, the lady did not long remain silent. She had hardly opened her mouth again when the cat flung herself upon her, all her claws extended. The lady recited no more for that evening.[1]

Once Renoir was reminiscing about a Dutch model.

"You've no idea how lovely that girl's breasts were — heavy and firm — and the pretty little fold underneath with a golden shadow.... I was so pleased by her docility and so delighted with her skin that caught the light so beautifully, that I half thought of bringing my Dutch girl to Paris... so long as someone didn't go and seduce her straight away, and she would keep that peach complexion for a bit (Renoir's favorite color for his nudes, Ed.). I told her mother, who seemed to be keeping a strict watch over her, that if she would let her come with me, I would see to it that the men would have no chance of running after her.

"'But then what's the use of her going to Paris, if you're going to prevent her from ***working***?' she asked.

"I tumbled at once to the nature of my 'virgin's' occupation when she was not sitting for me," Renoir concluded.

Recalling Rodin's classic sculpture, *The Kiss*, Vollard remembers admiring it when the writer Besnard, standing next to him, remarked: "But surely you see, it's merely two models. Those lovers have never slept together and they haven't the slightest wish to!"

Vollard tells of a Dutchman coming into his gallery and asking who Vollard thought was the greatest contemporary painter whose works he could purchase.

"To tell the truth," said Vollard, "it is impossible to decide who is the **greatest** painter, there are the greatest **painters** — Cezanne, Renoir, Monet, Degas..."

"Hold on. When I hear too many names at a time, it makes my brain seethe."

"In case of doubt Rabelais recommended the use of dice," Vollard suggested.

"My sister made me swear," the customer replied, "never to touch dice or cards."

1. The cat was Vollard's favorite animal. He had several of them who had the run of the house. In fact, in his will he bequeathed a sum of money to "the old lady and the lost cats in the public park." Could Vollard's attachment to cats reflect his rough, independent nature, preferring a pet with a mind and personality of its own rather than an obedient one.

"But if we put the names in a hat and drew lots, that wouldn't be gambling? Would it?"

The client thought that was a good idea and he wrote down on slips of paper the names that Vollard dictated to him: Cezanne, Renoir, Degas, Monet, Gauguin, etc. He also absent-mindedly picked a label with Van Gogh's name on it, which had been lying on the table, and put it into the hat as well. The first name he drew was that of Van Gogh. Then he decided to make another draw and Cezanne's name came up. Vollard sold him 30 of Cezanne's works and several by Van Gogh.

A few years later Vollard heard that the man's sister had entrusted her fortune to him to look after. When it was discovered that he had spent it all in Paris buying paintings, the purchases were submitted to experts and the man was examined medically. The experts were unanimous in declaring that the old paintings proved he was an ignoramus in art, but the modern ones, the Cezannes and Van Goghs, could only have been bought by a madman. The mental experts confirmed the conclusion of the art experts and the man was confined to a lunatic asylum. When he died the paintings were sold, fetching more than two million francs.

When news of this story got about, some people thought that only madmen had a flair for art. So several connoisseurs got together, collected a sum of money and sent some half-witted creature to purchase art for them. They sent one of their number to accompany him and arrange to send home the pictures the lunatic would select. But the latter spent most of his time in various Parisian "pleasure resorts" and soon exhausted the money. With that the venture came to an end.

Apropos of the above, Vollard tells of the parents of a boy who was growing up contrary and a bit looney. Someone advised them that since paintings by "loonies" fetched the best prices they should teach him to paint. So they put canvasses, paints and brushes within his reach and told him not to touch them. The unruly youngster immediately seized the canvasses and covered them with paint.

The parents took his output to a gallery owner and said: "We've come to show you some lunatic paintings."

"Look here," said the dealer, "do you take me for a fool? Lunatic painting is when you don't know if it's a portrait or a landscape or a still-life. Whereas look at this. Everything here is perfectly recognizable." He refused to take them.

The parents were thunderstruck.

"Christ," exclaimed the father, "that's nearly fifteen hundred francs worth of paint and canvas gone down the drain."[1]

Vollard dwells at length on the American writer and art patron, Gertrude Stein, who created one of Paris's most popular *salons* for indigent and expatriate artists and *literati*. Like Vollard, she too was prophetically ahead of her time in judging the works of the erstwhile novices.

Vollard recalls how in 1905 he had lent a Cezanne portrait of the artist's wife in a red armchair to the *Salon d'Automne* and how he would notice every time he went there, Gertrude Stein and her two brothers seated on a bench silently admiring the painting. When the exhibit was over and the painting was returned to Vollard's shop, Gertrude Stein and her brother, Leon, came to "bring me the price" for it.

"Now," Miss Stein said, "the picture is ours."

"They might have been ransoming someone they loved," Vollard remarked.

The Steins became good customers of Vollard. He once remarked that they were the only ones who bought pictures: "not because they were rich, but despite the fact that they weren't."

"Gertrude Stein," he wrote in his autobiography, "is a very attractive personality, in which the artist in her predominates. She writes for her own pleasure; if fame has come to her, it is certainly not because she sought it. There is nothing more lively, more fascinating than her conversation. Her eyes sparkle with intelligence. Their expression at times is mocking, but mockery is tempered with indulgence; if a spice of it creeps into her speech it is rounded off by a gay laugh at her own expense.

---

1. This reminds one of the story of the Art Institute in Chicago, perhaps apocryphal, which once put on an exhibition of abstract paintings to which it invited the art critics. Most of them praised the works with elaborate explanations of their merits. A few were neutral. Fewer still, panned the exhibition. It was revealed later that the paintings had been rendered by the chimpanzees at the Brookfield Zoo, who had been given several pails of colored paints, and then alternately daubed, splashed and smeared the canvasses put at their disposal

"To see her with her dress of coarse velveteen, her sandals with leather straps, and her general air of simplicity, one would take her at first sight for a housewife whose horizon is restricted to her dealing with the greengrocer. But you have only to encounter her glance to perceive in her something beyond the ordinary bourgeoise. The vivacity of her glance betrays the observer, the investigator whom nothing escaped. Yet one cannot withhold one's confidence from her, so disarming is the laugh she seems constantly to turn against herself."

Vollard once remarked in his autobiography: "how many times have I not regretted that nature has not endowed me with an easygoing, jovial manner!" Yet he had nothing to regret. His gruff, sometimes insulting manner brought him more attention than an easygoing way would have. Instead of courting public approval, he flouted it, and benefited in the process. As the American art critic Henry McBride once noted, "People got into the habit of going to his little gallery on the Rue Lafitte in order to be shocked — and as shock produces more outcries than satisfaction — it developed in a very short time that the Rue Lafitte outcries reverberated around the world. In the entire history of the art of picture setting, there never was such a comedy with a happy ending as this, for it all turned out as the prestidigitator wished. Cezanne was acknowledged in the public places to be great, vast prices were put on his productions, and Vollard became rich."

In 1906, just as Vollard was beginning to establish himself, Cezanne died. Vollard, however, managed to recover the master's remaining paintings from his widow. As for his second great discovery, George Rouault, matters did not go so smoothly.

Rouault was a truly revolutionary artist whose paintings fell into no known pattern or school. Vollard first and Šlomovič after him were fascinated by his art. Erich, as we noted earlier, created a strong rapport with Rouault; he gathered fifty of his engravings for his Yugoslav collection, more works than of any other artist. He left another half-dozen Rouault engravings in the Paris vault, as well as fourteen pages of poems by Rouault, one of them, quoted earlier, dedicated to Erich, written and illustrated in his own hand.

As for Vollard, he published three books featuring Rouault's illustrations; two of them were the last books he published. But he badly abused the artist's goodwill and patience by retaining several hundred of Rouault's works, which he had commissioned for other books but never published. As Vollard wrote, "with my habit of putting everything off, the years pass." In Rouault's case it was a good dozen years or more.

Vollard, as early as 1917, had given Rouault a studio on his premises from where he worked for many years. Rouault also signed a contract with Vollard which, in effect, controlled his entire output until Vollard's death in 1939. This agreement, Vollard felt, gave him the prerogative to demand more and more work from Rouault as the years went by.

Indeed, Vollard's lifetime habit of procrastination cost Rouault dearly, keeping him in dire financial straits for most of the period that he worked out of Vollard's premises. Rouault described the relationship as a "barbed-wire entanglement."

After Vollard's death, Rouault, ever restrained, remarked: "There were dark hours when I doubted I should ever see publication. If injustice has been shown Vollard let us agree that he had taste and a passion for making beautiful books, without breaking any speed records. But it would have taken three centuries to bring to perfection the various works with which, in utter disregard of earthly limitations, he wished to burden the pilgrim."

Vollard, at his death, left hundreds of drawings, sketches, and paintings commissioned from other artists for planned books. At least twenty-five volumes were in the works at the time of his death. In his lifetime he had published twenty books, six of them authored by himself.

Vollard's books were invariably limited editions of 150 to 350 copies. The volumes were meticulously proofread, edited and printed. (***illegible***). Since they were priced at $150 to $200 each, consequently not all editions were sold out. Today these rare books fetch anywhere from $1,000 to $15,000.

Many of the volumes contained anywhere from 50 to 100 original lithographs and other engravings, many of them detachable. Vollard presented Erich with copies of virtually all of his published books. Erich had at his disposal a wide selection of original lithographs which he removed and added to his collection as separate items.

Of the fifty Rouault engravings in Belgrade, nineteen were taken from the book: *The Reincarnation of Pere Ubu,* created by the controversial writer Alfred

Jarry. Ubu, a symbol of all the self-inflated bullies and humbugs of his time, suited Vollard as an excellent vehicle to vent his ever-active spleen against wide segments of the populace, especially officialdom. One of his favorite targets was French colonialism; Vollard's brother and heir, Lucien, was a colonial official in Vietnam. And who would be more suited to illustrate this satiric time than Rouault — that brooding, searching, contemplative artist whose favorite subjects, for commiserating with the human race and ridiculing it, were grotesque exaggerations of clowns, officials, prostitutes, priests, and judges.

In Rouault's writings collected by Erich are numerous acerbic attacks on Hitler and his Nazi ideology. During the war the Nazis, indeed, ransacked Rouault's home, from which he had escaped to go into hiding.

After the war Rouault had to sue the Vollard estate to collect his unused works, which the heirs did not want to surrender. In 1946, seven years after Vollard's death, the court ruled in his favor. Rouault then destroyed many of the works as not befitting his current style of painting.

Perhaps Rouault's greatest "tribute" to his patron was his portrait of Vollard. It was one of the more penetrating among many portraits of Vollard done by his artist-clients. In a wash drawing done in 1925, Rouault renders Vollard's disembodied head with his typically heavy black lines, leaving a large cogitative forehead, untouched by the brush, dominating the picture. The half-closed eyes look downward; together with the heavy jowls and tightly pressed lips, the painting conveys an overwhelming sense of inner strength, power of will, and... cussedness.

Among two portraits of Vollard done by Pierre Bonnard, one shows a seated Vollard holding on his lap his favorite domestic animal, a cat. His head falls forward in what looks like a deep sleep. A feigned sleep was, in fact, one of Vollard's favorite poses, enabling him to eavesdrop on those present and glean from them information which he would later put to use.

Among the engravings found in Erich Šlomovič's Paris safe are several other portraits of Vollard. One of them, by Picasso, was chosen by Vollard to illustrate the cover of *Recollections of an Art Merchant*. In a few well-defined lines, Picasso manages to achieve what one reviewer described as "a sublime simplification of the technique of drypoint engraving. Renouncing any pictorial accessories, Picasso evokes before our eyes the whole complex personality of Vollard...

seizing not only the creative passion but also the loneliness of the old fighter, his impulsive lucidity, his weariness, his resignation"... and, he might have added, his pugnacity.

Picasso did two other portraits of Vollard, one in the artist's cubist style. It comprises a complex series of interlocking geometrical designs from which the image of Vollard seems miraculously to emerge. No less miraculous is the fact that both Picasso and Rouault saw their subject in the same light, with the exaggerated forehead, the downturned look, the image of contrariness and restrained power.

Erich's eclectic collection provides further insights into the complex personalities of Vollard and the famous artists surrounding him. As mentioned earlier, in a rare Renoir self-portrait (found in the Paris safe) done in charcoal and dated 1915, a dedication by pen in the lower left-hand corner states: "To Vollard, my sympathetic pest."

Vollard, reportedly, had been after Renoir to do a portrait of him in an unusual costume, prompting Renoir's famous remark: "Do not insist any more, Vollard. You can fucking well dress yourself up as a toreador and I'll do your mug."

Clearly, Vollard was much more than a sharp businessman. Besides being a keen decipherer of human nature, he was a highly cultured man who understood the art enterprise in its deepest sense.

"When I opened my shop in the Rue Lafitte in 1894," Vollard wrote in his autobiography, "the Impressionist movement had won the day; but by then fresh adventurers were exploring fresh paths. For painting is not stationary. It cannot escape the urge to renewal, the incessant evolution that manifests itself in every form of art. At the same time it may be said with truth that each of these forms reacts upon the others, with sometimes one, sometimes the other predominating, providing the impulse for some fresh direction."

Erich Šlomovič, perfectly attuned to Vollard's understanding of art, to his ambitious, tenacious, and shrewd nature, no doubt reminded Vollard, in the sunset of his life, of his own youth, of the time when he set out to conquer the world of art that he had learned to love.

PART II

THE PARIS YEARS

Chapter XII

PARIS COURT PROBES COLLECTION'S ORIGIN

For years the French court has been wrestling with the question of the legitimacy of Erich's collection.

As noted in Chapter V, Vollard's heirs claimed that the collection was obtained by subterfuge. Vollard's brother and principal heir Lucien Vollard, they said, had loaned the works of art to Šlomovič, who was supposed to return them. No, said the Herzlers: Erich accumulated the collection over the years by his own means.

The Vollard side was represented by Mrs. Assunta Bertozzi Jonas, and after her death in 1984 by her nephew and only heir, Louis Sebastien. Mrs. Jonas was the widow of Edouard Jonas, a noted Jewish antiquarian and member of parliament who had escaped to America at the outbreak of the war; he had been a close friend and confidant of Lucien Vollard. When Lucien died in 1952 he left most of his estate, comprising his late brother's works of art, to Jonas. When the latter died in 1961, his wife inherited him.

Vollard's other heirs were his two sisters on the island of Reunion, where he was born, and Madame Madelaine de Galea, the unrequited love of his life. The sisters passed away after the war, both old maids without heirs. So did Madame de Galea, who left her estate to her only son Robert. He, in turn, left it to his only son Christian de Galea. The latter, who was alive and well during the course of the trial in Paris, seemed quite satisfied with some twenty valuable Vollard paintings still in his possession, including works by Renoir and Degas, and chose not to join Mrs. Jonas's suit.

On what did Mrs. Jonas and later her nephew, Louis Sebastien, base their case?

Their first assumption was that the bulk of the collection originated with Ambroise Vollard, as determined by the art experts who examined it. Next, that Erich was an agent of Vollard's and as such held art works from him in trust or on loan and not as his private possession.

Erich, reportedly, then "smuggled" the bulk of his collection out of France with the help of Yugoslav diplomats and hid the rest of it in a Paris safe. To further cover his tracks, they contended, Erich registered the contents of the Paris safe in his father's name.

Another indication of the collection's illegitimacy, it was claimed, was the incomplete series of photographs of the works of Odilon Redon found in the Paris safe. The fact that the other part of the series remained with the Vollard estate was a further indication of the doubtful nature of the possession, since art experts agreed that the photographs were of value as a whole and Vollard would never have given away a part of them.

Moreover, if most of the 190 items under litigation were bequeathed by Vollard, or given as a gift before his death on July 22,1939, as claimed by the Herzlers, then Šlomovič should have notified the administrators of Vollard's estate to that effect before his departure for Yugoslavia early in March 1940. His failure to do so, said Sebastien, obviated this claim and further showed the "clandestine" nature of the possession.

The project of mounting an exhibition of French art in Yugoslavia, argued Sebastien, was undertaken with the backing of Ambroise Vollard during his lifetime. It was on this basis that he loaned the works to Erich. This assumption was reinforced by the fact that Vollard helped Šlomovič to get many artists to autograph their works for him.

Furthermore, said Sebastien, the great confusion existing in Vollard's estate after his death allowed a further "misappropriation and plundering" of his works of art, a situation from which Šlomovič allegedly benefited. This looting, it was said, was carried out mostly by Martin Fabiani, the administrator of the estate of Lucien Vollard. Fabiani was capable of such depredations, as evidenced by his alleged collaboration with Nazi plundering of art during the war when he was in charge of the Vollard gallery in Paris.

Sebastien conceded that a dozen or more items in the Paris safe personally dedicated to Erich by Vollard and by various artists should rightfully belong to him.

According to French law (as in most Western countries), the possessor of property is presumed to be the lawful owner unless proved otherwise. In other words, the burden of proof was on the Vollards. The lower court felt that the Vollards brought no convincing evidence to prove their contentions and thus, in 1984, after three years of deliberations, awarded the contents of the Paris safe to the Herzlers in Israel.

Mrs. Jonas appealed; soon after, she passed away. After three more years, in 1987, the court decided that it couldn't decide since it did not know enough about art to determine its origin, its commercial vicissitudes, or its eventual owner. Consequently, it appointed an art expert to help it decide whether Erich's possession of most of the 190 items in the Paris safe was illegitimate, as claimed by Vollard's heir, or kosher as claimed by the Herzlers.

The report by the expert, Fare, which took three years to prepare, seemed to lean toward the Vollard side.

Fernand Cohen, the attorney for the Herzlers, didn't wait for the report. Shortly before it was submitted he traveled to Yugoslavia to collect material. After the report was submitted to the court on March 30, 1990, and seeing its paucity, Cohen returned to Yugoslavia for additional material.

What he found became the key to winning his case. Most of it was new and unknown to the parties in the Paris trial, including the court-appointed expert.

How did Fernand Cohen manage to obtain it?

By a simple stratagem.

On his first trip to Yugoslavia he approached the director of the National Museum in Belgrade, where the Šlomovič exhibition was being shown at the time.

"I need your help," he told him. "If I lose my case in Paris you'll be in trouble. It will mean that the court will have decided that Erich Šlomovič obtained his collection illegitimately. If so, the greater part of it, which is in your museum, will also be considered illegitimate. This will put the international spotlight on you and create a strong precedent for a claim against you by the Vollard heirs in France."

Fearing such a claim from France, much more than from the Israeli heirs who had already lost in the Yugoslav courts, the museum tapped its coffers and other sources, uncovering in the process crucial documents for Cohen and his clients.

Cohen's first task was to demolish the Vollard heirs' arguments.

The law concerning movable property, he pointed out, assumes that possession is equivalent to title obtained in good faith. The possessor does not have to prove title, unless the claimant can prove that his possession is neither innocent nor of common knowledge and that it is of a precarious or dubious nature. Moreover, according to article 2268 of the French Civil Code, "good faith is always presumed and he who claims bad faith must prove it."

The ignoring of this law by Vollard's heirs, said Cohen, exposed the "audacious" nature of Mrs. Jonas's initial claim, which was based on her conviction that since the majority of the objects under litigation belonged originally to Ambroise Vollard (a fact admitted by Cohen) they could not have left his patrimony and should remain part of it.

Asked to substantiate her argument, Mrs. Jonas claimed "with aplomb, but without bringing a single proof" that Erich Šlomovič was a broker (agent) for Ambroise Vollard and that after the latter's death he was entrusted by Lucien Vollard with organizing in Yugoslavia an exhibition in memory of the celebrated merchant. The exhibition was to comprise 429 works which Erich took with him to Yugoslavia in 1940 and also the 190 items which he deposited in safe No. 69-I at the Société Général Bank in Paris.

On the heels of this double claim, Cohen said, Mrs. Jonas, and later her inheritor Louis Sebastien, produced nothing in writing to prove the existence of such a contract or agreement, or any other document, between Erich Šlomovič and Ambroise or Lucien Vollard.

As a result, the first judge assumed good faith on Erich's part, especially after seeing the many items dedicated to him personally by the artists and men of letters. Since Mrs. Jonas still did not convince the court on appeal, it appointed the expert Fare to deal with her arguments (per its decision of February 26, 1987).

Fare, failing to discover the "slightest documentation" for the contentions of Vollard's heirs, addressed himself to the Société Général Bank, to the customs authorities, the archives of the police, and the cultural counselor of the French government. This "fruitless" and "flagrantly irregular" gathering of evidence, Cohen charged, produced only three items hostile to Erich Šlomovič. These were testimonies by two individuals who had known Erich personally — Daniel Wildenstein, son of a noted Parisian art merchant, and Dina Vlerny, model and consort of the sculpture Aristide Maillol, and a deposition from a certain professor of art, Sreten Maric. The latter had known Erich and had spoken badly of him to Kasanin, the director of the Belgrade museum, when the latter was deciding whether to show Erich's collection there or not.

These testimonies could not have succeeded in any case, Cohen contended, because they did not constitute "initial written proof" of a dubious ownership as required under Articles 1341 and 1347 of the French Civil Code.

I spoke to Paul Prompt, Louis Sebastien's attorney, about these contentions. A tall, blustery, back-slapping type of man, Prompt retorted that the presumption of ownership should never have applied in the first place since the other side never produced the necessary documents to prove possession by Erich Šlomovič, as required by French law.

Although the court did not accept Prompt's argument, Cohen decided not to rely on the presumption of ownership alone, as he was entitled to do. Instead, because of the "vacuity and one-sidedness" of the art expert, Fare, he decided to "present and analyze the many new and probing documents which [he had] collected in Yugoslavia." Not sparing the epithets, Cohen declared that these documents would "expose the inanity of the so-called proofs" brought against his clients.

The court should be aware, Cohen added, that the Herzlers had not limited their search to France and Yugoslavia: they had also approached the Hoover Institute at Stanford University in California, which possesses extensive documents from the Second World War, as well as Columbia University in New York, which has the archives of Prince Paul, Regent of Yugoslavia, up to March 1941. Both institutions, however, replied that they found no trace of Erich Šlomovič in their records.

When and where did the so-called mystery about Erich Šlomovič's acquisition, upon which the Vollard heirs based their case, begin? The misinformation, it transpired, began in Zagreb during Erich's exhibition there in 1940. It was disseminated by the extensive and frequently erroneous press coverage of the event and the man, given credence and oft-repeated up to the present day.

Paul Prompt gave copious quotes from these reports to reinforce his case regarding the "surreptitious and doubtful nature" of Erich's possession. He cited five press reports from the time of the opening of the exhibition in November 1940 which, he pointed out, was attended by, among others, the consul general of France in Zagreb, M. Gueyard. All the press reports cited by Prompt allege that Ambroise Vollard willed the collection to Erich before his death.

Since Vollard's will was written long before his death and did not mention Erich, this was an intentionally misleading smokescreen put up by Erich Šlomovič himself, Prompt contended.

Not so, retorted Fernand Cohen. The press gave no evidence to back this assumption; all the reports were based on hearsay.

"Had Monsieur Prompt made the effort to read more carefully the documents submitted by me to the court he would have noticed that only one newspaper quotes Erich in the first person. This was *Hrvatski Dnevik* of November 24, 1940, which quotes him as follows:

> "I first became interested in art at the age of 12. At the beginning I studied our [Yugoslav] artists. Later I went to France, London and Switzerland. In Paris I was constantly in the company of well-known artists, such as Bonnard, Maillol, Matisse, etc.... and I also knew well the noted publisher, Vollard. All of this together with my passion and love for art was my principal motivation for putting this collection together."

Not a word about inheriting it.

To reinforce the impression of an avid young collector of great talent and drive, capable of mounting the collection by his own efforts, Cohen goes on to cite other sources, including documents found in the safe of the Paris bank and examined by Fare. Among them is the text of a manuscript by the art critic Michel, the author of a book entitled *Les Montparnos,* in which he tells about "the great pleasure I had in writing these lines for the publication of the

Montparnos in the very intelligent and artistic translation by Mr. Erich Šlomovič" (Fare's report, p. 373).

On page 390 of Fare's report there is an autograph of the Russian painter Terechkovitch, who declared that he shared with Erich a common love for the art of Soutine (who was not part of the Vollard stable of painters) and that he had written these lines "for the book which Erich Šlomovič is preparing on me."

On March 20, 1981, the Belgrade newspaper *Politika* published an article by Sinisa Paunovič entitled "The Mysterious Šlomovič" which tells of Paunovič's acquaintance with Erich during the 1930s when he first heard his name and learned of his interest in art. He notes that a French artist, whom he probably met in Vichy in 1939, had described to him Erich's collection which reflected "a very high level of culture and knowledge of the plastic arts."

Paunovič adds that young Yugoslav painters residing in Paris said they were "fascinated by [Šlomovič]" and by his artistic knowledge; the Bulgarian painter, Papazov, spoke of him "in superlatives" and praised "his theoretical knowledge of the history of art" as well as his lack of commercialism, because it was obvious that he collected these works "out of his love for them and he dreamed of seeing all of them one day in a gallery which would belong to him either in Paris or in his own country."

These, Cohen contended, were the only objective items of information, based on proven documents and testimonials, which existed on the personality of Erich.

About the years Erich apparently spent in Paris, from 1935 to the beginning of 1940, information is even more scarce and what there is concerns only the year 1939 and the first months of 1940. There is no proof that he studied chemistry in Lyon or elsewhere, as contended in some of the Yugoslav papers in 1940 (it was his brother Egon who studied chemistry), nor that he visited England or Switzerland, except for evidence indicating that he might have been a live-in student at the College of Cannes between 1926 and 1931.

Paul Prompt, in his court appearance and in my conversation with him, claimed that Erich was an undercover agent for the Comintern and, like Tito, passed money and volunteers through Paris to the Loyalists in Spain. He used his art activities as a cover, Prompt averred. While this charge may have been one of the factors that impelled the producers of the *Donator* film to create a

Spanish Loyalist girlfriend for Erich in Paris, the police services who were questioned by Fare said that they did not find any information concerning Erich which could have justified Prompt's assumption that Erich had been an "agent for the international communist movement."

Nor was Prompt able to give the author any evidence for his accusations.

As for Prompt's claim, repeated in may press reports, that Erich acted as a broker or agent for Vollard, he could produce no proof of this either.

All the evidence points to Erich's single-minded pursuit of art and artists. During his last year in Paris (1939-40), for example, he registered for a course in the general history of art at the Ecole du Louvre. There is also ample evidence of his frequent visits to the studios of Maillol, Matisse, and other artists ("I frequently had to visit Matisse's studio at 6 a.m. because he started work very early"; exhibit No. FC67).

Based on the evidence from the autographs and dedications in his Paris collection, it appears that he was more interested in the creative and aesthetic aspects of the artists' works than in trading with them, Cohen claimed. (Footnote: "Nor is there any evidence to confirm the fable that he was a special secretary, a collaborator an agent for Ambroise Vollard... despite the fact that Mrs. Jonas and her successor Sebastien 'were respectively in possession of Ambroise Vollard's archives at the beginning of the present litigation'."[1]

The possession by the Wildenstein Foundation of part of the archives of Ambroise Vollard is attested to in Fare's report, together with his interview with Daniel Wildenstein about his recollections of Erich Šlomovič. Yet neither Mrs. Jonas nor Sebastien, Cohen noted, contributed to the argument a single document which could establish the existence of any professional bond between Ambroise Vollard and Erich Šlomovič.

Another "fable," still prevalent in Yugoslavia, was even believed by the Herzlers, as a result of erroneous information which they received in the course of their legal process in Yugoslavia in 1956. At that time they too assumed that Erich was an heir of Ambroise Vollard, when in actuality Vollard's will dates to 1911, before Erich was born.

---

1. The archives were subsequently donated mostly to the national museums, with the surplus being granted to the Wildenstein Foundation established by Daniel Wildenstein's family — and devoted to art research and propagation.

The theory that Erich inherited his collection from Vollard was first advanced by certain journalists on the occasion of the exposition of 1940. It was later repeated by Erich's artist friend Othon Gliha, who, Cohen charges, "let it be known that he had gained the confidence of Erich Šlomovič (as noted in the article in *List* on March 28, 1981, and again in the filmed interview during the exhibition in Zagreb in 1989). This same Gliha did not hide the fact that it was he who contaminated the scriptwriter of the film *Donator* [with this erroneous information]."

Nevertheless, in his filmed interview Gliha softened the matter by declaring: "There are many things which I have overlooked... as regards the will there are various theories and approaches... but I know absolutely nothing about them."

Cohen then proceeded to cast doubt on Gliha's reliability:

It should also be noted that Oton Gliha, who is today [1989] 76 years old, has become acquainted as a result of his friendship with Erich, with journalists, writers and cinema people, achieving a fame in the process which his talent as a painter never gave him. There is thus evidence that, imbued with the importance of his role in this story, he has been inclined to exaggerate and allowed a number of regrettable errors to creep into his testimony.

- He assumes, for example, that the vocation of a collector came to Erich at the age of 12 while hearing a lecture on Ambroise Vollard's biography, *Recollections of an Art Merchant*, forgetting that the book was written in 1937 when Erich was 22 years old.
- He places the Boulevard Jourdan where Erich lived [i.e., Hotel Ideal] near the Porte De Clignancourt, whereas it is located at the opposite end of town near Porte d'Orleans.
- He placed the gallery of Katia Granoff on the Blvd. Raspail whereas it was located at the Quai Conti. Oton Friesz, who Gliha says exhibited at Granoff's, was under contract since 1936 to the Max Kaganovitch gallery, which was located on the Blvd. Raspail.
- Gliha placed the Petrides gallery on the Rue La Boetie, whereas it was then located on the Avenue Declassé.
- He declared Petrides dead whereas he is still living.

In the introduction to the 1989 Belgrade museum catalog, Cohen pointed out, the art critic Vlado Buzancič proclaims that "Šlomovič inherited Vollard," but not without adding that the exhibition in Zagreb in 1940 aroused "an incalculable number of imaginary and moralizing versions, as well as café and salon intrigues about Šlomovič and his collection...."

Finally, the weekly *Nin* of Belgrade, in an introduction to an article on November 9, 1989, devoted to Erich, repeats the version that Erich was an heir of Vollard. It goes on to describe a scene at Vollard's funeral where his will is read, without apprising its readers that the scene was pure fiction and was taken verbatim from the movie *The Donator*. The magazine, Cohen charged, "did not even take the trouble to put in quotation marks the [movie] passage according to which Erich became heir to part of the collection."

Only a few articles do not allege that Erich was an heir of Vollard. One of them was by Paunovič in *Politika* on July 8, 1940 (four months after Erich's departure from Paris and four months before his Zagreb exhibit), in which he reveals the existence of the Šlomovič collection to the public for the first time. Paunovič mentions that "several years ago [Erich] undertook to collect artistic works" and that he was a close friend of the collector Ambroise Vollard, who died a year ago; **but he establishes no connection between these two facts**.

Similarly, in the article published by *Hrvatski Dnevnik* on November 25, 1940, which gives the only first-person quotes by Erich Šlomovič, there is not the least allusion to a will. Erich attributes his collection to his frequenting artists, to his acquaintance with the "celebrated publisher, Vollard," and to his "passionate love of art."

There is no indication anywhere that Erich himself was ever the source of information about his being an heir of Ambroise Vollard, a patently false claim which according to the attorney for Vollard's heirs was spread by Erich as a smokescreen to cover up the illegitimate nature of his acquisition.

Thus, concluded Cohen, are legends born and perpetuated.

Chapter XIII

THE BOMBSHELL

One of the most enigmatic items placed in evidence by Paul Prompt, Sebastien's attorney, was a letter allegedly written by Erich on March 23, 1940, shortly after arriving in Yugoslavia with his collection.

Prompt claimed that this letter constituted the initial written proof of the possession's dubious character, as required by Article 1347 of the Civil Code. The handwritten letter is postmarked Belgrade, and is addressed by the late Ambroise Vollard's brother, Lucien, at 14 Avenue Robinson, Chatenay Melabry (Seine), France:

Dear Mr. Vollard,

Excuse me for not writing to you sooner.

Everything went well. The people are frequently jealous, sometimes without reason. I have done everything as agreed. Per your desire I do not mention your name. This is for the best at the moment. You know the reasons.

I have also received letters from Paris from persons you know and which are likely to interest you as well.

I would be most happy if you would answer this letter. I would be very content to receive news from you. When I will be in Paris I will phone you but in the meantime I would appreciate your answer to this letter.

I will let you know in advance of my arrival in Paris.

Awaiting your response, I beg you, Mr. Vollard, to accept my most sincere salutations.

Devotedly,

Chlomovitch

Sebastien claimed that this letter indicated a prior arrangement between Erich and Lucien Vollard, namely, a confidential loan of the collection by Vollard for an exhibit in Yugoslavia which Erich was to return later, but which he did not or could not return because of the war.

No such thing, retorted Cohen. In the absence of any substantiating documents, such assumptions remained conjectures. Cohen had brought back documents from Yugoslavia, he claimed, which disproved this contention conclusively, clarified the allusions in the letter, and finally revealed how Erich had acquired his collection.

For the Vollard side, and for the court, Cohen's documents constituted a bombshell which more than any other evidence won the case for the Herzlers.

The first hints that such documents existed came in two articles published by the Belgrade museum. The first hint, Cohen discovered, was found in the introduction to a catalog for an exhibition in the Department of Engravings at the museum; the catalog was issued in March 1986 under the title "French Artists and the Parisian School." This special exhibit included many works from the Šlomovič collection. In the introduction to the catalog, Vanja Kraut, one of the museum's curators, writes, without revealing his sources, that "for reasons which only [Vollard] new and with an incredible generosity, Vollard saw fit to give from his collection a number of pastels and oil paintings to Erich Šlomovič, a Belgradian collector living in Paris."

A second hint came in another article, which appeared as an epilog to the more extensive catalog from the subsequent Šlomovič exhibition of 1989. Miodrag Kolarič, who was director of the National Museum during the 1960s, tells of hearing from a fellow artist, Svetolik Lukič, now deceased, how he made Erich's acquaintance in Paris "one or two years before the war." Lukič told Kolarič that, at Erich's invitation, he saw in his hotel room, located near the Gare du Nord, a collection of "oils, engravings and sketches by Degas, Renoir,

Pissaro, Cezanne, Derain and other famous French Impressionist and *fauve* artists. Upon inquiring about the origin of the paintings, Šlomovič explained that he was a "close collaborator and secretary to Ambroise Vollard, the famous gallery owner and that it was the latter who helped him gather the collection."

This testimony, which confirms in essence the story of Othon Gliha about his own encounter with Šlomovič and his collection in Paris, errs, like Gliha's account, in the location of Erich's hotel and in the description of Erich as Vollard's secretary, agent, or assistant. What is crucial, however, is that both witnesses date their meetings with Erich as occurring before Vollard's death, which can be deduced from the phrase "one or two years before the war" and from the use of the present tense to describe the so-called collaboration between Šlomovič and Vollard.

In the same epilog, Kolarič relates how Šlomovič proposed to loan his collection to the National Museum in Belgrade for an exhibition, as a result of which the "Museum made inquiries in France, via diplomatic channels, as to the origin of the collection." Kolarič adds further that "I had the occasion ten years later to meet Milan Kasanin, the director of the Museum before the war, who went himself to Paris where he met with the lawyer of the Vollard family who confirmed that the collection was legitimately owned by Šlomovič.

Unfortunately, Kolarič had no documents relating to these two episodes. Kasanin died in the late 1980s and his granddaughter, Zoja Bohič, who resided in Belgrade, informed the Herzlers' lawyer that her grandfather's archives were destroyed in the bombardment of Belgrade on April 6, 1941.

At this point Cohen came upon a third clue as to the existence of documents attesting to the nature of Erich's acquisition and ownership.

On March 4, 1990, the weekly *Ekspres Nedeljna Revija* published an article by Nikola Kusovač, a curator at the Belgrade museum, *which revealed for the first time* the existence of a crucial letter addressed on March 1, 1940, to Milan Kasanin by Predrag (Pedja) Milosavljevič, a painter and cultural adviser to the Yugoslav Legation in Paris (who died in 1987). The letter reported on an inquiry into Šlomovič's collection, undertaken at Kasanin's request, with Mr. Fabiani, "administrator of Vollard's inheritance."

In the course of his visits to Yugoslavia, Cohen heard about Kusovač's article, obtained a translation, and established contact with its author and with his superior, Jevta Jevtocič, the director of the Belgrade museum at the time.

He thus obtained on April 13,1990, a certified copy of the original letter of March 1, 1940, telling about Erich's acquisition, as well as copies of other documents, also certified, among which was an earlier letter on the same subject, dated January 30, 1940, from Milosavljevič to Kasanin.

These two letters were the bombshell which established how Erich acquired the major part of his collection and which, more than any other evidence, won the case for the Herzlers.

How and why were they written?

Having been bombarded by Erich to show his collection at the Belgrade museum, Kasanin, having heard supposedly negative reports on Erich from his assistant curator Pavle Vasič and from the art professor Breten Marič, decided to first check into the man, his collection, and its legitimacy before agreeing to such a request. For this purpose he asked an artist friend, Predrag Milosavljevič, to investigate the matter for him. As it happened, Milosavljevič had already written to him about Erich in January 1940, at his own initiative.

In Milosavljevič's first letter to Kasanin, dated January 30, 1940, he gives an account of a meeting he had with Erich, when the latter let him see his collecting, adding details on Erich's past and present:

> Dear Mr. Kasanin,
>
> I recently met in Paris a compatriot who has acquired a number of precious art objects of the 19th century from a personal collection and from the legacy of the late Ambroise Vollard. Since this collection is on a grand scale, of great importance and connected with the first professional art collector among us I think his case could interest us. It seems that he has also personally contacted the Prince Paul Museum.[1] His name is Erich Šlomovič. He is a Belgradian from Dorcol. I remember now that eight years ago, when he was a bachelor, he used to make the rounds of the ateliers of the Belgradian painters asking for

1. Subsequently the National Museum in Belgrade.

a drawing or an oil painting for a gallery (or museum) that he dreamed of creating in Belgrade. Not having succeeded in creating this gallery, he acquired a bad reputation in the artistic world. It seems that at the same time he got into a personal conflict with Petroč, Popovič and Vasič and owes them money for a portrait. After that he left for France.

According to his parents' wishes, he studied and matriculated in chemistry in Lyon. After that he spent a year and a half in London where he studied art history at the Museographie. During this period he was interested in paintings and books, especially in rare books for collectors.

In the framework of his occupation he made progressive contact with the best-known French art collectors by knocking at their doors as he used to do with ours. His ability and especially his passion for paintings and books seems to have received a better response than with us. He even became the friend of the old Ambroise Vollard and his brother, the lawyer at Versailles.

Rouault made a few drawings for him and wrote a large number of dedications. Matisse has dedicated to him one of his luxurious monographs on which he has signed all the reproductions.

Bonnard, usually inaccessible, received him in his atelier and was photographed with him, as well as Maillol. I have confirmed that he knew Utrillo, who is making for him now, from a postcard, a painting of the Belgrade cathedral. He also knows Le Corbusier, Soutine, Blaise, Cendras, etc. In his place I have seen letters, notes, photos, drawings and paintings from most of these people, which represent, not counting the collection, very important material.

When I met him the whole thing seemed so fantastic and incredible that it was difficult for me to hide my suspicions. I was in his apartment where I held in my hands and leafed through about 10 drawings and pastels by Renoir, especially young girls' heads, plus about 50 drawings and pastels by Degas, as well as large drawings of women, guitar players, or Renoir dancers, some magnificent Constantin Guys, Forain, Mary Cassatt, also portraits by Degas, a guitar player by Matisse — from an early period, a magnificent still life of a pitcher and fruit by Gauguin, two small sculptures by Maillol, drawings from Despiau, watercolors and lithographs by Laprade, a great variety of rare original lithographs in color by Cezanne, as well as a whole range of magnificent books edited by Ambroise Vollard, including the most precious books from the 19th century: *Parallelment, Daphne et Chloe, Fete Galante, La Vie de Renoir*, works of Villon, etc. etc. Šlomovič intends to transport half of his things to Belgrade, where he envisages organizing for the moment two exhibitions. If it will be so decided the Legation has agreed in principle to transfer this material with its own courier in order to protect it from war risks.

In the meantime, considering his past experience with us, Šlomovič is afraid that he will be badly received by our artistic world. He complains that he was just not lucky with us.

Although I have proposed to him a few times to contact the museum directly, he hesitated to do so after it had already refused a gift from him. He said that six months ago he sent a present with his brother, a large album (*The Reincarnation of Father Ubu*, written by Vollard and illustrated by Georges Rouault). The text was so luxuriously done that the initial selling price was 10,000 francs. The book was returned to him without even an accompanying letter and he assumed that the refusal must have been due to his previous differences with Vasič which must have left a bad impression.

It seems that this incident hurt more the pride of Rouault who [subsequently] sketched for Šlomovič [a poem of his with] a *gouache* drawing representing the head of Christ... with the following inscription: "To Mr. Erich Chlomovitch and not the Prince Paul Museum."

Please let me know if you have seen that album, or if there is any other reason that I do not know about to withhold the confidence he feels he deserves.

The attitude of the legation toward Šlomovič, who has already asked for its cooperation in transferring his things, will depend on your response. If I find out any new information concerning the Ambroise Vollard heritage, I will not hesitate to let you know, since the matter is very important.

Our collector stresses that he still has to receive other major items of importance and the trip to New York that he is planning for Vollard's brother will bring in millions.

I take advantage of this occasion to salute you cordially and respectfully.

P. Milosavljevič

Cohen asserted that the intention to transport half of the collection to Belgrade, implying that the other half would be left in Paris, constituted irrefutable proof, if such proof were needed, that the objects found in safe No. 69-I in the Paris bank were indeed deposited there by Erich Šlomovič.

Cohen pointed out that in the first paragraph of the letter, Milosavljevič stated that the objects of art "acquired" by Erich originated "from the personal collection and inheritance of the late Ambroise Vollard." But he does not attribute this affirmation to Erich himself. Instead he confines himself to stating further on that Erich had "become friendly with the old Ambroise Vollard and his brother, a lawyer from Versailles" (Lucien Vollard was actually a former colonial magistrate in Vietnam who resided in Chateny — Malabry.)

In this same letter by Milosavljevič an allusion is made to Erich's "bad reputation" which he acquired among certain artists in Belgrade during the period when he needed their support for the *Kolektanea*. More precisely, there is reference to a difference Erich had with an artist named Vasič "to whom he owed money for a portrait."

Erich had blamed Vasič for the refusal and return by the Prince Paul Museum of an album published by Ambroise Vollard and illustrated by Rouault, which Erich had sent to Kasanin as a gift via his brother six months earlier. It will be recalled that Kasanin had noted at the bottom of Erich's letter of October 30, 1939: "refused as a result of the oral report from Mr. Pavle Vasič."

Eric didn't give up. Three months later, on February 5, 1940, he once more sent a Vollard art album to Kasanin, this time through the good offices of the Yugoslav Legation in Paris. The album was one of Vollard's better-known publications, *The Reincarnations of Father Ubu*, written by Vollard himself and illustrated by George Rouault.

As Milosavljevič's letter indicates, it was he who suggested to Erich that he renew the offer of the gift. Impressed by Milosavljevič's report, this time Kasanin accepted it, hastening to register it on the same day in the museum's inventory of books.

As Vasič told the author of this book and as he wrote to Cohen for the record, he had once made a portrait of Erich for his *Kolektanea* project. "Considering his youth and my approval of the project, it was out of the question that I would demand the least payment," Vasič wrote. This statement, given to Cohen in 1989, in effect negates the rumor, echoed by Milosavljevič in his letter of January 30, 1940, that Erich owed money to Vasič for the portrait.

In his deposition for Cohen, Vasič added, "I heard no more about him or his project during the following years and I felt some resentment which brought me to express certain reservations about him [to Kasanin]."

Cohen then added: "But after having seen the description of the *Kolektanea* which appeared in the book by Neskovič, Vasič had the decency to admit his error.

Nevertheless, in his interview with the author, Vasič tried to convey the impression that he had said nothing negative to Kasanin about Erich when the latter asked him what he knew about the young man.

Predrag Milosavljevič's first report to Kasanin on the young Erich Šlomovič was just the frosting on the cake. The cake itself came in a second letter, dated March 1, 1940, a few short days before Erich's departure for Yugoslavia with the bulk of his collection. In effect, it was a report on Milosavljevič's investigation of Erich and his collection which Kasanin had requested. The following is its key passage:

Dear Mr. Kasanin,

...As concerns the Šlomovič case, I have learned the following. A certain M. Fabiani, of Italian origin, has been designated as the administrator of the possessions left by Vollard in his will. It is he who manages the entire collection and all of Vollard's interests. This gentleman today received the president of our association, M. Jeremič, whom I have charged with discreetly gathering information on our collector.

M. Jeremič touched on the first question of an eventual exhibition of Vollard's collection in Belgrade or Zagreb as Šlomovič had previously proposed. M. Fabiani replied politely that at this time, because of the war and the great risks involved, it would not be possible to mount an exhibition of Vollard's collection which incidentally has not yet been catalogued. The items are constantly in the process of being put in order: a large number of the paintings are in America or in the countryside at secure locations.

In addition, the Vollard collection comprises extraordinary artistic material and while it is a "virgin collection," as he says, it is in Paris where it must make its initial impact. The elderly Vollard is reputed to have been a very singular person, who held onto objects for commercial reasons, waiting for their price to rise.

Šlomovič is not an heir of Vollard. The objects which he has presently in his possession were given to him by Vollard during the latter's lifetime, because Šlomovič promised to create a sort of Vollard library as well as a small collection of French painters [emphasis added].

M. Fabiani declared that he did not maintain a relationship with Šlomovič and that [Erich] had been strictly forbidden to use the name of Vollard because none of Vollard's inheritance has yet been probated. At the same time Šlomovič is strictly forbidden from selling any of the art in Paris.

M. Jeremič believes that Šlomovič is effectively the owner of the objects which he found at his residence, but that Fabiani doesn't like him.

It is my guess that, taking into account the cold comportment of our collector and his great haste to transport the objects to Belgrade, he has more of a commercial interest to act in Belgrade than to help our painters, and that his desire to offer a gift of an object to the museum conceals a hope for personal success or some profit. Of course, one cannot reproach Mr. Šlomovič who will become, perhaps, a good merchant and who will inherit from Vollard at least his spirit.

Despite Fabiani's affirmation that Šlomovič has only a small number of items, that which I have seen is truly magnificent. Šlomovič has reproached me indirectly for delaying matters, in which belief, as you know, he is mistaken. I will be the happiest person if he truly carries out for our painters that which he promises them, and I informed you as well as Tabakovič of all his initial statements. Nevertheless, his behavior, in my opinion, is no longer in keeping with the manner in which he presented himself the first time.

Šlomovič today brought to the Legation four cases with his items, which he would like to transport personally to Belgrade, accompanied by M. Botorič. The ambassador, after acquainting himself with the information I received from M. Jeremič, has authorized the transportation of the items to Belgrade, on condition that a detailed list of the items will be given to the Legation.

> The Minister of the Royal Court [i.e., the Yugoslav royal government] has informed Minister Purič that the Court is interested in the Šlomovič collection but has demanded, as you have done, that we first obtain information on the proprietor's personality and his affairs. Taking into account all the circumstances, wouldn't it be preferable to transmit the containers by courier, after the Legation receives a written order from the Court?
>
> Sincerely etc.,
>
> P. Milosavljevič

The letters created a sensation in court.

But they didn't end the debate between the contending parties. They only raised its tone a few decibels.

Chapter XIV

UNRAVELING THE MYSTERY

On the surface, the submission to the court of the two letters from Paris to the director of the Belgrade Museum didn't faze Louis Sebastien and his attorney Paul Prompt. But it soon became apparent that the letters' contents had put them on the defensive. From now on their fight would be a rearguard action.

Their first reaction was to claim that the letters only strengthened their previous contentions about the dubious and clandestine nature of Erich's possession. The letters, they said, proved that Erich had managed to conceal the irregularity of his collection in order to get the Yugoslav Legation to help him "sneak" it out of France.

Sebastien presented examples of Vollard's alleged stinginess in order to throw doubt on the contention, contained in the letters, that the art merchant had given such a large number of items to the young Šlomovič as a gift. Sebastien continued to insist that Erich was an agent for Vollard and as such was entrusted with the items. At most they were loaned, not given to him. Moreover, no document had been found confirming the granting of a gift to Erich.

Furthermore, Erich's behavior in Yugoslavia, as reflected by his enigmatic letter to Lucien Vollard and by the press stories about him, showed that he had spread false information about himself, notably his claim to have been an heir of Vollard. Nor had he bothered to inform the custodians of the Vollard estate about his possession, something he should and would have done had the possession been legitimate.

Finally, Sebastien implied a possible collusion between Erich and Fabiani, the chief administrator of the Vollard estate. Fabiani, he alleged, was untrustworthy. He had spirited several hundred paintings out of the country to the United States in October 1940 and had collaborated with the Germans during the war. The implication was that Vollard's estate was mismanaged after his death by his brother Lucien and by Fabiani, a situation which Erich took advantage of to acquire from them numerous works of art by dubious means.

And indeed, eight months after the letter was written, when Erich put on his exhibit in Zagreb, he made sure not to mention Vollard's name in the catalog, except as the publisher of the art albums in the collection. Unlike the catalog for the aborted 1981 Paris auction, whose title was "Erich Chlomovitch Collection; *Provenance* [origin] *Ambroise Vollard,*" the title on the Zagreb catalog was "French Art, *From the Collection of Erich Šlomovič.*"

Erich's undertaking not to mention Vollard's name also explained his enforced silence as to how he had acquired the collection, a silence which created an aura of mystery around it and led to so many speculations in the press and by his friends.

As for the proscription against selling or, by implication, exhibiting any of the items in Paris, this was in keeping with the desire of the Vollard heirs, as mentioned by Fabiani, to guard their exclusivity to be the first to exhibit any part of Vollard's collection once it was collated and classified. This restriction did not apply to Yugoslavia, where Erich felt free to show his collection and even to sell a dozen items from it to help cover expenses.

Regarding Erich's remark in his letter to Lucien Vollard, "People here are frequently jealous," he did indeed encounter plenty of that, especially from colleagues in the art world, some of whom passed on their antipathy to Kasanin.

The Herzlers' attorney next proceeded to confound Sebastien's other contentions one by one.

The claim that Ambroise Vollard or his heirs had "loaned" the collection to Erich so that he could mount a Vollard exhibition in his native land was "demolished" by Fabiani's remark that "because of the war and the great risks involved it was not possible to show the Vollard collection, and that furthermore it was not yet classified."

Erich, indeed, had dreamt of mounting a comprehensive Vollard exhibit in Yugoslavia, but the project was not realizable for the reasons invoked by Fabiani and therefore was not adopted by Vollard's heirs either. At the most, Erich could mount an exhibition of those items which Vollard had given him as a gift.

The claim that Vollard would never have granted such a valuable gift was also belied by subsequent evidence of art experts who demonstrated that the collection was not as valuable as imagined, especially in 1939 when it was given to Erich. This was stressed by the curators of the Belgrade museum in their articles in the 1989 catalog, where they pointed out that only thirty items from the Belgrade collection were considered of sufficient artistic merit to keep on permanent exhibit. The rest, they said, while of great value to art experts and historians, especially when studying the totality of any artist's works, were more in the nature of *art de chambre*, i.e., minor works.

Regarding the Paris collection, the art critic of the Brussels newspaper *Le Soir*, reporting on March 27, 1981, about the Šlomovič auction in Paris, wrote:

> it seems that this collection contains very few paintings; among them only one work of the *fauve* painter, Andre Derain, has historical importance.... In addition to this painting, there is a rather mediocre small Cezanne of Emile Zola of mostly anecdotal [exclusively concerned with detail] interest and *A Bouquet of Flowers* by Louis Valtat, [all of which] would probably not have been sufficient to justify all this ado if the collection hadn't included the impressive number of etchings and handwritten manuscripts illustrated by the greats.

Fernand Cohen's conclusion: "The collection of Erich Šlomovič seems to have been accumulated from a didactic viewpoint, for the needs of the museum he dreamed of building in his country, not for commercial purposes."

Derain's *fauve*-period painting, which in the later 1980s reached a price of some $1 million, had little value when Erich acquired it in 1939, since the Fauvists were not then recognized as representing a historical transition in the world of art. The bulk of the collection comprised lithographs and other types of serial reproduction which, while they are considered "original" art works, are generally reproduced from the stone or the metal etching in quantities of one hundred or more pieces; the stone or metal etching is subsequently destroyed. Vollard, who had scores of such identical reproductions, would have had no problem parting with one from each artist for the benefit of Erich's future museum in Yugoslavia.

The value of the entire collection, as estimated by the auctioneers Lenormand and Dayen in 1981, was only 3,382,950 French francs — $626,000 at the time. This was three times the estimate of the bank two years earlier. By the end of the 1980s the auctioneers' estimate would have had to be multiplied at least 20-fold, giving the collection an entirely different value from what it was worth in 1939 when Erich acquired it.

Ambroise Vollard's will was handwritten in 1911 and never changed, so that it could never have mentioned Erich Šlomovič. The will was officially deposited with the authorities on July 24, 1939, two days after Vollard's death in a car accident. This is confirmed by the protocol of M. Marnhac, a Parisian notary, who mentions that the items were sealed on July 25, 1939, at Vollard's home on 28 Rue Martignac. Then, in innumerable sessions beginning on September 11, 1939, several thousand paintings were inventoried and deposited in a sealed storage. According to the Vollard heirs, in a document submitted to the court, the total number of art items found in Vollard's collection after his death was *5,232!*

No wonder that Fabiani described Vollard's gift to Erich (amounting to anywhere from 400 to 600 items) as comprising "only a small number of items."

Cohen stressed Fabiani's apparent antipathy to Erich, as expressed in the remark of the Yugoslav investigator that Fabiani "did not maintain a relationship" with Erich and "doesn't like him." Despite this antipathy, Cohen pointed out, Fabiani did not try to deny Erich's ownership, or do him harm in any way.

Thus, while Fabiani could not deprive Erich of the legitimate gift given to him by Ambroise Vollard before his death, he could distance himself from Erich and forbid him from using Vollard's name in connection with his collection. This would assure Fabiani's primacy as the true custodian of Vollard's legacy and his principal successor, an ambition he realized during the war.

Did Erich "sneak" his collection out of Paris, as Sebastien claimed? The facts indicate otherwise. As Cohen argued before the court, the Yugoslav ambassador in Paris, Mr. Purič, in effect confirmed the legitimate, public, and unequivocal character of Erich Šlomovič's collection when he authorized its transfer to

Yugoslavia through the good offices of the Yugoslav Legation in Paris. Moreover, he allowed Erich to travel together with the collection, accompanied by Minister Botorič, a senior diplomat in the Legation.

Cohen also pointed out that the expert Fare, after having questioned "different witnesses in the prewar art trade," concluded that art works could in 1940 circulate freely over frontiers without administrative formalities or special permits.

Thus, in applying to the Legation of his country Erich sought assistance, not concealment.

Cohen next dealt with some of the doubts, expressed by Milosavljevič in his second letter, about Erich's general reliability. This concerned the possibility that Erich would not keep his promise, as reported in Milosavljevič's first letter, to help the painters of his country by donating a work by Renoir for the foundation of an artists' center in Yugoslavia in the name of Djura Jaksič.

"It is, therefore, not without interest," Cohen continued, "to reassure the court about Erich's fidelity to his ideals and obligation."

In her article in the 1989 Belgrade museum catalog, curator Irina Subotič wrote that "it is well known that Erich wanted to build in Belgrade for the Yugoslav artists the house of Djura Jaksič, where his collection would eventually have been exhibited."

Furthermore, on March 29, 1941, two days after the coup d'état which toppled the Prince Regent Paul and brought Yugoslavia into the war, Erich acquired a building plot in Belgrade for which he paid in cash. In the circumstances of the moment, this acquisition could not be explained either by the desire to invest or by a plan to build a personal residence. It must have been the first step on the road toward implementation of his project to build an artists' house and a museum to house his collection. As noted previously, this aim was further confirmed by his artist-friend Oton Gliha.

Irina Subotič, in her above-mentioned article, undoubtedly gives an answer to the question which Milosavljevič put to himself, namely, whether Erich would keep his promise to donate a work by Renoir for the benefit of the Yugoslav artists.

She wrote: "It would be interesting to discover the origin of a work by Renoir, donated by Moise Pijade to the National Museum in 1947, knowing the friendship between Erich Šlomovič and the artist-politician and the fact that in 1940 Pijade made a portrait of Šlomovič, the possibility that the drawing by Renoir might have been given by Erich to Pijade as a present or in exchange for the above portrait, should not be excluded." According to Gliha and other witnesses, Erich did give gifts of paintings to various friends during and after his Zagreb exhibition.

So much for the alleged unreliability and stinginess of the young art collector.

But what about Erich's impecuniousness? This was stressed by the Vollard heirs throughout the trial in order to show the unlikelihood of his ever having acquired art works on his own. To support this contention they cited the appearance, in the course of a television program on France's *Atenne 2* channel on April 19, 1981, of a certain Mr. Leibovici, a one-time acquaintance of Erich's. To back his claim that Erich did not have "considerable financial means," Leibovici recalled that whenever he met with Erich in a café, he himself usually picked up the bill.

Fare devoted much time to researching, viewing, and transcribing this interview with Leibovici, which was also included in the program on Erich by Belgrade television on March 6, 1990. The interview, Cohen pointed out, constituted the only support for Fare's conclusion that Erich had "often been described as an impecunious student."

More light on the enigmatic interview with Leibovici was shed by a journalist, Dominique Durand, who had become interested in writing a biography of Vollard. In the process of his investigation he obtained, through Fare's report, the address of Leibovici, and went to interview him.

According to Leibovici, he had met Erich in Paris's Montparnasse quarter between 1935 and '36 when Erich was thirty years old. He described him as having "a very Hebraic appearance." Erich, he said, was wont to go to cafés frequented by Russian emigrés, and spoke Russian; Leibovici assumed he was himself one of the Russian emigrés.

But Erich was born in 1915 and in 1935 was only twenty years old. Also, the photographs of him found in his collection do not indicate a Semitic type at all, and his scholastic documents show that he studied German, French, and Latin but never Russian. Moreover, his family lived in Yugoslavia for many generations and never had any Russian antecedents.

This was typical, Cohen concluded, of the sort of evidence which the Vollard heirs brought to court.

Chapter XV

DENYING THE VOLLARD HEIRS' CONTENTIONS

A key witness in the Paris court case was Christian de Galea. A tall, lean, handsome man with a shock of wavy white hair, he was the grandson of Madelaine de Galea, Vollard's unrequited love and one of the main beneficiaries of his will.

Ambroise Vollard was the godfather of Madelaine's only son, Robert, who was Christian's father. Rumors had abounded for years that Christian's father was the illegitimate son of Madelaine de Galea and Ambroise Vollard.

Not so, Christian told the author. "My grandmother," he said, "was happily married to a diplomat stationed for many years in Leningrad. My father, Robert, and I are definitely legitimate."

Madelaine de Galea had come from the same island of Reunion that Vollard came from and had known him there. She preceded him to Paris and was his close friend and confidant during his early years of struggle in the city.

Christian denied that Vollard was homosexual and consequently could have had a homosexual relationship with Erich Šlomovič, a rumor meant to explain Vollard's generosity to Erich. Vollard had lady friends, Christian recalled, though he does not remember any of them residing in the house with him.

The main "residents" there he recalled were three cats, who had the run of Vollard's large mansion at 28 Rue Martignac. Christian, who was twenty-two years old when Vollard died, recalled him as a man who was very "gentle" with the people he liked and very rude with those he didn't.

Vollard was also very discreet, even secretive. He was tough with buyers but not necessarily with painters. He could be most generous with friends. Christian, a successful architect, still possessed "a score or more" of paintings bequeathed by Vollard to his grandmother, among them several by Renoir and Degas.

He recalled one story in particular which his grandmother told him about Vollard. The latter had been scheduled to fight a duel with another person over a cause that she did not remember. Vollard, who had a slight lisp, asked the duel's second to stop the count for a moment so he could take off his hat; he feared it would get damaged. Each side then fired three shots simultaneously and missed.

Madelaine de Galea died in 1955, six years after Vollard, leaving her estate to her only son Robert. It included Vollard's summer home and numerous works of art. Robert's son Christian appeared content with what his father had left him and had no interest, he said, in becoming a party to the Šlomovič court case.

He was, however, called as a witness.

On the stand he confirmed that during the entire proceedings concerning Vollard's inheritance, which stretched over several heirs and several years, no one had ever claimed that Erich was an heir or an absconder This applied equally to: Ambroise's brother and principal heir Lucien, who died in 1952; to Edouard Jonas, Lucien's heir, and to Robert de Galea, both of whom died in 1961; and to Paul Cezanne, the son of the artist, who served as an executor of Ambroise Vollard's will. Cezanne died in 1946, seven years after Vollard.

Nor did Martin Fabiani, who managed much of the inheritance on behalf of Lucien Vollard's estate, and who lived until 1988, ever accuse Erich of misappropriation or demand the return of his collection.

All of these people, Cohen pointed out, had every reason to pursue Erich and recover his collection if they thought it had been part of a loan to be returned or had been obtained illegitimately, as claimed by Sebastien and his late aunt, Mrs. Jonas.

It is obvious that Robert de Galea, and later his son Christian, would have had every interest in recovering any part of the Šlomovič collection that rightfully belonged to their inheritance. Cohen concluded that their abstention from doing so, together with the other heirs, Lucien Vollard and Edouard Jonas, constituted clear proof that Erich's six hundred or so works were legitimately owned by him and were never part of Ambroise Vollard's inheritance.

Martin Fabiani, in his book *When I Was an Art Merchant,* gave further refutation to the rumors about Vollard's supposed homosexuality. He wrote (on pp. 71-72) that Vollard "was always discreet about the women of his life," but one day by coincidence after he was seen going into a small hotel, he told his brother Lucien that "the most important woman for him at that time lived in that hotel."

Fabiani continued: "This scoffing man, of much cynicism, and with a dissimulating faculty, knew how to keep a secret. He had a big love in his youth. It was on his native island of Reunion that he fell in love with a young lady. But [being young and without independent means] he was not in a position to pursue it. He later left the isle and when he arrived in Paris he found that the object of his love had married and was now called Madame de Galea."

Fabiani related further (pp. 73-75) that when he once sold two paintings and a pastel of Degas on behalf of Vollard, the latter gave him a most generous commission: "four still lifes by Renoir."

The journalist Jacque Guenne, in an article entitled "The Truth About Vollard" which appeared in a Swiss literary review in May 1944, told about his long-standing friendship with Vollard, whom he depicted as a virtual thesaurus of art, and then concluded: "While Vollard displayed the virtuosity and professionalism of a consummate gambler in his work, he was an amateur in all that is implied by the words 'unselfishness and love.'"

In his biography *Recollections of an Art Merchant,* Vollard reproduces in the appendix a letter he had written to Edmond Jaloux, in response to an article written by some academicians in which it was asserted: "If Maillol was able to live well for many years, it was thanks to the generosity and intelligence of Ambroise Vollard."

Not suffering from false modesty, Vollard may have been flattered by the word intelligence but not by the word generosity. He writes: "As far as [the term generosity being applied to] the relations between a merchant and an artist, it is like ascribing generosity by a buyer toward a seller for having purchased land from him on which the buyer expected to find gold."

The Herzlers' attorney's next move was to demonstrate that Šlomovič had acquired the bulk of his collection before Vollard's death on July 22, 1939, and not after. This would destroy one of the Vollard heirs' major contentions: that Erich had obtained his collection through possible collusion with Fabiani or alternatively on loan from Lucien Vollard during a period of great confusion and maladministration following his brother's death.

The first evidence that Erich already possessed the bulk of his paintings before Ambroise Vollard's death came in the article by the artist Miodrag Kolarič in the 1989 Belgrade catalog. There Kolarič recalled seeing the collection in Erich's hotel room "one or two years before the war." That, of course, would place the encounter before Vollard's death on July 22, 1939.

But what about the contrary evidence of Erich's friend Othon Gliha, Sebastien pointed out, who told how he first encountered Erich in the autumn of 1939 after which he saw his collection in his hotel room. That would place this encounter after Vollard's death. Opening the door to the alleged illegitimate acquisition from Vollard's estate.

Not so, said Cohen, who investigated the circumstances of this first encounter between Gliha and Erich. Gliha recalled that this meeting took place at an exhibition of the artist Oton Friesz at the Katia Granoff gallery on the Blvd. Raspail in Paris (see the transcript of Gliha's television interview in Chapter X). But it is known that this painter had a contract with the Max Kaganovich gallery located on the same Blvd. Raspail ever since 1936, and not with the Katia Granoff gallery which was never located on this boulevard.

Cohen took the trouble to determine whether, and at which gallery, Oton Friesz held an exhibition in 1939. He discovered that there was no such exhibition. The last exhibition of this painter in Paris, before the war, took place at the Max Kaganovich gallery in June 1937. He held another exhibition in New York in October 1937, and a later one in Paris in March 1941 at the gallery of Petrides, with whom he had a contract.

The meeting between Gliha and Erich could not have taken place in Paris at that latter date since by then Erich had transported his collection to Yugoslavia; nor could it have been in 1937, which was two years before Vollard's death.

A similar deduction was made by Momcilo Stevanovič, then-curator of the National Museum in Belgrade, in his preface to the Denis Rouart album *The Unknown Degas and Renoir* (in the Belgrade museum). Stevanovič avers there, without citing any source, that Vollard had given to Erich, as a "gift," a large number of art works "several years before his death."

This deduction provides additional proof to the statement in the letter of Milosavljevič to Kasanin on March 1, 1940, that the collection which Erich transported to Yugoslavia in March 1940 was his personal collection. Further proof was provided by Milosavljevič in his earlier letter addressed to Kasanin, namely, that he had already seen the collection in January 1940 and that it came from a live Ambroise Vollard and not from his inheritance, held at the time by his brother Lucien.

It is also useful to recall, Cohen continued, that the court's seal affixed to the entire collection at Vollard's home, just three days after his death, showed that it had been previously inventoried in the presence of a court notary and immediately placed in safes rented in various banks. *Not a single piece from Erich's collection was ever listed in this inventory as belonging to Ambroise Vollard's estate.*

If Lucien Vollard would have known that any part of Erich's collection belonged to his late brother's estate, he would not have failed to inform the notaries accordingly, who would then have included the items in their inventory. All this would have contradicted the affirmation by Fabiani of the gift by Ambroise Vollard to Erich, which Fabiani made on March 1 to the Yugoslav investigator and transmitted to Kasanin.

Lucien Vollard reported on March 22, 1940, to his two sisters on the island of Reunion that the estate had been divided and that the paintings belonging to him and to them had been divided among the heirs, without citing a date when all this had taken place. It must have been close to the above date, however, since Fabiani had declared three weeks earlier, on March 1, 1940, that the Vollard collection could not be exhibited because it had not yet been classified.

Only if Lucien Vollard would have intentionally deceived his sisters by telling them that he sold their patrimony, while holding back part of it for Erich Šlomovič, without informing Edouard Jonas, who had the power of attorney for the sisters, would the scenario painted by the Vollard heirs hold water.

The next major task of the Herzlers' lawyer was to deal with the adverse testimony of Prof. Sreten Marič submitted to Fare in response to questions Fare had posed to him. In his letter, Marič, who was eighty-five years old at the time, tells how Erich had written to him from Paris toward the end of 1939, asking to meet with him upon his return to Yugoslavia.

Marič, who was a professor of art for most of his life, did not know Erich at the time. The latter had apparently obtained his name from fellow artists.

In April 1940, a month after Erich's return to Yugoslavia from Paris, Marič visited him at his home at 35 Dobracina St., which he describes as being in Dorcol, Belgrade's "poor Jewish quarter." There he entered a "modest apartment... with small rooms" where he was astonished to see works by Renoir, Degas, Picasso, Matisse, and Derain, piled one on top of the other, as well as a large number of Vollard art albums and five or six bronzes by Degas together with seven or eight by Maillol and Rodin.

I was stupefied standing before so many works of art. When I asked Mr. Šlomovič how he had acquired them, he showed me correspondence he had had with the various artists and told me that he had gone to Paris to acquire a stamp collection in the course of which he had the opportunity to enter the artistic milieu and that he had received the works as gifts from these artists, principally from Ambroise Vollard.

When I asked Mr. Šlomovič why he had invited me, he said he wanted to sell, at a good price, these works to the museum in Belgrade. He thought that since I was a well-known professor of art at that period I could make contact for him with the director of the museum, who was a close friend of Prince Paul, who was well known as an art collector. Mr. Šlomovič also hoped to receive a small pension from the museum.

Marič then tells how he approached Kasanin, and since neither knew anything about the origins of Erich's collection, he advised Kasanin to first have the police investigate the collection's legitimacy. But Kasanin was preoccupied at the time with safeguarding the museum's contents against the dangers of the impending war, and never got around to acting on the suggestion.

Marič's sister, who was married to Erich's friend the noted cartoonist Pjer Krizanic, was also quite amazed by the extent of the collection, Marič remarks.

Marič then recalls hearing about Erich's subsequent exhibition in Zagreb and speculates about reports that Erich was ready to give the collection to the city of Zagreb in return for a modest honorarium. Marič then concludes his testimony with the remark: "He was a peculiar character, that Šlomovič. At a time when he was offering his entire collection to the state, he gave his closest friends a mediocre lithograph by Cezanne, *The Picnic on the Grass*, of which he had many copies. He gave a present to my sister and I also read in the Zagreb press that he gave presents to two painters there."

Marič then cites newspapers in 1940 from which he had culled articles on Erich Šlomovič.

Cohen ripped this testimony apart.

Marič, he said, gave himself more importance than he deserved. Othon Gliha, the artist and close friend of Erich's, never once mentioned Marič in his recollections of the important people to whom he had introduced Erich upon his return from Paris. Nor did Marič's name appear on the list of persons invited to the opening of the Zagreb exhibit.

As for the Šlomovič family living in a very modest apartment in Belgrade's "poor Jewish quarter," Cohen remarked:[1]

> In fact the Šlomovič family lived in a middle-class apartment in a beautiful stone building [see photo opposite], decorated with statues, on Dobracina Street, in one of the nicest residential quarters of Belgrade. Marič's description [can only] provoke the amusement of all Belgrade citizens who know that at least up to the end of the Turkish occupation there was no longer a Jewish quarter in Belgrade, neither poor nor rich.
>
> ...Marič's statement that Erich had gone to Paris to gather a stamp collection... is so ridiculous and concocted that it can only help to disqualify its author."

Having thus set the scene, Marič arrives at the main subject, which consists of pretending that Erich Šlomovič, because he hardly knew anybody, had asked [Marič] to contact the director of the Prince Paul Museum. Marič also contends that Erich wanted to sell his collection at a good price, against "a small pension," as if he was in a hurry to get rid of it.

Erich didn't need Marič's intervention, Cohen pointed out, since half a year earlier, in October 1939, he had already established direct contact with Kasanin.

1. Much of the ensuing expositions from the Paris court proceedings are taken verbatim from Fernand Cohen's brief. Others are paraphrased or elaborated by the author.

In January 1940 when the Yugoslav Legation in Paris intervened in Erich's favor with Kasanin, the latter accepted Erich's gift. Meanwhile, Predrag Milosavljevič was able to write on March 1, 1940, to Kasanin that the Minister of the Royal Court (i.e., the Royal Yugoslav government) had informed the Yugoslav ambassador in Paris that "the Court was interested in Šlomovič's collection."

"Erich, who then forwarded his collection from Paris to Belgrade in the company of the Court Minister, did not need an unknown professor to create a relationship with Milan Kasanin," Fernand Cohen argued. Furthermore, it had already been established by the testimony of Prof. Pavle Vasič, who was then deputy director of the Prince Paul Museum, that Erich had proposed to exhibit his collection and not to sell it.

Better still, Marič places his meeting with Erich in April 1940. Thus, his intervention with Kasanin could only have been after that. But he did not know that at the time when he pretended to have advised Kasanin to instigate a police investigation, the latter had already possessed for several weeks the information [he needed on Erich] which Predrag Milosavljevič had transmitted to him on March 1, 1940, and which had resulted in the help of the Royal Court and the Paris Legation in transferring the collection to Yugoslavia.

Finally, Marič remarks perfidiously that the Prince Paul Museum and then the city of Zagreb, which had received a similar proposal, had both rejected the "gift" of Erich Šlomovič. He made believe that he had asked himself as to the mysterious reason for such a rejection. But Pavle Vasič explained [in his written statement submitted to Cohen] that the exhibition desired by Erich did not take place because of the political and military situation, which had made it ill-timed for that period.

In an article included in the catalog of the present [1989] exhibition one can read that in 1940, "there was a special psychosis in Zagreb. Clans and parties confronted each other; war had already seized most of Europe and was drawing near to Yugoslavia as well. Anguish and fear infiltrated at all levels... this is one of the reasons why Erich Šlomovič did not succeed in establishing his museum of modern French art in Zagreb.

The court [Cohen concluded] will not fail to dismiss Marič's testimony, not without censuring it severely.

During my last trip to Zagreb and Belgrade in 1992, I heard from several individuals who had known Erich personally, or who had interviewed people who knew him, that Erich had had an affair with the wife of his artist-friend Pjer Krizanič. She happened to be Marič's sister.

Could resentment over this affair have motivated Marič to bad-mouth Erich? Fernand Cohen believed that it was a principal cause.

Chapter XVI

MORE REVELATIONS IN PARIS

After having traveled to Yugoslavia in April 1990 to see the Šlomovič exhibit at the Belgrade museum and interviewed Mara Albahari, I went to Paris the following year. There, I spent the entire month of May trying to find out what had transpired on the court case there, then in its ninth year, and to locate people still living who might have known Erich and Vollard.

I had gone to Paris to conduct an investigation for a book. What transpired could merit a book on the investigation.

I began my investigation with a call to Shlomo Malka, deputy editor of the monthly *L'Arche*, France's leading Jewish publication.

"Do you know anything about the case of the Šlomovič art collection?" I asked.

"No, but perhaps you should try our art critic, Perre Assulin."

Assulin said he remembered the matter vaguely. "Call Jean Demartini," he suggested.

"Who's he?" I asked.

"He's a Frenchman, not Jewish, who's been on a personal crusade for several years now to recover art works plundered by the Nazis in World War II. He's especially interested in art treasures which were later misappropriated by collaborators, public bodies, or governments and are today in private homes or museums. The original owners or their heirs, of course, know nothing about their whereabouts. If they do know they hardly ever succeed in surmounting the complicated legal procedures involved in recovering their possessions."

Demartini had helped to save the lives of a Jewish couple named Schloss while serving in the French underground during the war. They were members of a wealthy Jewish family which had collected a great art treasure before the war.

When they passed away childless after the war, they bequeathed most of their collection to Demartini whom they had virtually adopted. When he went to collect his inheritance, he discovered that of 333 works of art in the original collection, 185 had disappeared during the war. Further investigation revealed that many were dispersed around the world in various museums and private collections. One of them, a Rembrandt, he traced to the Carnegie Museum in Pittsburgh. Another, by Franz Hals, he recovered by court order from the American Newhouse Galleries stand at the 15th Biennial Exhibition of Antique Dealers in Paris in October 1990.

Demartini was by now on a personal vendetta not only to recover his misappropriated patrimony but to expose similar cases. As a result of his efforts major articles appearing in the world press, including a fourteen-page cover story in France's leading weekly newsmagazine *L'Express* in its issue of December 20, 1990.

When I met him in Paris in May 1991 he was seventy years old, a distinguished-looking, hawk-eyed gentleman still full of fight.

"Yes," he said when I first called him, "I heard of the Šlomovič collection. There's a newsman in Paris, in fact, who's working on the story. His name is Phillip Sprang. His phone number is 488-23300. If there's any other way I can help you, please feel free to call me."

I immediately called the number he gave me and set an appointment to meet Phillip Sprang the following afternoon at the Café Flore in the St. Germaine de Près quarter.

I arrived a little late and found him standing on the sidewalk outside the café, looking concerned but not resentful. Before me was a young man with a pair of large glasses covering part of a big forehead, exuding a warm smile and extending a firm handshake. He was wearing a leather jacket and carried a weather-beaten leather briefcase bursting with notebooks, pamphlets, books, and papers.

We went inside and took a quiet table on the second floor. Phillip worked for the leading Parisian newspaper, *Le Figaro*, as a part-time commentator on food and restaurants. He had learned the restaurant trade during several years as a waiter and *maitre de* at a leading French restaurant in London. The job at *Le Figaro* was for "the bread and butter," he said; his real love was investigative reporting, which he did for *Le Figaro* and other journals.

Demartini had interested him, as he had interested other newsmen, in the subject of art treasures stolen in World War II. One day when scanning the back files of the Paris newspapers on this subject he came across the Šlomovič story, which had been covered extensively by the local press after the discovery of Erich's collection in a Parisian bank safe in 1981. Phillip had been working on the story for several months now, having followed the French court proceedings and interviewed the principal contenders. He knew very little about the Yugoslav part of the saga.

The nice thing about Phillip Sprang was that he was old enough to treat the story seriously and young enough to be idealistic about it. He was neither blasé nor cynical, the endemic maladies of long-time newsmen. He showed a schoolboy's enthusiasm and a bulldog-like determination to discover the truth and see justice done.

I told him what I knew and took him to my hotel room to show him the documents I had collected, especially from Yugoslavia. He showed me his documents and promised to get for me the protocol of the Paris court, including its last decision of October 3, 1990. It was from him I heard, for the first time, that the court had decided to split the Paris collection between Erich's heirs in the United States and Israel and to award eight works of art and six art albums to Vollard's surviving heir, Louis Sebastien.

The following day Phillip called to tell me he could barely sleep the night before from the excitement of meeting me and hearing the rest of the Šlomovič story for the first time.

From that day on Phillip and I kept in touch daily, comparing notes, documents, and interviews.

After meeting Phillip my next task was to find people who had known Erich during his Paris years. There were only three in Paris still alive. One was Paul Petrides, the former Cypriot tailor who became friendly with many famous artists while fixing their shirts and trousers. In 1929 Petrides set up his own art gallery and eventually became the exclusive agent for the Montmartre artist

Maurice Utrillo. As recalled by Othon Gliha, Erich had purchased several Utrillo paintings from Petrides.

In 1979 Petrides had a run-in with the law. He was sentenced to three years in jail and fined 2,100,000 francs for falsely authenticating a Utrillo painting. Further legal complications over the years kept him under a cloud, and the closest I could get to him in Paris was to speak briefly with his son at the family's very posh art gallery in Rue Faubourg St. Honoré. Fortunately, Fare had managed to reach Petrides and record his testimony; more on that later.

The second person who had known Erich was Dina Vierny, model and consort to the sculptor Aristide Maillol. She had encountered Erich on several occasions when he visited Maillol's studio. She was never in town when I visited Paris; fortunately, Fare obtained her testimony as well.

The third person was Daniel Wildenstein, who had met Erich on several occasions when he had come to visit his father's art gallery on business. Wildenstein, who was also interviewed by Fare, eventually agreed to meet with me, but only after several phone calls and a thorough probing by his secretary.

His home, more properly the family estate, was located at 57 Rue le Boetie (the *t* is pronounced like an *s*) in the center of Paris, around the corner from the exclusive art galleries and fashion shops of the Rue Faubourg St. Honoré. The house was bought in the 1870s by Daniel Wildenstein's grandfather, Nathan, and used for many years by his father, George, as both a home and headquarters for his flourishing art business.

Being Jewish, the family escaped to the United States before the German invasion of France. There, George Wildenstein and other key artistic personalities persuaded President Roosevelt to set up the Commission for the Protection and Salvage of Artistic and Historic Monuments in Europe, which was eventually attached to the U.S. army with the mission of salvaging art plundered by the Nazis.

Fortunately for the Wildensteins, most of their collection was preserved and recovered after the war. Eventually the family established the Wildenstein Foundation for preserving and nurturing art, based partially on their own extensive art collection. Daniel Wildenstein, while still dealing with art, had spent more and more of his time over the years breeding and raising racehorses.

The two-story family mansion, with attic, was sandwiched between massively built 19th-century edifices housing a mixture of apartments, shops, and commercial offices. The mansion had a concave frontage and was the only building on the block with an iron fence and a driveway-parking lot up front.

One entered the premises through a black, decorative wrought-iron gate, electronically operated from the inside, a large one for cars and a smaller one for individuals. After properly announcing myself through the intercom, the gate was unlatched and the butler emerged from a side door to usher me into a richly furnished waiting room through whose transparent white curtains a large garden decorated with statues and creeping vines revealed itself.

The royal elegance and silence of the salon contrasted sharply with the crowded street and noisy traffic outside.

After the "customary" wait of several minutes, Daniel Wildenstein entered. Formally dressed in a business suit, trim, of medium height and carrying a cane, everything about him bespoke formality and propriety, coldness and calculation.

"Yes, I knew Erich Šlomovič," he began, in response to my question. "I must have seen him twenty or thirty times. He was an *intermediere*... a runner," he added with a voice of disdain and a motion of dismissal by a hand that had been resting, along with his other hand, on his cane. His pose — the cane between his knees, where it served as support for his hands and upper body — reminded me of an English gentleman at the horse races.

"There were scores of runners in those days," he volunteered.

"What's a runner?"

"Those are the small-time brokers who work for art dealers or artists on commission. They get about ten percent commission. As I remember, Šlomovič worked mostly for Vollard."

"What sort of impression did he make on you?"

"Not very good. I didn't like the type. Maybe we bought something from him; I don't remember. He never brought anything important. But he seemed to understand art well. How do I think Šlomovič gathered his collection? I don't know. Lucien Vollard had a drug habit [which he brought back with him from Vietnam where he had been a colonial magistrate]. Perhaps Šlomovič was able to influence him and others who handled Ambroise Vollard's inheritance to sell him items from the collection cheaply."

"What were those paintings worth in those days?"

"I bought some twenty paintings from Vollard at $40 each, mostly Vlaminck and three by Derain from the *fauve* period. Today each one is worth anywhere from $5 to $10 million. In 1939 we put on a Bonnard exhibit. The highest price was $3,000 but nothing was sold. The better Renoirs in those days were worth $12,000. Šlomovič obtained the cheaper Renoirs, mostly portraits which cost $1,000 or so. Today they're worth $75,000 or more. The Renoirs in his Belgrade collection are junk [!]."

Being on the subject of prices, Wildenstein inquired about my connection with the Šlomovič family in Israel and promised me a commission if I could help him acquire any works from the collection once the court case was concluded.

By this time the atmosphere had warmed up a bit and Wildenstein seemed to unbend, ever so little, from his stiff and formal composure. He was married (for the second time) to an Israeli woman, he said, but had never visited Israel. "The Jews," he remarked, "were never good at painting. It was proscribed in the Bible.[1] Besides, they're too intelligent. Most of the great painters, except for Da Vinci, were stupid. The only exceptions were Modigliani and Chagall, both Jews, but they were apart from the mainstream."[2]

"Do you think there could have been a homosexual relationship between Šlomovič and Vollard?"

"Not at all. My father knew Vollard well and would have known. He never mentioned the possibility. Vollard had an illegitimate son with De Galea. His grandson, Christian, is still living today. I remember Vollard well. He was one of the most difficult persons I've ever seen. He never gave away paintings to anyone... not five pence. When he sold paintings he always got his money first. He wouldn't give away the right time of day.

"We bought two paintings a week from him. We never got what we wanted. If we'd ask for a Renoir we'd get a Cezanne. But he had great culture and good taste. Vollard was in our home every week and we also visited him frequently."

When I asked Daniel Wildenstein if he knew others in Paris who had known Vollard or Erich, he lifted up the phone resting on the marble table at his side,

1. "Thou shall not make a graven image."
2. Other noted Jewish painters of the time were Chaim Soutine and Camille Pissaro in Paris, Isaac Levitan in Russia, and Max Lieberman in Germany.

gave some instructions, and a few minute later the butler entered with a note which he handed to his master.

As Wildenstein rose to usher me out, he handed me the note. On it, neatly typed out, were the names, addresses, and phone numbers of Maillol's model, Dina Vierny, the art gallery owner, Paul Petrides, and Christian De Galea. He also mentioned the name of an elderly gallery owner, Alfred Daber.

I left Wildenstein with a bad feeling from the deliberately negative picture he had painted of Erich and a bad taste from his offer of a commission should I help him purchase paintings from the Šlomovič collection.

In his written testimony given to Fare Wildenstein repeated much of what he told me, but with some differences and additions.

Fare had approached Wildenstein after seeing two letters discovered in the Paris safe, from the artist Maurice Vlaminck addressed to Erich on December 4, 1939, some five months after Vollard's death. In one letter Vlaminck gives his opinion of a painting of which Erich had sent him a photograph. In the other letter he notes that he seldom comes to Paris, and adds: "As to you wish to acquire some paintings [of mine], you could call on… George Wildenstein, 57 Rue la Boetie…. I am writing to him and telling him about your wish…. He owns some of my selected recent works… [you can call on him] in full confidence."

Wildenstein told Fare that Erich was "part of Vollard's entourage and enjoyed his confidence." He added that Vollard would offer his father and him "the best and most representative works of the Impressionist artists." As for the "less important, minor works, he would not offer them to us."

But after Erich had asked Vollard to allow him to deal in these lesser works, he would come to the Wildensteins' home to offer them for sale. Vollard allowed him to earn the usual commission.

Question: Do you believe that the rapport between Vollard and Šlomovič was no more than simple friendship and collaboration?

Answer: This is a most delicate question as far as it concerns Vollard's friendship with certain "particular" persons and which could account, in part, for the items which Erich Šlomovič possessed around the time of his departure for Yugoslavia. I might add that my recollection of Šlomovič is sufficiently precise to tell you that it led me to consider him as an intriguer, an ambitious and not very sympathetic personality.

Question: Since it seems that Šlomovič lived from the commissions he earned selling Vollard's paintings, can you explain how he obtained such a large number of works found in his Paris and Belgrade collections?

Answer: I remember very well the "economical" character of Vollard and it seems most unlikely that he would part gratuitously with such important works. He might have offered some books, a few sketches and lithographs. That is quite possible. But that he would offer to sell important works under extremely generous terms seems to me impossible. Personally I'm inclined to presume that Šlomovič made his acquisitions of works, which are today considered important and were also important then, by dubious methods.

Question: Do you believe that if Mr. Vollard had entrusted the works to Mr. Šlomovič for the purpose of organizing a retrospective of French art in Belgrade, we would be able to find some documents with the customs authorities indicating the true ownership of the works?

Answer: I can bring you evidence that before the war paintings could be exported freely and there were no formal requirements which might have produced information as to the official nature of the exportation.

Fernand Cohen blasted this line of questioning and the reliability of the testimony itself. At the same time he instituted a lengthy legal battle to have the evidence struck from the record for never having been signed by Wildenstein. Although the court did not accept this technical argument, since the testimony was subsequently signed, it did take into account some of Cohen's other arguments.

Daniel Wildenstein, who prides himself on possessing one of the most important art libraries in the world, couldn't show any bookkeeping records which would establish the existence of the copious commercial relations which he and his father supposedly had with Ambroise Vollard directly or through Erich Šlomovič.

It is symptomatic that the name Wildenstein is not once mentioned in Vollard's autobiography *Recollections of an Art Merchant*. It is still more remarkable that Daniel Wildenstein's biography in *Who's Who* mentions that he was born in 1917, that he received his high school diploma in 1936 and college degree in 1938; that he later studied at the Ecole de Louvre, before getting married on the day after the declaration of war when he, no doubt, was mobilized like all the young Frenchmen of his age.

This same biography places the beginnings of his professional career in New York in 1940, without any mention of activities before that date, in the family business or generally, and no professional activity in France before 1956.

This information makes it very doubtful that Daniel Wildenstein knew Erich Šlomovič except perhaps at the Ecole de Louvre (where they had both registered during the same term in 1939-40), essentially because it has not been proved that one of them was engaged in any professional activity at that time. Wildenstein exaggerates when he imputes to Ambroise Vollard and Erich Šlomovič a homosexual relationship.[1] None of this famous merchant's biographies ever made such an allegation and people who were close to him, like Christian de Galea and Martin Fabiani, dismissed this possibility.

The same is true for Erich Šlomovič, whose entourage knew about several feminine adventures he had. Nobody ever pretended that he might have had other attractions. The implication to the contrary by Daniel Wildenstein is not accompanied by any proof, just like his other statements, nor does it contain the least circumstantial details. Wildenstein's statement is therefore calumny, as attested by Christian de Galea, Vollard's grand-godson.

There are still more decisive proofs. The expert Fare had doubtless forgotten that he had transmitted to the lawyers of the parties the letter written to him by Daniel Wildenstein on March 9, 1988, in which he said: "I remember vaguely Mr. Šlomovič but remember Vollard better, a great friend of my father's and my family. I do not know whether I am able to give verification on this point, but I should be happy to be of service if possible."

"It couldn't have been said better," Cohen remarked.

Despite this disclaimer, Wildenstein's testimony taken by Fare begins with the words: "I very well remember Mr. Šlomovič…."

It has already been proved that the witness was unable to submit any proof for the basis of his statements regarding the existence, before the war, of a close commercial relationship between his father's gallery and the gallery of

1. In his interview with the author, as we saw, Wildenstein denied that Vollard was homosexual.

Ambroise Vollard. Nor was any such proof provided from Vollard's commercial archives or in his autobiography.

Whereas all persons who knew him, mainly the lady Vierny, stressed Erich Šlomovič's charm and the sympathy he inspired, which was proved by the relationship he was able to develop with Vollard, Maillol, Bonnard, Rouault, Leger, Le Corbusier, Matisse and so many others, Wildenstein alone ascribes to him a not very sympathetic personality. This rounds out his previously explained disqualification as a reliable witness.

Confronted with the testimony of Christian De Galea, submitted by the Herzlers, Sebastien was compelled to admit that Daniel Wildenstein was mistaken in stating peremptorily that Ambroise Vollard had "particular friendships."

It doesn't seem necessary to condemn any further this witness, who is not worthy of being one, because Mr. Sebastien has done it himself. Wildenstein was guilty of "being helpful" rather than admitting that his recollection of Erich Šlomovič was much too "vague" to allow his collaborator [Fare] to describe his evidence as an "authentic and principal" testimony.

As a parting shot, Cohen pointed out that Fare was employed by the Wildenstein Foundation on a research project at the time he took Daniel Wildenstein's testimony.

As mentioned, the second witness in Paris who had known Erich was Dina Vierny, of Jewish origin, model and reputed paramour of the sculptor Maillol. Fare decided to approach her after noting the many photos in the Paris safe that showed Erich visiting Maillol in his studio. Also found was an autographed manuscript by Maillol dedicated to Ambroise Vollard, eight days after his death, with the following inscription in the lower left-hand corner: "Mr. Erich Chlomovitch has given me the last letter addressed to me by Vollard. Maillol."

When Fare approached Dina Vierny she was the owner of an art gallery in the St. Germaine de Pres quarter and the custodian of a museum dedicated to Maillol's works. In Cohen's words, her "anatomy today abundantly adorns the Tuileries gardens" where several statues of her by Maillol are interspersed throughout the park. They depict a strong, heavy-set figure of imposing proportions, bringing to mind a woman wrestler.

In her written testimony, Miss Vierny recalls how Erich used to frequent Maillol's studio in the suburb of Marly le Roi on Sunday mornings when Maillol customarily received artists and young people who wanted to speak with him and seek his advice. The period was 1939-1940.

Šlomovič was a young man who did not have the means to buy art. Consequently he never bought anything from Maillol. But he had a grand idea: to organize one or several exhibits of contemporary French art in his country. For this idea of an exhibition he had works of art entrusted to him.

It was difficult for a young man like Šlomovič to become friendly with Maillol, who was one of the great sculptors of the 20th century and among whose friends were André Gide, Matisse, Bonnard, and Vuillard. Nevertheless Šlomovič often visited Maillol, who was amused by his audacity and loquaciousness.

Erich Šlomovič never bought anything from Maillol and his name doesn't appear in his archives, but he sincerely admired Maillol's works and Maillol once gave him one of them as a gift which he dedicated to him.

I don't recall if he ever got what he wanted from Maillol, that is, if he succeeded in having Maillol entrust to him works for exhibiting in Yugoslavia. On the other hand, those works which were given to him did not belong to him because he never paid the artists for them.

In further responses to Fare's questions, Miss Vierny noted that Erich had come to Maillol's upon Vollard's recommendation. She did not know if Maillol eventually loaned works to Erich, though his conversation constantly revolved around that theme. "It was a possibility," she added, "since Vollard had loaned works to Šlomovič, at least that's what Šlomovič alleged."

Regarding Erich's personality, the witness described him as "sympathetic, at the same time passionate about art and resourceful."

She then speculates about his relations with Vollard and his financial status: "He convinced Vollard to entrust him with works of art. His financial sources were unknown. But one could see that he had no money, like most of the young men before the war, and like me as well, a young student who loved art, worked for Maillol, but also was unable to buy any works of art."

The idea that Šlomovič convinced Vollard to lend him art works for an exhibition, which he later held in Yugoslavia, Miss Vierny testified, "seemed to be quite an exploit considering that Vollard was a distrustful type. But Šlomovič knew how to inspire confidence. At least that's what we supposed. I can add that Vollard quickly adopted the idea because he believed in the benefit of exhibitions."

Miss Vierny then adds in handwriting as an afterthought: "But I cannot confirm that [Vollard] really loaned him the works."

Cohen seized on this handwritten comment to nullify the witness's previous speculations about Vollard lending art works to Erich. She was at fault, Cohen pointed out, in concluding that Erich had no money without giving further details, adding only that "this could be seen."

"Her capacity for guessing reached its peak," Cohen charged, when she cited the fact that Erich bought no art works from Maillol as proof of his impecuniousness, but in the same breath she said that all the young people who came to visit Maillol came to talk to him and get advice, not to purchase art works.

Fare had never bothered to meet Miss Vierny, Cohen pointed out. Instead, he sent her a written questionnaire with a good deal of "leading" questions. But the lady's conscience allowed her to be led only so far, Cohen added; thus she included the written disclaimer at the end of her testimony.

Her testimony, Cohen concluded, was "so inaccurate and contradictory as to make it insignificant, so that the court can neither take it into account nor dwell upon it."

The most confusing and least forthcoming of the three witnesses who had known Erich in Paris was Paul Petrides, the Cypriot tailor-cum-art dealer who at the time of his testimony was trying his best to keep out of the public gaze after several run-ins with the law.

The following is Fare's summary of his interview with Petrides, which was held at the latter's gallery on the Faubourg St. Honoré on December 17, 1988.

TO THE QUESTION: What are your recollections of Mr. Erich Šlomovič?
HE RESPONDED: In 1939 Erich Šlomovič came to see me in my gallery from time to time. He told me he was a friend of Vollard and that the latter had given him art works for his museum in Yugoslavia. I never saw him together with Vollard. He

offered me works for sale but I never bought anything from him. Erich Šlomovič was not a collector. I didn't know him very long.

TO THE QUESTION: How many times did you see him?
HE RESPONDED: Three or four times.

TO THE QUESTION: Did you know Ambroise Vollard?
HE RESPONDED: I knew him by sight but never had any dealings with him.

TO THE QUESTION: Did you have any commercial or professional dealings with Erich Šlomovič?
HE RESPONDED: Erich Šlomovič never offered to sell me any paintings and I never discussed the subject with him, since because of his age and his status as a stranger I distrusted him.

TO THE QUESTION: Did you ever offer to sell him paintings?
HE RESPONDED: Although he told me he was interested in Utrillo, he never proposed acquiring any of his works.

TO THE QUESTION: Was Erich Šlomovič known as an actual or potential buyer or collector within the milieu of the art merchants?
HE RESPONDED: As far as my acquaintance with him went, he was not known as a collector or active buyer during his sojourn in Paris. I don't remember him doing any business in Paris.

TO THE QUESTION: Did he appear to you to have the reputation of, or to have been engaged as, an art broker?
HE RESPONDED: I don't think so. He never spoke about it or proposed doing business with me. Besides, I never would have bought from him because I was afraid.

TO THE QUESTION: Was he known among the art galleries in Paris?
HE RESPONDED: It seems to me, no. It didn't seem that he had a reputation for doing business in the art world.

TO THE QUESTION: Do you believe that he was a connoisseur in the matter of paintings?

HE RESPONDED: No. I don't believe so. He was new on the circuit. He was not in the milieu.

TO THE QUESTION: Do you believe that he knew Fabiani and did business with him?
HE RESPONDED: I don't believe so. He wouldn't have had an understanding with Fabiani because he could eventually become a rival, a competitor in his relations with Vollard, especially as far as his pretending that Vollard had given him paintings.

TO THE QUESTION: Who else could give me information on Erich Šlomovič who is still a living witness to that period?
HE RESPONDED: No one. Maybe you can try Katia Granoff.[1]

TO THE QUESTION: In conclusion, what general impression do you have of Erich Šlomovič?
HE RESPONDED: The impression is of a person I saw three or four times. After the war someone, who told me he was a friend of Erich Šlomovič's, said that the latter had told him about me as an art merchant and that he had been arrested by the Germans during the war and killed because he was Jewish.

Fare recounts how, after this interview, he wrote to Petrides asking for clarification of an apparent contradiction whereby Petrides stated at the outset that Erich had "offered me works for sale but I never bought anything from him," whereas slightly later he says that Erich "never proposed to sell me any paintings."

Six months later, after several reminders, Petrides responded but without answering the question, remarking instead that because of his advanced age (eighty-eight years) and the long time that had passed, his recollections of Erich were vague.

Fare characterized Petrides' responses as reflecting "extreme prudence... distrust [and a] quasi-obsession with secretiveness," all a result, no doubt, of his frequent difficulties with the law.

1. By that time (1990) the famed art gallery owner and patron had passed away.

With such an opening, provided by the expert himself, Fernand Cohen jumped in with both feet. In his request that the court dismiss Petrides' evidence, he argued, among other things:

> The interview with Petrides is especially revealing of the methods used by the expert Fare. Mr. Sebastien seems to disapprove of these methods when, in criticizing the discoveries of the Herzlers, he writes on page 54 of his conclusions that one must make sure "that the questions put to the interviewee shouldn't prejudge the answer and deprive the witness... of his independence of mind and freedom of expression."
>
> ...The expert asked Petrides if Erich Šlomovič was "known as an actual or potential buyer or collector within the milieu of the art merchants." To this Petrides replied that to his knowledge he was not known as an active collector or buyer during his stay in Paris and that "he did not remember that he did business in Paris."

The object of the next question was to discover whether Petrides had the impression that Erich Šlomovič "was reputed to have acted as an agent." In light of the preceding answers the wording of this question must seem tendentious insofar as, beyond his direct knowledge, the witness was asked to convey impressions or to spread gossip regarding someone else's reputation.

Petrides replied: "I don't think so. He never spoke about it nor proposed doing business with me. Besides, I never would have bought anything from him because I was afraid." Instead of asking Petrides to explain his fear, the expert put another question which had already been answered in another form: "Was Šlomovič known in art gallery circles in Paris?" Petrides answered in the negative.

This [Cohen charges] did not hinder this singular inquisitor from asking once more whether Erich Šlomovič "was a connoisseur of paintings" to which once again Petrides replied negatively.

Becoming aware of the fact that his method of interrogation and of transcribing the answers had led to apparently contradictory replies, because Petrides had stated on the one hand that Erich Šlomovič had submitted to him paintings to buy and on the other hand that Šlomovič had never suggested doing any business with him, the expert unsuccessfully tries to obtain a second session with this eighty-eight-year-old man whom he seems to have disturbed.

From Petrides' answers one can understand that Šlomovič never suggested to sell him paintings in his possession which, he explained, had been given to him by Vollard. On the eve of the war this would have exposed the prudence of this former Cypriot tailor (who during the war registered his gallery in the name of his French wife). The fact is that Erich Šlomovič never proposed to him, as an agent, any paintings belonging to a third person.

Despite his efforts, the expert, whose questions do not cease to appear loaded with prejudice, did not even succeed in getting Petrides to testify that he had heard it said that Erich Šlomovič was an agent.

Mr. Sebastien, rather than renouncing the use of such testimony, which was of no use to anybody else, does not fear to claim that this testimony showed that "Erich Šlomovič was a poor man who did not inspire confidence."

Such a deduction is so ridiculous that it is not worth dwelling on any further. It must only be remembered that Petrides thought that Erich Šlomovič was a friend of Ambroise Vollard's, that the latter "gave him art works," and that to his knowledge Šlomovič was nobody's agent.

Cohen does not mention that Petrides' memory failed him on another point, namely, that Erich had bought some Utrillo works from him, as testified by Othon Gliha who was a witness to the transactions.

There are three Utrillos in the Belgrade museum's Šlomovič collection, all obviously acquired by Erich on his own recognizance since Vollard never had any Utrillos in his collection.[1]

1. In his autobiography, Vollard tells how by the time he became interested in Utrillo, the price of his works had gone sky-high.

Chapter XVII

VOLLARD'S INHERITANCE IN A KNOT

Louis Sebastien, as explained earlier, was Ambroise Vollard's heir three times removed. Edouard Jonas inherited what was left of the collection from Lucien Vollard, Ambroise's brother. Jonas died in 1961, leaving the paintings to his widow. She died in 1986, in the course of the Paris court case, leaving what was left of the collection to her nephew, Louis Sebastien. By that time the Vollard collection, originally comprising 5,232 works of art, had dwindled down to several hundred pieces.

What had happened to this great compendium of paintings, art albums, and memorabilia over the years? The Šlomovič collection of some six hundred items, obtained before Vollard's death, is the largest single collection traceable to Vollard still extant. What about the other 5,232 pieces? Who got them? Where did they end up?

Although these mysteries cannot be unraveled in detail, a rough picture can be drawn.

The problem begins with the fact that Vollard wrote his first, last, and only will in 1911 when he had precious little to distribute. In a fit of optimistic generosity he bequeathed a life pension to his three sisters, living on the island of Reunion, 100,000 francs to his brother Lucien, and 200,000 francs to his unrequited love Madelaine de Galea. He named Madame de Galea and Paul Cezanne as his executors. By the time Vollard died in 1939, neither was alive and their respective sons took over as executors.

Vollard also bequeathed four paintings to the city of Paris, including two portraits of himself by Renoir and Cezanne. He left money to an institute which looked after stray cats and 50,000 francs to prize-winning inventors of children's toys.

In his handwritten will Vollard instructed that the monies be raised from the gradual sale of his paintings, to be spread out over a period of at least six years in order to assure the best possible prices.

Vollard had no idea when he wrote his will in 1911 that his collection would be worth a great fortune upon his death twenty-eight years later. Following his death, his brother Lucien asked his close friend and confidant, Martin Fabiani, to administer the distribution of the inheritance. Fabiani had been one of Vollard's agents and assistants and knew the collection well. Madame de Galea appointed her own expert to work alongside Fabiani in making the valuations.

Because, with war clouds gathering, the time was not propitious for selling art work, the parties decided to make an assessment of the property and art work, and divide the inheritance according to each party's share in the will.

De Galea received Vollard's country estate and the balance of her two-thirds share in the form of paintings. Lucien took his one-third share in paintings, amounting to some 1,500 in number.

Within two years after Vollard's death, Fabiani had purchased a large part of Lucien's share at, reportedly, a ridiculously low price. He then spirited some of the paintings out of Paris for safekeeping in the countryside and shipped off several hundred others to Canada. These were confiscated on the high seas by the British navy and returned to the Vollard estate after the war.

During the war Fabiani remained in Paris and ran an art gallery from Vollard's mansion at 28 Rue Martignac. He also published several art albums, based on works which artists had left with Vollard for that purpose; Vollard had never completed these albums. According to the author Jean Paul Morel, who was at work on a biography of Vollard, Fabiani never compensated the artists for their works. He also kept some of their original lithograph stones and metal plates from which he continued to make engravings, also without compensating the artists.

After the war Fabiani was arrested and accused of collaborating with the Germans. One of the charges was that he sold to them, at bargain prices, art works plundered from Jews. With the help of three noted lawyers and some highly placed friends, including the communist writer Louis Aragon, whom he had helped financially with several publishing ventures, Fabiani apparently managed to wiggle out of the charges.

Notwithstanding his sale to Fabiani of an undisclosed number of paintings, Lucien Vollard was still left with enough works to spare for various donations: eighteen to the city of Paris, 120 to an art museum in Reunion, and scores of others to a museum in the Swiss town of Winterthur.

When Lucien died in 1952 he left the bulk of his estate to Edouard Jonas, who had returned to Paris after the war and had become his close friend and confidant. Jonas was a successful antique dealer, a member of the French parliament, and honorary director of the museums of the city of Paris.

The two surviving Vollard sisters in Reunion gave Jonas a power of attorney to recover their share of the inheritance, the bulk of which, they claimed, had never been received. Nothing, reportedly, came of this.

Fabiani, who continued as an art gallery owner for many years, died in 1989, leaving behind him a large estate and a cloud of suspicion over his wartime record and his handling of the Vollard estate.

Over the years the Vollard estate was the subject of numerous litigations. At one point Madame de Galea's son, Robert, sued claiming that his family had been short-changed in the distribution. The municipality of Paris lost its suit to recover the paintings bequeathed to it by Lucien Vollard, which had been lost during the war. And the artist George Rouault, with whom Erich had excellent relations, sued the Vollard estate to recover hundreds of paintings he had left with Vollard for several art albums which Vollard never published; Rouault won the case.

Except for the Šlomovič collection and other individual items in various museums, it is doubtful that more than two or three hundred works of art originating from Vollard remained intact in private hands — namely, Christian de Galea, the grandson of Vollard's lifelong lady friend, and Louis Sebastien, the heir of Lucien Vollard twice removed.

I met at length with Sebastien and his attorney, Paul Prompt, to hear their side of the story.

Louis Sebastien, seventy-six, lived with his wife in one of those numerous high-rises that dominate the skyline of the La Defense complex in the northern confines of Paris, overlooking the Seine where it makes one of its more extensive convolutions around the city. They had just returned from England, where they had reportedly made one of their periodic sales of art works still left over from the Vollard collection.

It was during the confusion shortly after Vollard's death, claimed Sebastien, that Erich managed to obtain most of his collection. Notwithstanding evidence to the contrary which Fernand Cohen brought back with him from Yugoslavia, Sebastien continued to insist that the documents did not disprove his original contention that most of Erich's collection was loaned to him by the heirs and administrators of the Vollard estate (i.e., Lucien Vollard and Martin Fabiani), and that the war prevented him from returning the works — or, alternatively, that he obtained his collection from them for a song, by collusion and underhanded means.

This new castle in the sand was soon washed away by Cohen's arguments.

Chapter XVIII

REINFORCING THE HERZLERS' CASE

During my month-long stay in Paris my most productive meeting was with Fernand Cohen, the attorney for the Israeli heirs. Since he had not replied to my queries directed to him before my arrival in Paris, I held off calling him until my last week in town. I calculated that the more material I would be able to accumulate on my own the harder it would be for him to refuse to meet with me. An incomplete dossier in my hands would be more dangerous to his cause than a full one.

I was thus pleasantly surprised by his cordial reception. He invited me to meet with him in his plush office on the Champs Elysées, on a Saturday morning, when things would be quiet.

A secretary announced my arrival and he, as the continental gentleman he was, negotiated the twenty-meter-long corridor up to the reception area, to accompany me to his office which was around the corner in another corridor. He ushered me into a spacious, high-ceilinged, carpeted room, lined with the usual legal volumes. A large desk piled with files stood by the windows, partially concealed by transparent drapes reaching from the high ceiling to the floor.

Behind the desk was an adjoining door to the suite of the head of the law firm. Count René de Chambrun, former adviser and legal counsel to the U.S. air force in France, was the scion of an aristocratic French family descended from the Marquise de Lafayette. The only shadow in this otherwise cloudless sky was Chambrun's marriage to the daughter of Pierre Laval, prime minister of the Vichy Government in World War II, executed after the war as a collaborator with the Germans. The marriage by itself would not have tainted Chambrun had it not been for his periodic attempts to defend his late father-in-law's record.

Cohen had joined Chambrun's firm as a senior partner in 1989, by which time Chambrun, already advancing in years, had considerably cut back on his workload. The Šlomovič case was one of the firm's lesser ones, yet occupied a disproportionate part of its time. As Cohen told me, "I took on the case because of its emotional and intellectual interest for me, especially as a Jew. It also drew me because of its connection with the Holocaust and because of the miserable fate of the surviving family, up to the present day.

"There have been so many falsehoods and misrepresentations spread about Erich Šlomovič and his collection that I felt I must destroy the legends and myths that have grown up around the case.

By the end of June 1990, three months after Fabrice Fare submitted his report to the Paris court, the two attorneys for the contending parties submitted their rebuttals.

Cohen's presentation, on behalf of the Herzler family in Israel, covered 190 pages and included more than one hundred exhibits. Paul Prompt's rebuttal on behalf of Louis Sebastien covered 130 pages, accompanied by a lesser number of exhibits.

Cohen pointed out that in the course of the court proceedings, Sebastien's attorney submitted 370 selected documents from Vollard's archives, including receipts, contracts, correspondence, invoices, credit notes, statements, orders, delivery notes, and declarations of turnover. They covered most of Vollard's mercantile career up to his death in July 1939. Many of the documents referred to Vollard's lending of works to organizers of exhibitions. Others confirmed deposits with merchants, librarians, or agents, mentioning in the process various agents who acted on Vollard's behalf.

Yet none of the documents mentioned the name of Erich Šlomovič, nor was there a trace of any salary paid to him. The obvious conclusion was that he was neither an agent, a secretary, nor a salaried employee of Vollard, as claimed in numerous press stories and testimonies over the years as well as in Sebastien's brief.

Despite the plethora of documents submitted by Sebastien, he was unable to produce a single one showing the existence of any commercial relationship between Vollard and Erich. Cohen was at pains to stress this point, since it meant that civil, not commercial, law would apply.

According to Articles 2230, 2238, and 2279 of the Civil Code, Sebastien was obligated to bring proof, such as a loan by Vollard to Erich, to destroy the legal presumption of Erich's legitimate ownership, Cohen pointed out. The Civil Code, of course, was to the advantage of the Herzlers, who for their part were exempted (by Article 1352) from submitting any proof of the legitimacy of Erich's ownership.

Had Sebastien proved his claim that Vollard had loaned the art works to Erich, commercial law would have applied and such proof would have fulfilled the legal requirement of doubtful ownership. This, in turn, would have destroyed the presumption of lawful possession by Erich and the burden of proof would no longer have rested on Sebastien's shoulders.

"Sebastien tries to feign ignorance of these rules," Cohen charged, "going so far as to accuse the Herzlers of being incapable of producing the key to the safe, *as if the crematory ovens might have spared such articles*.

"Trying to squirm out of this obligation to bring literal proof or at least initial proof, as required by law, and to benefit then from the right to prove by any means the justice of his allegations, he prefers to state simply that the matter is commercial, since according to him Erich Šlomovič was an agent for Vollard. This statement has the form of a postulate but it is not founded on any document issued by the Register of Trade nor in any written book or register, or commercial document," Cohen concludes.

Cohen's tongue-in-cheek summary:

> Mr. Sebastien's conclusions, extending over more than 130 pages, running counter to the truth but presented with professed aplomb, show, by their abundance and by the great number of arguments, the embarrassment of the author and his contempt for the facts and documents of the case.

The Herzlers have been poorly rewarded for the seriousness and clarity of their own documents.... They had to compete with the lacunae and insufficiencies which Mr. Sebastien himself imputes to the Fare report. Furthermore, it is inappropriate that Mr. Sebastien allowed himself to criticize the conditions under which the Herzlers, Israeli citizens of modest means, were able with the help of their lawyer to obtain for the court completely objective items of information which neither Sebastien nor the judicial expert was capable or desirous of obtaining for the court.

Having been thus challenged by Mr. Sebastien, the Herzlers intend to prove that he has continued to use evidence which, in effect, can only be characterized as phony.

Cohen also pointed out that none of the documents submitted by Sebastien showed any transaction with the Wildenstein gallery. Their name, in fact, appears nowhere, neither in the documents submitted by Sebastien nor in Vollard's autobiography.

In these circumstances, Cohen remarked, "one must note the total inability of Daniel Wildenstein to provide any substantiation for his erstwhile collaborator, the art expert Fare, of his following testimony: *'I remember well Mr. Šlomovič, with whom I met on numerous occasions before the war since* my father and I had many commercial relations with Ambroise Vollard.... *Many times my father and I would visit Vollard in his home where we acquired Impressionist works of which he was an expert.'*

In a desperate attempt to counter these arguments and prove that there was a commercial relationship between Vollard and Šlomovič, Paul Prompt, Sebastien's attorney, submitted to the court two signed receipts for a Vollard art album, *Cirque de l'Etoile Filante*, allegedly containing notations by Erich. The volume was sold by Vollard on April 18, 1939, to a Mr. Lauck, a stranger who was passing through Paris, for a price of 6,000 francs of which 1,000 was paid on the same day and the rest on the following day, upon delivery. Prompt submitted in evidence a handwritten note by Lauck promising to pay the money due, on which was written: "gravures sur bois" (woodcuts) and "eaux fortes" (original etchings). Prompt attributed the latter words, written by hand, to Erich Šlomovič. This supposedly proved that Erich acted as an agent in the above transaction.

Cohen's reply:

> "The above-mentioned handwriting, when compared, even by an amateur, to Erich's handwriting in his letter to Matisse, also produced in evidence by Sebastien, is completely different. In fact

> one can find the word 'gravures' in the letter to Matisse, thus providing a decisive comparison.
>
> "Even if Erich had written these words, which is doubtful, they wouldn't have been able to involve him in the transaction except as a translator, but surely not as an agent. The handwritten receipt for the advance of 1,000 francs is in a different handwriting, and the receipt for the balance is typed out and not signed. Finally, in the absence of any date there is nothing to give Sebastien the right to state that these words were written on April 19, 1939."

So much for the so-called proofs of a commercial relationship and a loan of the collection to Erich by Ambroise Vollard before his death. And what of Sebastien's claim that the loan was granted after Ambroise's death by his brother Lucien, the man from whom Sebastien derived his inheritance.

To prove this assertion Sebastien invoked the enigmatic letter which he claimed was addressed from Belgrade on March 23, 1940, by Erich to Lucien Vollard. As Cohen pointed out in his earlier arguments, this letter no longer was ambiguous because its significance was clarified by the letter of March 1, 1940, by Predrag Milosavljevič to Milan Kasanin. In it, Fabiani is cited as mentioning the prohibition on Erich's using Ambroise Vollard's name in connection with Erich's personal collection.

One seeks in vain in the letter of March 23, 1940, Cohen argued, the slightest allusion to any loan of art works or any indication of an alleged loan. The existence of such a loan was a pure guess on the part of Sebastien. Nor did Sebastien explain why Lucien Vollard never answered the letter, as Erich had pressed him to do. The absence of such a response was even more glaring, Cohen charged, considering that Lucien, being a former magistrate, would not have missed the opportunity to confirm formally the granting of an important loan, given originally without written confirmation. Moreover, until Lucien's death on February 3, 1952, despite the fact that the distribution of Ambroise Vollard's estate lasted until 1949, there was no indication that Lucien knew anything about the tragic death of Erich Šlomovič. Nevertheless, he made no claim and undertook no investigation to locate him and recover the alleged loan. Neither did he reveal to the other inheritors, nor to the French notary of the inheritance, the existence of Erich's important batch of art work, which should have been taken into account in the distribution of the inheritance.

"The fact that he remained silent on this question for twelve years constitutes irrefutable proof that the alleged loan did not exist," Cohen concluded.

On this aspect especially, said Cohen, Sebastien's "audacity" was striking. This gentleman obstinately imputes fault to Erich Šlomovič for not having made any statement to the notary in charge of Ambroise Vollard's inheritance and then pretends that this abstention confirms the illicit nature of Erich's possession.

"But according to the law only a person entitled to an inheritance — which Erich Šlomovič was not — has to declare, to those making the inventory, the possessions of the deceased which he holds, as well as any gift made to him by the deceased.

"This type of argument by Sebastien," Cohen declared, "justifies characterizing him as an imposter."

Another reason that Lucien could not have loaned art works to Erich is that the legacies awarded to Vollard's heirs comprised funds, not art works. It is unlikely, therefore, that before Erich left for Yugoslavia during the first days of March 1940, "Lucien Vollard could have disposed of any of the art works included in his brother's inheritance. In any case, they had been sealed by court order since July 25, 1939, three days after Vollard's death, and were later placed, on September 12, 1939, in three sealed safes in Parisian banks."

To shake this argument, Louis Sebastien submitted extracts from Martin Fabiani's book *When I Was an Art Merchant* which relate how, during the occupation, the author had entered the cellars of Ambroise Vollard's residence in order to remove (for the *Letters Francaise* newspaper) a large quantity of lead letters for typesetting. Sebastien commented that this episode showed "how easy it was for Martin Fabiani to enter the Ambroise Vollard gallery, including its cellar, and to remove from it whatever he wanted to." The implication is that Fabiani could have done likewise when Vollard's collection was supposedly sealed by court order after his death.

However, as Cohen points out, Erich had left for Yugoslavia before the German invasion of France in May 1940. Subsequently, during the entire occupation, Fabiani, at the request of the inheritors, stood guard over Ambroise Vollard's residence from which all the art objects had been removed and sequestered in safe places.

According to the declarations by Fabiani to the Yugoslav investigator on March 1, 1940, reported the same day by Milosavljevič — that is, on the eve of Erich Šlomovič's departure for Yugoslavia — the inheritors had refused to authorize the organization in Yugoslavia or an exhibition of the Vollard collection, which for the time being was scattered and unclassified.

Furthermore, Milosavljevič explained that on the very day Fabiani's declarations were made, March 1, 1940, Erich Šlomovič had brought his collection to the Legation, where an inventory was to be made of all the items he wanted to take with him to Belgrade.

It is thus impossible that Šlomovič could have, in a day or two, convinced Lucien Vollard or Fabiani to reverse their earlier decision and to entrust him, without written approval, with several inheritors, legatees, executors, and court representatives who had an interest in the inheritance and who never uttered a word against such an alleged act.

Cohen gave four other reasons why Erich could not have conspired with Fabiani and Lucien Vollard to obtain large number of art works from them. These concern the fact that the bulk of Erich's collection was already in his possession before his alleged collusion with Vollard's heirs and that he never made a secret of it:

- Milosavljevič related in his first letter of January 30, 1940, five weeks before Erich's departure for Yugoslavia, that he had been able to view "recently," at Erich Šlomovič's residence, the latter's collection, enumerating the tens of Renoirs and Degas paintings, the Forein and Cassat and others which were later found in the Parisian bank vault and in the Yugoslav part of Erich's collection.
- Milosavljevič wrote in the same letter that "Erich Šlomovič intends to transport part of these items to Belgrade" (i.e., two months before his departure for Yugoslavia he already made no secret of his intention to take the art works out of France).

- The Yugoslav painter Lukič, residing in Paris, had already "a year or two before the war" viewed Šlomovič's collection, the opulence of which he had described to Kolarič, director of the National Museum of Belgrade (i.e., they were obtained during Vollard's lifetime).
- The Yugoslav painter Gliha, who had resided in Paris until December 1939, had, despite some circumstantial errors, also described his encounter with Erich Šlomovič's extensive collection. This recollection proves that Šlomovič's collection had been constituted in its known form *before* the death of Ambroise Vollard. The collection was probably completed at the latest in January 1940, when it was seen by Milosavljevič. At that time all of Vollard's works belonging to his inheritance were sealed as they had been since July 25, 1939, three days after his death.

To reinforce his case Cohen next proceeded to analyze some of the more unusual items in Erich's Paris collection, especially those dedicated to him by Vollard and the numerous artists. The task was not difficult since all 190 items had been carefully researched and described in the catalog of the abortive sale prepared by the auctioneers, Lenormand and Dayen.

At the outset, Cohen criticized the auctioneers and Sebastien for abusing the term "Provenance (origin) Vollard." Since Vollard's name added magic and value to a painting, it was no surprise, Cohen remarked, that the above gentlemen as well as art historians and merchants continued to abuse the term "Origin Vollard," thereby implying that Erich's collection belonged to Vollard.

In this connection Cohen also blasted Sebastien for what he termed his "intellectual dishonesty"; his "pretending to analyze" Fare's findings as if they confirmed that the works under litigation were part of Vollard's "artistic collection." Such a conclusion made no sense because the "artistic collection" of any merchant is intended for changing hands.

"Insidiously," Sebastien alleged in the first paragraph of his argument, the detailed examination of the objects in litigation had permitted all the parties, including Fare, to conclude that, except for certain small items, the entire contents of the safe came "directly" from the Ambroise Vollard gallery.

The surreptitious introduction of the word "directly" on pages 272 and 294 of his report, which is sought in vain in Fare's findings, was sufficient alone to justify the accusation of intellectual dishonesty, Cohen charged. On the contrary, Fare wrote in the conclusion of his report (p. 427) that "everybody agreed that the majority of the works originated within the perimeter of Ambroise Vollard (except, for example, the drawings by Cocteau, personal correspondence and documents, and perhaps the works of Utrillo...)."

This enumeration, although it is incomplete, has the merit of including Utrillo, whose works were never part of Vollard's collection and only one of which, a gauche watercolor, appears in the Lenormand-Dayen catalog (p. 180). At the same time, four important paintings by Utrillo appeared in Šlomovič's Yugoslav collection. Vollard relates in his autobiography how he missed this artist, whose works were already too expensive by the time he had the opportunity to admire them. Yet even Petrides, author of the definitive catalog on Utrillo, errs when he identifies three paintings by this artist found in the National Museum in Belgrade as belonging to the "former collection of Ambroise Vollard, former collection of Erich Šlomovič, Belgrade, National Museum of Belgrade" (the third one is ascribed to the same source but without mention of Šlomovič).

Among all the exhibits submitted to the debate by Sebastien the only mention of a work by Utrillo appears in the transaction concluded on March 22, 1949 between Edouard Jonas, acting as a proxy representative (of the Vollard sisters) on the one hand, and Martin Fabiani and Lucien Vollard on the other. In this transaction it is stated that a painting by Utrillo appeared in the list of items that were shipped by Fabiani to the United States before the German invasion of France and then seized by the British navy, but that it belonged to Fabiani personally.

To strengthen his claim that a large number of works should rightly belong to Vollard, Sebastien noted that they carried on the reverse side the letters "PH" signifying that they were photographed by Vollard. Concurrently, he claimed that the inscription "PV" on the reverse side of certain other works signified that these, too, were "photographed by Vollard."

It would be surprising, Cohen suggested, if PH and PV meant the same thing. He challenged Sebastien, however, to point to a single item in litigation among the 190 items of the Lenormand-Dayen catalog on which Fare found the inscription PV.

As for the inscription PH, it was only found on the reverse side of items 38 and 40 (monotypes by Degas), 182 (portrait of Emile Zola by Cezanne), and 185 (woman with engravings by Forain).

Sebastien, Cohen said, must possess a strange sense of arithmetic to pretend that four is a "large quantity" in relation to 190. He also showed very little respect for his readers in asserting that PH meant "photographed by Vollard."

His "vigilance failed him" when he did not mention that No. 3 in the catalog (*The Beautiful Girl or Love at Forty,* a book published by Vollard and illustrated by Raoul Dufy) carried the initials AV and RD, evidently corresponding to the initials of the editor and the illustrator, respectively, or that No. 57 (*The Unknown Masterpiece* by Balzac, illustrated by Picasso), which nobody contested as having been published by Vollard, carried the initials AV.

But it was not these picayune details which focused the attention of the court, but rather the broader canvas of Erich's relations with the leading artists of the time. Since Sebastien also claimed numerous items which had been personally autographed for or dedicated to Erich, Cohen, in opposing these claims, was able to open a wide window on Erich's relations with the artists. In the process a new aspect of Erich's personality emerged — that of a young art collector hell-bent on obtaining whatever he could, while he could, from the great artists of his time.

Chapter XIX

THE AMAZING MR. ŠLOMOVIČ

OR: ERICH'S ACQUISITIONS FROM ARTISTS

Although most of Erich's collection admittedly originated with Ambroise Vollard, the young entrepreneur was no laggard in amassing many items on his own.

His most concerted effort began shortly after Vollard's death on July 22, 1939, and continued until his departure for Yugoslavia in March the following year. During this period Erich managed to obtain artists' autographs on works already in his possession as well as original autographed drawings and documents, poems and palettes, gifted and dedicated to him. Aside from art works he was especially interested in reflections by the artists on their youth, their philosophy, and their art. This was in keeping with his lifelong preoccupation with the artist's creative processes, which he felt were no less important than the creation itself.

He struck while the iron was hot, when both Vollard's memory and the memory of his close relationship with Vollard were still fresh in the minds of the artists he approached. It is quite possible that to advance his cause he mentioned his intentions of creating a museum in Yugoslavia and publishing a book dedicated to Vollard's memory. This was in addition to his plans for publishing albums on the French school of painting and on the artists Rouault and Matisse, among others.

Among the outstanding items gathered by Erich during this hectic period are five autographed drawings by the playwright, poet, and artist Jean Cocteau, two of them dedicated to Erich. One of them is a drawing in china ink and colored crayons of the head of a faun. At the bottom is the inscription: "Souvenir of a cruel world, to Erich Chlomovitch from his friend Jean Cocteau, Sept. 1939." At the top of the drawing Cocteau had written, in large flowing letters, "Harper's Bazaar."

The faun, reflecting a mischievous spirit, was supposedly inspired by Cocteau's homosexual lover, the French actor Jean Marais. A second sketch by Cocteau, a self-portrait in china ink on tracing paper, is also dedicated, with the inscription "To Erich, a souvenir from Jean, Sept. 1939." A large *Merci* (thanks) is scribbled on the side. In a third sketch, also of a young faun, dated a few days after Vollard's death, Cocteau wrote: "Do make drawings like this."

Erich's richest lode of material came from George Rouault, including the earlier-mentioned fourteen pages of handwritten poems, a detailed reply to a twenty-six-point questionnnaire Erich had sent the artist, a special poem and drawing dedicated to Erich, and two handwritten pages about Rouault's approach to his art, not to mention several paintings and etchings in the Paris collection and fifty works in the Belgrade museum.

Erich also managed to obtain a handwritten manuscript by Marc Chagall, dedicated to Vollard, in which the artist describes his arrival in Paris in 1910. The contents are taken from Chagall's autobiography *My Life*, written in 1931. In the text are two pen drawings, both signed. Also included in the collection is the letter written by Vollard introducing Erich to Chagall.

The original text which Chagall gave to Vollard tells of his attempt to leave Paris, and then his discovery of French painting and his life at la Ruche, the complex of artists' studios known as "the beehive."

"Only the great distance between Paris and the city of my birth," Chagall writes, "prevented me from returning there immediately.... It is only the Louvre which ended these hesitations. Walking around the long hall of Manet, Delacroix, Courbet, I desired nothing else.... At that time I didn't look for the meaning of art, only the professional skill in execution."

Also found among the memorabilia in Erich's safe was a manuscript signed by Chagall and the sculptor Charles Despiau. In the first sentence Despiau writes: "When I work it doesn't matter to me whether what I do is good or bad. The only thing that matters is that I do what I want." Just under this inscription, illustrated by a small sketch by Chagall, are the latter's words: "Only an honest and free heart has its own logic and its reason."

To this is attached Vollard's letter to Chagall introducing Šlomovič.

In pursuance of his fascination with the creative forces in art, Erich also managed to obtain the following handwritten and signed quotes from the artist Fernand Leger: "Modern life in all its aspects must be the true ground from which we draw the constructive elements of our plastic expression. All which surrounds us, including fragments and even the most modest visual events, are precious and usable.

"Imagination is superseded by reality, but that which the world ignores is the new reality which surrounds only those of us who are artists, sensible enough to discover it — while others must wait to understand it."

These documents are accompanied by a sketch in pen and black ink of Leger's palette with seven tones of aquarelle paint, all noted (green, yellow, blue, etc.). A similar drawing of a palette was obtained from Matisse.

Not missing an opportunity to expand his collection, Erich obtained a written explanation of the art of Jules Pascin from his former companion Hermine David, and from Lucy Krohg who had exhibited his works in her Paris gallery every year. The former added at the bottom of her recollections: "I write these lines at the request of Mr. Šlomovič for the book which is shortly to be published."

Chapter XX

COHEN v. SEBASTIEN

An intimate look at other memorabilia gathered by Erich during this period was afforded by Fernand Cohen in the Paris courtroom when he took exception to Sebastien's including in his claim at least eighteen items which had been specifically dedicated to Erich. Sebastien's "effrontery" in claiming these obviously personal items of Erich's, Cohen remarked, was a further example of the "free use of his imagination."

Here are the more representative items among those Cohen cited:

Original Engravings

- Eight etchings by Marc Chagall for Gogol's book *Les Ames Mortes* (Dead Souls), published in Vollard's name after his death, with a handwritten note from Chagall that Erich Šlomovič had received them from Ambroise Vollard (Nos. 34 and 35 in the Lenormand-Dayen catalog).
- An etching by Pierre Bonnard carrying his handwritten and signed annotation: "I recall with pleasure my collaboration with Vollard." It is dated July 25, 1939, that is, two days after Vollard's death (No. 44).
- A color drawing of Matisse's palette, mentioned by Erich in the letter he wrote to this artist on March 17, 1941, indicating that he had "left it in Paris in a safe" (No. 51b).
- A number of title pages and prospectuses for art albums published by Vollard, including some superfluous pages from these albums, with handwritten annotations by him. One is dated July 19, 1939 and includes a dedication by

Lucien Vollard to Erich Šlomovič. Another has an annotation by Pierre Bonnard, dated July 25, 1939 (No. 64).

- Five etchings based on drawings by George Rouault for the book *Circus of the Shooting Star* and a prospectus for the book *The Reincarnations of Pere Ubu,* all carrying, in the handwriting of the artist, the confirmation that they were given by Ambroise Vollard to Erich Šlomovič (No. 83).

Photographs

- A photograph of the portrait of Madame Paul Guillaume, wife of the well-known art merchant, by Marie Laurencin, dedicated by the subject to Erich Šlomovič (No. 87).
- A number of photographs showing Erich with Blaise Cendrars, Chagall, Le Corbusier, Maillol, Leger, Matisse, and Rouault, some of which are dedicated to Erich or his brother Egon who took the pictures (Nos. 88 and 89).
- A photograph of Ambroise Vollard, dedicated by Lucien Vollard: "To Erich Šlomovič I give this photograph of Ambroise Vollard in remembrance of my brother who was his friend. Paris, Feb. 26, 1940" (No. 92).

Documents and Autographs

- An autographed drawing of the palette of Pierre Bonnard, dated July 26, 1939 (three days after Vollard's death), manifestly done for Erich Šlomovič (No. 106).
- A copy of the letter written on July 20, 1939, by Ambroise Vollard to Marc Chagall recommending Erich Šlomovič, which the author gave to him for presentation to Chagall personally (No. 108).

(*Note by Cohen*: "Mr. Sebastien has the effrontery to write that this letter shows that Erich Šlomovič intended to organize an exhibition of Chagall in Yugoslavia. But it is sufficient to read the photocopy [of this letter] to find that Ambroise Vollard limited himself to writing: 'I take the liberty to introduce Mr. Erich Šlomovič, who promotes French art in Yugoslavia and would be honored if you would agree to grant him some moments of your time for a talk.'"

- A note by Maillol in homage to Vollard nine days before the latter's death, with the added remark at the bottom: "Mr. Erich Šlomovič handed me the last letter Vollard wrote to me" (No. 115).

This note, apparently given to Erich by Maillol for personal delivery to Vollard, elicited a response which Erich brought to Maillol. Erich then got Maillol's original note back from Vollard's estate and brought it to Maillol for autographing. This exchange of notes, with Erich acting as go-between, further confirms the close relationship Erich had with Vollard.

A number of sample documents, including pages and prospectuses connected with Vollard art albums, were apparently handed over by Ambroise Vollard a few days before his death to Erich with numerous remarks addressed to him. Their content, suggested Cohen, indicates an obviously didactic and quasi-paternal attitude by Vollard toward his young protégé. These include:

- One or several handwritten pages from each of the following books by Ambroise Vollard: *Sainte Monique, Listening to Cezanne, Renoir and Degas, Recollections of an Art Merchant,* and *The Reincarnation of Father Ubu.*
- Two copies of *Sainte Monique,* one of which carries a dedication: "To Mr. Erich Šlomovič in homage... sketches by Pierre Bonnard," signed by Ambroise Vollard; and also in his handwriting, dated July 19, 1939, an explanatory annotation: "Where you see a saint sacrificing her own salvation in order to ensure the salvation of her son." The other copy carries, in Vollard's handwriting, the statement that the illustrations are by Bonnard, and Vollard's signature following the admonition: "Learn the meaning of the sentence, 'I prefer forgiveness to sacrifice' (Saint Matthew)."

These annotations by Vollard contradict the statement in Sebastien's conclusions that Vollard had never dedicated any of his works to Erich. When these mentions are compared with others made by Vollard on the same day, July 19, 1939, on pages extracted from his books, their didactic and paternal overtones become obvious. The following are some more examples of prospectuses and pages taken from Vollard volumes:

- On pages from the following books, Vollard writes, "Take some time regularly every day for this precious reading": *The Small Flowers of St. Francis, Gaspard of the Night, The Life and Works of August Renoir, The Imitation of Jesus Christ.*
- On a page from *Les Pastorales de Longus*, he writes: "When I had the luck to find a Pierre Bonnard as illustrator." A week later on July 25, 1939, already three days after Vollard's death, Bonnard adds in his handwriting: "When I had the luck to find a publisher like Vollard."
- In *Parallelment*, there is a page on which Vollard wrote in his handwriting the first line of a ballad by Verlaine and declared: "the first work I published."
- In *The Unknown Masterpiece*, there is a page on which Vollard wrote and signed in his handwriting: "an unknown masterpiece which is also a masterpiece by Picasso I am so happy to have published."
- In *The Mimes of the Courtesans*, illustrated by Degas, Vollard wrote on one page over his signature: "A book of our times."

These documents, which have no commercial value and are not suitable for exhibition, said Cohen, prove definitely that in contradiction to the "obsessive statements" of Sebastien, Erich Šlomovič's relationship with Ambroise Vollard was not mercantile. They show convincingly that Vollard's feelings toward Erich were those of a master toward his pupil.

But that was not all:

- Item No. 121 from the Lenormand-Dayen catalog comprises four pages handwritten by Vollard from his autobiography, apparently accompanied by the autobiography itself and by a handwritten and signed note by Lucien Vollard: "Mr. Ambroise Vollard had promised Mr. Erich Šlomovič this book in homage but since he died by accident it is being handed over by his brother, Lucien Vollard."
- A handwritten note by Ambroise Vollard, dated July 20, 1939, inviting his Royal Highness, Prince Paul, Regent of Yugoslavia, to visit his private collection. Vollard must have written this letter at Erich's suggestion and then entrusted it to him for handing over to Prince Paul personally in Yugoslavia.

Cohen adds: "The claim by Mr. Sebastien for possession of the objects 64 and 83 in the Lenormand-Dayen catalog, although they clearly belonged to Erich as testified in the dedications by Lucien Vollard, Bonnard and Rouault, can be explained by the fact that the expert Fare in his report about the objects under litigation notes erroneously that No. 64 is 'without particular mention' [of Erich's name] and that No. 83 had 'no particular mention.'"

Such errors, Cohen noted sarcastically, "no doubt contributed to justifying the severity of the judgment regarding the competence of this singular expert."

The expert also "distinguished" himself, Cohen charged, in connection with item No. 105, consisting of a batch of seventy-nine photographs of works by Odilon Redon. Their numbering, which runs through No. 133, makes it appear that the series is incomplete. The Lenormand-Dayen catalog mentions that seventy-two of the seventy-nine photos are signed and carry a legend on the reverse side in the artist's own hand.

Fare wrote in his report: "Such a collection is exceptional and inestimable for an art historian, an editor or an important art merchant." Here he had a good opportunity to mention that the Wildenstein foundation had undertaken to publish a well-edited catalog of Redon. He then added: "to break up such a collection is uncommon because it would become unusable. Where are the missing photos? It seems that their disappearance cannot be the result of a voluntary act."

Sebastien repeats this insinuation by the expert, and writes on page 63 of his conclusions: "The follow-up on the missing numbers, containing the same legends in the same handwriting, is in the hands of Mr. Sebastien. It is not customary to sell half a collection, all or nothing [*sic*]. The presence in the safe rented by Erich Šlomovič and registered in the name of his father, of only part of Odilon Redon's collection, testifies to his haste and throws very serious doubts on the legitimacy of his acquisition."

To strengthen his arguments Sebastien submitted twenty-eight numbered photographs which he claimed were printed on the same paper as those found in the bank safe, thus completing the series. He also submitted twenty-four unnumbered photographs, which he claims to have printed on different paper, all made from the negatives kept by the Vollard heirs.

Cohen explained the incomplete nature of this series by recalling the anarchic conditions under which the Société Général Bank proceeded on October 24, 1946, to open safe No. 69-I. At that time it placed its contents in a container and transported the container to the Governmental Department of Safekeeping in Paris. In 1975 it transferred the contents to Nantes; it then opened the safe again in February 1977 and in March 1979. On the latter date, a detailed description was made of the contents for the first time.

This negligence leads irresistibly to the conclusion of accidental destruction or theft of the missing photos, the importance of which nobody at that time recognized. These photos are mentioned for the first time in the descriptive document made on November 7, 1980, in Nantes by Lenormand under the vague label "exceptional collection of photographs signed Redon," and estimated at a value of 5,000 francs.

Nothing, Cohen stressed, allowed one to claim that Erich Šlomovič had not put into the safe the 133 photos which seem to constitute the complete series. Nor does anything permit one to dismiss the hypothesis that the missing photos were taken by Šlomovič to Yugoslavia and lost in the course of the tribulations of his collection, following the railway accident in which his mother died and which was described in detail by Neskovič.

The long and fastidious enumeration of the items in litigation, which Sebastien thought was useful, giving pointless details such as dimensions of the paintings, the number of editions of the books, or the characteristics of the printing of the etchings, did not achieve its objective, contributing instead to disqualifying his arguments.

"Mr. Sebastien apparently counted on the fatigue of his readers and blithely continued to accumulate more errors," Cohen concluded.

Regarding the etchings by Chagall — listed as items Nos. 34 and 35 in the Lenormand-Dayen catalog — Sebastien claimed that they had neither the signature of the artist nor any mention of the number of the proof. He thought this proved that Vollard was unable to get rid of them because they were imperfect and unfinished. But it had already been noted that all of these etchings had certification in Chagall's handwriting and that they were given by Ambroise Vollard to Erich Šlomovič.

To prove Šlomovičae's duplicity and mercantile character, Sebastien stressed that it was strange that, leaving for Belgrade and establishing his residence there, Erich left in Paris many autographed documents even though he said that he had intended to write and publish different books based on these documents. Sebastien "feigned to forget" that he had himself submitted to the court a letter from Erich, written from Belgrade on March 23, 1940, to Lucien Vollard, in which Erich expressed his intention to return to Paris where he would have followed up on those projects.

"In fact," Cohen averred, "Erich left Paris in March 1940 with the intention of returning. Like most of his contemporaries he had not foreseen the invasion of France in May, 1940 nor the occupation of Yugoslavia in April 1941. Nor had he foreseen the circumstances which compelled him to hide for several months in a Serbian village before being arrested, imprisoned, and killed for the sole reason that he was Jewish."

One of Sebastien's less successful attempts to cast doubt on the legitimacy of Erich's ownership was his emphasizing that Erich had rented the bank safe in the name of his father, Bernard. This, he insinuated, was just one more attempt to hide his misbegotten possession.

Cohen argued that the use of Bernard's name, mentioned for the first time in 1946 by the Société Général Bank (which negligently lost the contract for the rental of the safe), was justified for two reasons. First, there was an administrative custom in Yugoslavia of preceding a person's first name with his father's first name. Second, Erich departed for Belgrade soon after renting the safe and planned to stay there with his parents. He therefore made sure to leave with the bank the name and address of his father, the person through whom he could be contacted in those troubled times. His last known visit to the safe was after February 26, 1940, about a week before his departure for Belgrade, as proved by a photo bearing that date, found in the safe and listed as item No. 92 in the Lenormand-Dayen catalog (which details the 190 items found in the safe). The photo, of Ambroise Vollard, was given as a souvenir by Lucien Vollard to Erich on the eve of his departure for Belgrade.

Sebastien unwittingly contradicted his own contention that Erich surreptitiously stashed his possessions in the Paris safe when he presented in evidence a letter written by Erich from Belgrade on March 17, 1941, to Matisse.

In it Erich writes: "Although the reproduction of the palette is not bad I regret that I do not have the original here. I left it in Paris in a safe." The palette is listed as item No. 51b in the Lenormand-Dayen catalog.

At this point, Cohen caught Sebastien with his "moral" pants down as well. Using his "favorite form of disinformation," said Cohen, Sebastien submitted as "exhibit 13" a copy of a letter he had written to a Mrs. De Guebriant, a specialist on Matisse. After asking her about the relationship which could have existed between the great artist and Erich Šlomovič, he wrote: "The inheritors of Erich Šlomovič say that the good relationship [between the two] had caused Matisse to offer him the *Guitar Player,* which had been exhibited in 1904 at the first Matisse exhibition sponsored by Vollard.

Sebastien's insinuation in his letter to Mrs. De Guebriant, Cohen charged, constituted pure invention, "odiously aimed at provoking the reaction of Madame Guebriant." The latter's reply, in the form of a letter dated June 14, 1990, was duly submitted to the court. In it she expressed her indignation: "It is impossible that Matisse gave Erich Šlomovič the painting *Guitar Player Standing,* found in the safe of the Société Général; Matisse only gave a few paintings as gifts in the course of his life and would never have done so without a dedication."

Cohen challenged Sebastien's attorney, Paul Prompt, to show where and when it had ever been claimed that Matisse had offered this painting as a gift to Erich. This procedure, Cohen remarked, "is characteristic of the perfidy practiced by Sebastien [and his attorney] in order to mislead the court, all because they are conscious of the inanity of their other allegations."

The incident reminds one of the old saw about the lawyer asking an innocent defendant: "When did you last stop beating your wife?"

After committing this "legal barbarism," Cohen continued, Sebastien tried another tack to prove Erich Šlomovič's clandestine activity. This was indicated, Sebastien charged, by his failure to inform the notary in charge of the Vollard inheritance about the existence of his collection. But if Erich held the collection legitimately he would have had no reason to inform the notary.

Sebastien next tried to distort the contents of the letter which Cohen brought from Belgrade in which Predrag Milosavljevič told, on January 30, 1940, of his first and recent meeting with Erich. Sebastien "rejoiced" to find in this letter further "proof" of surreptitiousness: namely, that Erich had not contacted the staff of the Yugoslav Legation in Paris earlier. But nothing indicates that he did not have a longtime relationship with other members of this Legation.

It was sufficient to remind Sebastien, Cohen stated, that the many dedications made to Erich Šlomovič by well-known painters and writers show that he was leading anything but a clandestine existence in Paris. Moreover, he openly showed his collection to his compatriots Lukič, Gliha, and Milosavljevič, the latter being a painter and also an official of the Yugoslav Legation.

If this were not sufficient proof, the information given to Fabiani on March 1, 1940, by an emissary of the Yugoslav Legation about Erich's imminent departure for Yugoslavia with his collection constitutes the most convincing evidence of all that Erich had nothing to hide, not even from an incontestable representative of the Vollard inheritance. If there was anything illicit about his collection, the Vollard heirs had every opportunity to stop him from removing it from France.

At this point Cohen caught Sebastien in another contradiction. Sebastien had earlier described the transporting of Erich's collection by diplomatic courier as illicit. Then, in his conclusions, he inadvertently detailed the risks, caused by the state of war, which such transport entailed, namely, the necessity to cross Fascist Italy and Nazi Austria in order to reach Belgrade. It was precisely this situation which justified Erich's request from his country's diplomatic representatives to help him and not any desire on his part to use the diplomatic courier to cover his tracks.

This request was all the more innocent insofar as at the time, as noted earlier, there existed no customs regulations that might have required a declaration to the French authorities of any exportation of art objects. On the contrary, Fare reported: "Regarding the question which I have addressed to various witnesses dealing with art commerce before the war, it transpires that during that period no formalities were required regarding international commerce in objects of art. These art objects, whether belonging to merchants or private individuals, circulated freely across the frontiers."

Sebastien fared no better in trying to use the declarations which Erich allegedly made to Yugoslav newspapers upon his return to his country as additional proof of the illicit nature of his ownership.

"If he had made the effort to read more carefully the exhibits and documents submitted by the Herzlers," Cohen noted, "he would not have failed to recall that *Hrvatski Dnevnik*, in its November 24, 1940, issue, on the day of the inauguration of Erich's exhibition in Zagreb, was the only newspaper to quote Erich in the first person. There Erich gave an accounting of how he had gathered his collection by pointing to his interest in painting since he was young, his passionate love of art, his period of study in Paris, London, and Switzerland, and his frequent visits to Vollard and the great painters in Paris."

Erich Šlomovič was in no way responsible during that period for the many legendary newspaper accounts about him. In fact, he never presented himself as the heir of Vollard, an erroneous allegation repeated for decades in other journals and in the film *The Donator.*

Sebastien, Cohen noted, managed to ignore the fact that Šlomovič acted like a man who had nothing to fear from publicity (the exact opposite of clandestinity as stipulated by the law regarding doubtful possession) when he organized in Zagreb his remarkable exhibition, inaugurated on November 24, 1940, in the presence of numerous personalities including the consul general of France. The exhibition continued to attract public and press attention for three months.

"With a disarming lack of logic," Sebastien did not even hesitate to include in the category of illicit actions, which according to him would taint Erich's ownership, the cautious and discreet behavior manifested by the Belgrade museum in refusing to show his collection there.

In this connection it should be noted that the Belgrade museum exhibited the Šlomovič collection for the first time in 1950, judiciously avoiding any identification of the collection with his name, describing it instead as "New French Art From the Collection of the Belgrade Museum of Art." At that time the legal status of the Šlomovič collection had not been determined (this would only be done in 1969), and the museum did not want to endanger its title to the collection by identifying it with its original owner.

However, the name of the exhibition and the works by Daumier, Pissarro, Renoir, Degas, and Bonnard which it presented would necessarily have attracted the attention of experts and interested persons like Lucien Vollard, Robert de Galea, and the Jonas couple who were all alive at the time.

This is also true for subsequent exhibitions in Belgrade and Zagreb in 1957, '58, '61, '63, and '65 under the headings:

- Degas, Rodin, Renoir: Drawings and Pastels From the Collection of the National Museum
- Exhibition of Drawings by Forain, Bonnard, From the Collection of the National Museum
- Odilon Redon
- Renoir, Degas From the Collection of the National Museum

In addition, the Belgrade Museum contributed individual paintings to exhibitions in:

- the United States and Austria in 1960
- Japan in 1967
- Austria and the Soviet Union in 1968

Because of their number, titles, and importance, these exhibitions could not have gone unnoticed by the Vollard heirs, well immersed by that time in the world of art.

But the most open display of the Šlomovič collection in Belgrade came in 1966 with the publication in Serbo-Croatian, and in 1967 in French and English, of an art album by Denis Rouart, the French art expert, in collaboration with Momcilo Stevanovič, a former curator of the Belgrade museum. The album, entitled "The Unknown Degas and Renoir in the National Museum of Belgrade," clearly identifies Erich Šlomovič and Ambroise Vollard as the progenitors of the collection. In fact Stevanovič, in his introduction to the album, goes into great detail about Erich, including his relations with Vollard and with various artists of the time. The author was the first person to guess the truth, namely, that Vollard, during his lifetime, gave the bulk of the collection to Erich as a gift.

A further exposure came in July 1969 with the publication in the Yugoslav press of the series of articles by Bora Neskovič telling how he had uncovered the collection. The French newspaper *Le Figaro* picked up the story and revealed to the French public for the first time the identity of Erich Šlomovič and the odyssey of his collection. A three-column headline in *Le Figaro* of July 23 announced: "A Fabulous Collection of French Paintings Discovered in Yugoslavia; Bequeathed by Vollard to a friend, they disappeared during the war."

Five days later, on July 28, the same newspaper followed up with another story headlined "The History, Vicissitudes and Mystery of the Fabulous Chlomovich Collection: Many unanswered questions about Vollard's donation to his Yugoslav collaborator." The story goes on to speculate about Erich, the mystery of his acquisition, his disappearance, and so on.

Subsequently, numerous exhibitions of the Šlomovič collection were held in:

- Prague and Belgrade, 1971
- Belgrade and Ljubljana, 1972
- Belgrade, 1974 and 1977
- Ljubljana, 1977
- Belgrade, 1981, '82, '84, '86, and '87
- Stockholm and Tokyo, 1988

By this time Erich Šlomovič's name was prominently displayed. But none of the Vollard heirs ever reacted or tried to take action to recover what they subsequently claimed was rightfully theirs.

The Vollard heirs also had an opportunity to take legal action during the thirteen years (1956-1969) that the Herzlers' case dragged on in Yugoslavia; yet they remained silent.

Nevertheless, Sebastien and his attorney, Prompt, "have the audacity to criticize the Herzlers for having failed to inform [Sebastien's] late aunt and Vollard heir, Mrs. Jonas, of the proceedings which they undertook in Yugoslavia and to associate her with them," Cohen pointed out.

Cohen reviewed the Yugoslav case briefly to indicate that Sebastien had added presumption to neglect by trying to base himself on the false claims and perverted decisions of that case. He did so despite being aware that the Yugoslav state prosecutor abandoned his intention to base his case on the alleged donation by Erich's mother of her son's collection to the Yugoslav state for lack of valid proof of such a generous intention.

This alleged donation was just one more fable among the many spread about the person and the collection of Erich Šlomovič.

In the end, as we saw, the Yugoslav court scandalously applied an exceptional law which placed a one-year limitation on suits for recovery of property lost in the war. Since Erich's heirs had not filed a claim within this one-year limitation, the conclusion was that Erich had "abandoned" his property, which thereby became state property. This so-called "abandonment" was due, of course, to no other cause than the arrest and murder of Erich, his father, and his brother.

Cohen then reminded the court about the letter he had obtained in Belgrade written by the head of President Tito's Bureau on March 14, 1972, in response to the appeal by the Herzlers after all legal means had been exhausted. In this letter, Tito's bureau chief notified the Belgrade City Council, which had sued for ownership of the collection, that he believed the Herzlers had been victims of a serious injustice by the use of indefensible arguments. It was important for Yugoslavia's international reputation, he wrote, to indemnify the heirs as much as possible.

This appeal remained a dead letter.

The French court, Cohen concluded, was thus able to appreciate the audacity of Mr. Sebastien, who does not confine himself to reproaching the Herzlers for not having included his late aunt, Mrs. Jonas, in their case in Yugoslavia but by a twisted logic also imputes to them a mythical donation to the Yugoslav state which resulted from the adverse decision in that country's courts. He, therefore, demands that they be condemned to pay him the sum of one French franc for damages and interest, pending final determination of the value of the collection being kept by the Belgrade museum.

For all these reasons [Cohen concluded], Mr. Sebastien's appeal should be faulted, declared null and void, and all the claims of the Herzlers, who have waited eight years for justice, should be accepted in full.

Additionally, Cohen demanded that his clients not be charged with paying the bank's storage costs because of its negligence in handling the safe and its contents. Therefore, they should also be freed of paying the expenses of the abortive auction ordered by the bank.

He also demanded a return of the 106,000 francs obtained from the sale of items to cover court expenses and asked that Sebastien be charged with paying his clients 160,000 francs for the expenses they had incurred in the course of the case.

In a separate appeal, Cohen argued against the right of Zdenka Šlomovič to any part of the inheritance. As will be recalled, Zdenka left Yugoslavia in 1954 and went to live in Hollywood, Florida. Whereas the Herzlers were aunts and first cousins of Erich's from his mother's side, Zdenka was a first cousin from his father's side.

Cohen based his case against Zdenka on the unproved argument that she had already received compensation, before leaving Yugoslavia, through the intervention of Moise Pijade.

As for the Yugoslav consulate, it had filed a brief with the French court at the beginning of the proceedings in 1981, on behalf of the four Israelis and Mara Albahari. It eventually withdrew from the case when it saw that none of the direct heirs (Mara was not a direct heir), whom it pretended to represent, were Yugoslav citizens.

That, at least, was the official reason for withdrawing. More to the point was the fear that should the Yugoslavs lose in the French courts, a precedent would be set which could be used by the litigants to sue for the treasure in Yugoslavia.

Nothing illustrates the perfidy of the Yugoslav authorities in this charade better than the fact that their petition to the French court was filed on behalf of the very heirs whose claim the Yugoslav courts had previously rejected. They had also conveniently forgotten that even Marshal Tito's Bureau had described the Yugoslavian disinheritance procedure of the Yugoslav communist state as a serious miscarriage of justice.

Chapter XXI

THE DECISION

When the Paris Court of Appeal reached its final decision on October 30, 1990, it had three major litigants to deal with: the Herzlers in Israel, Zdenka Šlomovič in the United States, and Louis Sebastien in Paris. It also had to decide on the claim of the bank, which was demanding 30,895 francs ($5,600) for storage fees and related expenses and 400,290 francs ($74,000) for the auctioneers Lenormand and Dayen, who had prepared the abortive auction of the collection at the bank's request.

The court reviewed Cohen's main contentions one by one, elaborated on them, and accepted virtually all of them.

In its thirty-seven-page decision the court states, among other things:

> It is... established that Erich Šlomovič's ownership of the works in litigation was public in January 1940 and even in 1939. His ownership was not ignored by the heirs of Ambroise Vollard since the latter's brother, Lucien, was closely acquainted with him. In his letter of March 1, 1940, Predrag Milosavljevič mentions information collected from Martin Fabiani, who participated in the administration of the Vollard gallery, who declared that Erich Šlomovič had "only a small number of things," this estimation being explained by the immensity of the Vollard collection.
>
> The public nature of the possession could not have disappeared by the storage of the objects in the bank safe. This storage was imposed by the exceptional circumstances of the war period and by Erich's trip to Yugoslavia. Moreover, Erich mentions the existence of

> the safe in the letter he wrote to Matisse on March 17, 1941. The exportation of the other objects by diplomatic mail does not affect the present litigation.
>
> Thus, the illicit nature of the ownership is not proved.

Consequently, the court decided to divide the collection fifty-fifty between the Herzlers and Zdenka Šlomovič, but only after deducting fifteen items for Sebastien. This included six art albums, two photographs, three portraits of Vollard, and works by Renoir, Bonnard, and Forain.

The main reason: since these items were personally dedicated to Vollard, Sebastien should benefit from the doubt that Vollard might have preferred to keep them in his possession.

In the revealing words of the court:

> Two photographs are dedicated to Ambroise Vollard, one by August Renoir and the other by Emile Bernard and Elizabeth Altarriba. These are personal souvenirs which are nontransferable and which exclude, if it is not expressly mentioned, irrevocable relinquishment.

Among the drawings there is a self-portrait of Renoir wearing a cap, carrying the dedication of its author to Vollard: "My sympathetic pest." This personal manifestation of affection excludes the gift by hand of the object.

Among the prints there are portraits of Ambroise Vollard done by Dufy, Picasso and Renoir. None of these watercolors and lithographs is dedicated to Erich Šlomovič in contrast to [other works].... Taking into account the number of other dedications collected by Erich it may be concluded that he would not have failed to have dedicated to him the portraits of his spiritual patron if they had been given to him.

It is also significant... that no portrait of Vollard appears among the 352 foreign works in the Šlomovič collection in the Belgrade museum. From this fact it can be deduced that the undedicated portraits of Vollard left in the safe of the Société Général Bank were not destined for Erich Šlomovič and do not belong to his inheritance.

Among the books which the expert had observed, he noted in connection with the illustrated album, *Father Ubu's War,* that this was the publisher Vollard's personal copy and that it included many original drawings of which the reproduction in engravings had been made with zinc plates now owned by Mr. Sebastien. Moreover, the comparison between the books and the manuscripts leads to the presumption that there was a liberal intention and a gift by hand only for the dedicated books, whereas the others were possessed in a doubtful manner.

The expert did not find any [signatures or dedications] on nine of the ten canvases in the inventory. However, when he examined Forain's painting, *The Woman With the Prints* and the canvas and the frame, which are original, he found an old label on the frame mentioning, "Gallery A. Vollard." This indication of ownership by the Vollard gallery on only one of the paintings in litigation is incompatible with a gift by hand of the painting and determines the ownership of this work by Mr. Sebastien.

On the other hand, it is impossible to deduce that the other objects in litigation were not given by hand, neither on account of their exceptional value nor on account of the suspicion of fraudulent action which the previous decision of this court irrevocably excluded....

As a result, the claim should be partially considered by attributing to Mr. Sebastien batches 2, 3, 5, 7, 8, 8b, 42, 58, 78, 79, 87d, 91, 105, 171 and 185; the other objects under litigation belong to the inheritance of Erich Šlomovič. [emphasis added]

The court also awarded the seventy-nine controversial photos of the works of Redon to Sebastien, saying that these were an incomplete part of a series of 133 photos apparently divided up by mistake. The court, thus, did not accept Fernand Cohen's argument that the photos were either lost by the bank during the frequent opening and transfers of the safe's contents or had been removed by Erich, taken to Yugoslavia, and lost there during or after the war.

As the court put it:

> The expert expressed his astonishment about the dividing up of this series which in its entirety would have been of inestimable value for an art historian, an art publisher or art dealer. The amputation of this series prevented its use.

Mr. Sebastien submitted 28 photographs of the same series. Even if the series remains incomplete the resemblance of the negatives proved that the series was divided up by error and that it was not meant to be dispersed; thus there has not been a gift by hand of this batch (No. 105).

As for the bank, the court decided, after criticizing it for mishandling the collection, that the Herzlers and Zdenka Šlomovič should share equally in paying its expenses, including the cost of preparing the auction, plus interest beginning from 1982. The cost of the expertise was to be shared by all three litigants, including Sebastien.

The court also ruled that the trustee, Mr. Gondre, should administer the distribution of the items and that if the litigants could not agree on how this would be done he would auction off the collection and divide the money.

In the interim, the French Ministry of Culture notified the parties that it considered two paintings as national treasures which, though they could be sold, must not leave the country. These were the *fauve* painting by Derain, which graced the cover of the Paris catalog, and *The Guitarist* by Matisse.

Going, apparently, on the Las Vegas principle that there is always a jackpot there for someone to win, *all of the parties* appealed the decision to the Supreme Court of France. As is customary in Western jurisprudence, the supreme court decides on matters of law, not fact. Thus, the basic decision as to the rights and division of ownership seemed likely to remain intact.

If, however, the court found a misapplication of the relevant laws or any other legal faults, the case would be returned to the Court of Appeal for reconsideration.

Thus, the battle had been joined once more. Nevertheless, both the Herzlers and Cohen, realizing for the time being that Zdenka had both the law and justice on her side, entered into negotiations with her to reach a compromise. At the same time, Cohen found the basis on which the court had awarded Zdenka fifty percent to be strange, to say the least.

The French court surprisingly accepted the Yugoslav court's decision, which arbitrarily set the date of Erich's, his father's and his brother's death as May 16, 1946. Since the mother had died before that, Erich thus remained owner of his property until his death together with his father and brother. However, according to French law if deaths are simultaneous, which was the case here, the youngest (i.e., Erich's brother Egon) becomes the heir. Since Egon had no progeny, French law decrees in such cases that the inheritance is to be divided equally between the maternal and paternal sides.

Cohen and the four Herzlers entered negotiations with Zdenka for a compromise even though Cohen had appealed this reasoning. One suggestion was that since there were five heirs, each should receive a fifth. Zdenka Šlomovič was ready to accept less than the fifty percent awarded to her but not the twenty percent proposed by Cohen and his clients.

Chapter XXII

THE LIFE AND DEATH OF VOLLARD:

PROBING THE MYSTERY FURTHER

Although the French court case largely cleared up the mystery of Erich Šlomovič, it created a new enigma, that of Ambroise Vollard.

It also left a nagging question.

Was Vollard, a reputedly tight-fisted, tough-minded businessman, capable of giving such a generous gift to an individual like Erich who was outside the circle of his own heirs? In searching for an answer during my busy visit to Paris in May 1991, I discovered several people who knew Vollard personally.

The first was Daniel Wildenstein. As will be recalled, he described Vollard as "one of the most difficult people I've ever seen. He never gave any paintings to anyone... not five pence. When he sold paintings he always got his money first. He wouldn't give away the right time of day."

Was this the real Vollard? Or was it an image Wildenstein was trying to create in order to cast doubt on Erich's ownership? It was this later impression which remained with me after my interview with him: It was also the opinion of Fernand Cohen, who argued persuasively that Wildenstein's testimony was inconsistent and unreliable.

When, at the end of my interview with Wildenstein, I asked him if he knew anyone else who had known Vollard personally, he mentioned, among others, an elderly man named Alfred Daber who "used to run an art gallery and had some dealings with Vollard, I believe."

When I called Daber, he invited me to visit him in his eighth-floor apartment which was the top floor under the eaves, in an elegant apartment house off the Place Periere, just northwest of the Etoile. He was a spry ninety-two-year-old raconteur, with a mischievous look in his eyes and an animated way of talking. Even his daughter, who helped to translate his more slangy expressions and who had probably heard his stories many times over, couldn't resist a chuckle now and then.

"Vollard?" exclaimed Daber as if he were appraising the Eiffel Tower for the first time. "Yes, I knew him... but not as well as I would have liked to. He was a very cunning man. He would hold onto his paintings. He wouldn't sell them easily. When he talked to you he would grab your lapel and remark about the quality of the material. This would give him time to size you up and figure out a proper response to whatever you asked him.

"I was a young man in those days — it was in the late '20s — and I was trying to set up an art gallery in Paris. I didn't have much money and I wanted to meet Vollard. I thought he could help me make contacts in the art world and find some bargain paintings, and so on.

"He received me in his bedroom. He was wearing one of those funny-looking, old-fashioned, pointed nightcaps and he seemed to have a cold. He spoke little since he was hoarse. He let me do most of the talking... and asking. But his answers were noncommittal or else boiled down to vague promises.

"As I was leaving I looked backward and what did I see sticking out from under the covers? Both of his feet with shoes on. The old bugger had been putting on an act... all of it, so he wouldn't have to talk much or give me any commitments.

"Vollard became famous via the people he knew," Daber continued. "He understood human psychology. He would listen to what others would say about paintings, learn their thoughts... he was very skillful in getting information out of them and they never realized that his knowledge came from them."

Vollard didn't always "discover" new artists who later became famous, Daber contended. "Take the sculptor Maillol. Some amateur once brought a statue by Maillol to Vollard. Vollard put it aside for a few days and forgot about it. One day a customer came in, got all excited, bought it and said: 'Look, I've discovered a new sculptor.'"[1]

"I once bought three aquarelles by Cezanne from Vollard. I sold one to Ivar Churchill, Winston Churchill's cousin. He paid 50,000 francs for it and then turned around and sold it right away.

"Do you know how Vollard died? He liked to cook, especially specialities from his native island of Reunion. So one day he cooked up a large batch for lunch at some friends' place, put it in a large iron pot, and got into his car to have his chauffeur drive him there. He put the pot on the back shelf of the car just behind the back seat. On the way the driver had an accident and the iron pot crashed into the back of Vollard's head.

"Killed by a Reunion stew," remarked Daber.

As a further recollection of Vollard, Daber remarked, "George Rouault was a great friend of his, but Vollard was not sincere with him," and then as a parting shot: "Vollard would have sold paintings to Saddam Hussein." (As we saw in Chapter XI, Vollard procrastinated interminably on planned albums of Rouault's work and cost him dearly.)

Louis Sebastien confirmed the circumstances of Vollard's death.

"I visited him on his deathbed at the hospital in Versailles. He had had a brain concussion but he was conscious. He died several days after the accident."

Sebastien's father was an opera singer and had been friendly with Vollard. Sebastien first met him in 1929 at the age of fourteen and then used to visit him periodically at his mansion on Rue Martignac. Vollard had been impressed by the young man's knowledge of art, which he had gained by frequenting museums, and he gave him several autographed albums as gifts.

"Vollard never thought of death," said Sebastien. "He had never arranged for a burial plot, so when he died my family buried him in our family plot at Bagneux outside Paris.

"Vollard was shrewd," Sebastien recalled. "He always tried to get the best deal he could from the artists. He came from peasant stock. He was tough but he had a good heart. He was the opposite of mild-mannered. Nevertheless, he was

---

1. This story may be apocryphal, since it is known that Vollard first exhibited the unknown Maillol in 1902 after being introduced to him by the painter Vuillard. Thereafter Vollard made a great success with Maillol's terra cotta statues by casting them in bronze.

the perfect host. He was always trying to induce artists to give him works for various albums he planned to publish, but he never got around to a lot of them."

A slightly different image, a sort of split personality, emerges from the testimony of Vollard's grand-godson Christian de Galea. In an interview with the author (see Chapter XV), de Galea described him as "very gentle with people he liked and rude with those he didn't... tough with buyers but not necessarily with painters... [and] most generous with friends."

It is this description which probably comes closest to the truth. Simply stated, Vollard possessed that very human condition of contradictory traits: at once tough and gentle, rude and courteous, tight-fisted and generous. Here certainly was a man who, at the age of seventy-two, was capable of giving the most generous of gifts to a twenty-four-year-old Erich Šlomovič. Erich, with his passion and unerring eye for art, his limitless ambition to nurture it and disseminate it, reminded Vollard of his own youth.

Chapter XXIII

BETRAYAL IN BACINA

In following the footsteps of Erich, I had been fueled at the outset by journalistic curiosity. As the years went by it had become a panoramic pilgrimage, from the zenith of mortal achievement and creativity to the nadir of human tragedy.

In February 1992, I decided to retrace Erich's last journey. I was determined to visit the village of Bacina where Mara and the Šlomovič family had hidden, and to speak to any persons still alive who had known or helped them.

The civil war between Serbia and Croatia had died down by then and so, despite warnings from friends and family, I proceeded to that torn country with the feeling that it was now or never. My trip took me from Israel to Zagreb, and then to Belgrade. To reach the Serbian capital from Zagreb one had to make a long rail detour via Budapest: the only way to get around the war-torn border between Serbia and Croatia.

In Belgrade I was fortunate to find Alex (Fredi) Mosič, vice-president of the Federation of Jewish Communities in Yugoslavia and chairman of the Jewish Museum there, whom I had met two years earlier on my first trip to Yugoslavia. He agreed to be my guide and interpreter. Fredi was a fourth-generation Belgradian, a veteran of the Partisans, a former executive with a government-controlled oil company, a born linguist, and a mine of information. These attributes were graced by an accommodating manner, invariably accompanied by a broad smile.

We took his car and drove two hundred kilometers southeast to Bacina, most of the way along a broad four-lane expressway, brushed from time to time by the railroad tracks which had borne the train that carried Roza Šlomovič and Mara's two children to their deaths.

We turned off the highway at the district town of Varvarin, from whence Mara and Roza had boarded the fatal train for Belgrade on December 31, 1944. Six kilometers to the west, through flat farmlands, lies the village of Bacina. We reached it at noon. Before us stood a typical Serbian farming village with its small, square, uniform homes topped by red tiled roofs and surrounded by small yards set off by cement fences, all cast in the same quilt-like mold.

The village had hardly changed its appearance, I was told, since Erich and his family had hidden there fifty-one years earlier. Then it boasted three thousand residents; today it had 3,800. Then as now most of the population worked at farming, raising wheat, grapes, and assorted fruits.

The asphalted streets were covered with a thin layer of dust mixed with straw and other remains of harvested crops, blown off from the occasional tractor or horse-drawn buggy passing by. The town square was more like a triangle — a three-pointed intersection housing a grocery store, a café, and a hardware shop. A block away stood the Orthodox church painted a bright yellow, with its square twin spires dominating the scene.

We entered the grocery shop in the town square, and after a few words from Fredi all present understood what we were seeking. The proprietor had begun to give us directions when a gangly, middle-aged man with the weathered face of a farmer offered to take us to the people who had hidden the Šlomovič family during the war. But first, he suggested, he would take us to the municipality which was just around the corner, less than a hundred yards away.

As we emerged, we passed by one of the village's few two-story buildings with a café on its ground floor and with an apartment above. It overlooked a small stream barely trickling by. As we crossed the bridge over the Stabar our guide pointed to the apartment with the balcony and told us: "That's where Mara and her two children lived."

Past the bridge we turned right. Thirty meters away on our left stood a typical square-shaped house with a worn wooden door at its center and two square windows on either side.

"This," our guide pointed, "is the Spasič home where the Šlomovič family lived." One side of the house shared a common windowless wall with a two-story building next door. The other side faced a large empty lot, followed by another, larger square house, standing by itself on a raised cement platform. It differed from other houses only in its larger dimensions and its rose-colored coat of paint. This was the municipality. The plaque outside said it had been built in 1915, the year Erich Šlomovič was born.

We entered a large room, sparsely furnished with two simple desks, several cabinets, and photo of Tito on one of the walls. At one table sat a young man working at an old typewriter, who rose to greet us. He was the town secretary, we were told; the mayor was not there at the time.

The wartime mayor had passed away many years ago. In this room, on a winter day in 1942, a German officer in charge of a punitive expedition had asked that mayor if there was anyone in the village who spoke German and could act as an interpreter.

"In the house next door," the mayor had said, pointing to the Spasič home where the Šlomovič family was living. It was these incautious words, uttered spontaneously, that doomed the Šlomovičs.

How it happened and what transpired afterward were told by Dusan and Branca Zivadinovič to whom our guide took us next. To get there we retraced our steps. As we again passed the Spasič house where Erich and his family had hidden, our guide said: "We'll go there later, after we talk to the Zivadinovičs."

As we recrossed the bridge, we turned right onto a dirt road running along the bank of the stream and then turned off after fifty meters into a group of modest homes, in one of which lived the couple we were seeking.

Dusan Zivadinovič and his wife Branca came out from their backyard utility shed to greet us. Upon hearing of my mission their faces assumed a friendly mien and they invited us to sit on the small balcony at the entrance to their house. Branca took off her shoes, entered the house and soon emerged with Turkish coffee and cookies.

Dusan, now seventy-six, and Branca, now seventy-two, had befriended the Šlomovič family upon their arrival in Bacina. Branca, together with Dusan's father, had built the double wall in which Erich had hidden his paintings. Simple folk with simple manners, their story unfolded in keeping with their character, straightforward and unembellished.

Before moving into the Spasič home next to the municipality, Dusan recalled, the Šlomovičs first lived at the home of Dusan's neighbor Ristič. Across the street lived Dusan's brother, Adam. It was Adam and Erich's father, Bernard, who together hatched the idea of hiding Erich's paintings in a double wall.

We walked over to Adam's yard, to the utility shed. His widow greeted us and took us through a narrow passage to her dwelling, a replica in miniature of the village homes. It had a window and a single door, offset to the right. The door was one yard from the wall. It had been decided to build the false wall in that space, thus creating an enclosure of some thirty centimeters to accommodate Erich's collection. Erich had stored the paintings and art albums in three iron containers about one meter square by thirty centimeters thick. He also prepared a metal cylinder into which he had rolled a large number of paintings. As Dusan's wife demonstrated, anyone entering the shed could hardly perceive that the inner wall to his right was twelve inches closer to the door than the outer wall.

The idea was to create a hiding place, apart from the Šlomovič living quarters, so that if any of the family were arrested the treasure would not be found with them.

"One day, several weeks after his arrival, Erich brought the containers to be hidden," Dusan recalled. "I didn't know what was in them and didn't ask, but I knew it was something valuable. Only after the war I heard it was an art collection."

The containers were put in the kitchen of Adam's home one evening while Dusan's father and wife prepared the bricks and cement to build the wall. It was a cold winter day towards the end of 1941, Branca recalled. "The bricks were frozen. It was necessary to thaw them so that the cement would stick to them. My father-in-law put the bricks to heat in a big receptacle with burning wood. We put the iron containers in place and built the wall around them, then we spread the plaster, which also had to be heated because of the cold, and painted it all white in such a way that no one could tell that something was hidden there. The whole operation took three hours.

"Yes, it could have been dangerous," Branca admitted, "but we didn't think of that at the time."

In an interview on Yugoslav television several years earlier, the late Adam Zivadinovič recalled how he guarded the cache and the secret throughout the war. "After the Germans took the Šlomovičs away I was not afraid. If the Cetniks [the anti-Partisan royalist underground] would have known about it they would have cut off my head and burned my house."

Dusan recalled Erich as "very pleasant, good-humored and communicative," a slightly different portrait than that drawn by most others who observed a very withdrawn, taciturn young man. The confinement to the village and the lack of any rewarding activity had apparently impelled Erich to seek Dusan's company.

"Around that time I joined the Communist Party," Dusan recalled, "so I found I had something in common with Erich. We were both persecuted, he as a Jew and I as a communist. Erich was not involved in politics, and he was not a communist, but he was interested in what was going on. We used to discuss current events a lot. He was oriented more to Western democracy. He also told me of his interest in art.

"The family stayed in their home a lot and didn't move around much, but Erich would come to my shop from time to time. I had a shoe shop in the same building where Mara lived. I made mostly native *panak* shoes. Erich's brother used to visit me more frequently. He was a chemist and he specialized in leather, so we had a lot in common."

As for the arrest of the Šlomovič men, Dusan's story paralleled that of Bora Neskovič but with some important additions.

"When the mayor pointed to the Šlomovič family as possible interpreters for the Germans, he didn't reveal that they were Jews," Dusan said. "Nevertheless, it was a mistake on his part. That's how the Germans found Egon, and when his father Bernard went to look for him they took him too. Erich was not around at the time. They took them to Krcin in the Juhor mountains.

"In the meantime someone in town told the Germans that there were Jews hiding in Bacina and when the German expedition came back the same evening, other German soldiers were waiting for them at the entrance to town to arrest Egon and Bernard. They then went back to the house and found Erich and arrested him together with another Jew by the name of Pinto who was also hiding in Bacina. Even if the men hadn't been taken as interpreters they probably would all have been arrested anyway because someone had revealed that there were Jews hiding in the town."

"Did the Germans come to Bacina again?" I asked.

"Twice, once to requisition goods and another time to take hostages when an Italian plane crashed near our village. The Cetniks had ransacked the plane and the Germans demanded that everything be returned or else the hostages would be shot. They returned the equipment and the hostages were released. After that we weren't bothered by them."[1]

"How did the Šlomovič family support themselves?"

"They did various work in the village but they also had jewelry and gold which they sold. Also, Mara used to take agricultural products, mostly meat, to Belgrade and exchange them for textiles, costume jewelry, and other items which she would sell. It was a bit dangerous since everything required permits and just about everything you had to do to survive was illegal.[2]

"When Branca and I decided to get married — it was in November 1941 — I had an adopted brother in Varvarin who offered to be my witness.[3] But Erich said: 'You've been very nice to me. You've done a lot for us. I would like to be your witness.' I accepted his offer.

"From that moment on he became like one of the family because with us, in our village, an adopted brother or a witness is like a real brother. He was a very fine person. I don't have enough words to praise him.

"After he and his father and brother were taken away by the Germans, our son Bratislav was born and Erich's mother, Roza, would spend every day in our home looking after him. She took care of him for three years and became his godmother. The Šlomovičs were good people."

At this point I asked Fredi to ask Dusan why he was ready to accept a Jew and a virtual stranger as the best man at his (Christian) wedding.

"I can't ask that question," Fredi answered.

"Why not?"

---

1. This was because Tito's Partisan struggle, which had begun somewhat west of Bacina, had moved ever westward and northward, outside its general area.
2. It was this activity which earned Mara the appellation "Black Marketeer," mentioned by Neskovič in his book. It was a misnomer, considering the harsh struggle that was necessary to survive in those times.
3. Similar to a best man.

"I'll tell you later," he replied with a furtive glance at our hosts.

After we left them and were on our way to the home of Vera Spasič, I reminded Fredi of the question and asked him why he wouldn't translate it.

"You've got to understand these people, Victor," he replied. "They're Serbians. You'll hardly find anti-Semitism among them, especially among peasants like Dusan. Besides, they're spontaneous and sincere, and if they like someone it's all the way, no reservations. That was the case with Erich. They'd be insulted if I'd ask them such a question."

I had flown over this country during the war, heard of the Partisan struggle, one of the greatest and most successful in World War II. Several of my comrades had been shot down and then saved by the Partisans. I had admired them tremendously, but only at a distance, as an abstraction.

Now, as I heard Fredi's words, the abstraction suddenly became real. I began to understand a prime reason for the Partisans' success. Yugoslav peasants like Dusan Zivadinovič were not just the salt of the earth; they were the earth itself, solid, unyielding, and giving of themselves unstintingly.

Dusan accompanied us to the home of Vera Spasič. Greeting us at the door stood an old, wrinkled lady, her head covered with a kerchief, framing what seemed like a permanently saddened expression. She was eighty-three years old at the time and had been widowed for several years. She took us to the rear of the house to a small room which served as both a guest room and dining room.

The house had a single corridor, leading from the front door to a back door. All the rooms led off from the corridor: a bedroom, a bathroom, and a kitchen on the left, another bedroom and the living room/dining room on the right.

The Šlomovič family, all four of them, had lived in the first room to the left. It still contained the same furniture that had been there fifty years ago: twin beds with brass-tubed bedsteads, joined together and covered by thick, maroon-colored brocade bedspreads. The two sons slept on cots at either side of the door.

The back door led to a cluttered yard with chopped wood and tools tacked haphazardly under a waist-high shelter. An unused well with an old hand pump stood at the far end of the yard. The family would work in the back yard, Vera Spasič said, tanning pig hides to earn some money. But they seemed to have other means, she added.

Vera remembered the evening in the fall of 1941 when the mayor came to her home together with the village priest to ask her to take in a Jewish refugee family which had fled the Germans. "I was alone. My husband, Dusan, worked in another town as a court clerk and came home only on weekends. They told me that the family was staying in another home in the village but there was not enough room there. They were very decent people, the mayor said. I told him that I didn't know. I couldn't decide without my husband. But they said: take them, don't worry... you have nothing to fear. You won't be sorry.

"So I took them in without consulting my husband, and when he came home a few days later I told him what had happened and he had no objection. He received them very nicely. Later I felt very sorry for them. I could imagine what it meant to flee the Germans. I put myself in their place... if such a thing had happened to me. And after all, I had a large house with two small children while those who were suffering didn't even have a roof over their heads.

"The young man [Erich] was very calm, elegant, and self-contained. He was a bit sad and spoke little. But his brother and also his father were more open and spoke more freely. It was as if Erich knew what was awaiting him.

"Erich hardly left the house, but his brother, Egon, was much livelier and would go out and walk around the village, visit the café, and so on. Erich would play with our children. He liked children very much. He used to make sketches at home. His mother told me that he was an artist, that he had a lot of art works, and that he had hidden them at the home of Zivadinovič in the chimney.

"His mother, Roza, stayed home most of the time and did the cooking. She and her husband tried to speak in the local dialect so they would not be given away. They also changed their names to the local versions. She called herself Ruza and her husband, Bernard, called himself Bercil.

"Once when an Italian plane crashed near here and the Cetniks cleaned it out and the Germans took hostages to make them return everything, Roza and I went to hide with a relative near here. When the whole thing was over we came back. I carried a shovel so I'd look like a peasant coming back from the fields. On the way a German soldier pointed his rifle at me, but I managed to run off."

"How was Erich caught?" I asked.

"On the same day that the father and brother were taken off by the Germans into the mountains, a local villager came to our house with two soldiers looking for Erich. They searched the house and found Erich sitting on his bed. Roza and I were in another room when the German soldiers entered. Roza ran to the bedroom when she heard them taking Erich, but he was no longer there. She went to the door and saw him being led away. But she dared not follow.

"She came back to me and started crying bitterly. After that she used to cry every day. When she'd sit down to eat she'd say: 'I'm eating here, getting my fill... but what is happening to my people?'

"The men were held in Cuprija, so Roza and Mara would go there every Saturday to bring them food and a change of underclothing. They were there for three months and then were taken away. Roza was broken and Mara would come every day to visit and help her."

"Weren't you afraid that the Germans would come and arrest you and Roza as well?"

"Yes, I was afraid all the time that they might catch us and punish me for hiding a Jewish family. But it seems that the traitor only denounced the men, not the women. Besides, the Germans were busy elsewhere and didn't bother us after that except for the incidents I mentioned before."

"Who betrayed the Jews in Bacina?"

"The man who accompanied the two German soldiers when they arrested Erich."

"Who was he?"

Vera hesitated for an instant and then gave his name. Fredi wrote it down for me to be sure I would get it right: Sreta Mihajlovič Kamenarač.

"What do you know about him?" I asked.

"At the beginning of the war," Vera related, "he had been a member of the local government militia. They had been defeated by the Germans so he soon joined the Cetniks and then in 1944, toward the end of the war, he switched sides and joined the Partisans. After the war he joined the Yugoslav army and became an airplane mechanic and later a pilot in the air force. Later he was a pilot for the Yugoslav national airline. He died two or three years ago, in 1989 or 1990, I believe."

"Wasn't he ever tried as a war criminal?"

"No, he was never tried or punished."

During this period Roza came into contact with her sister Hilda (nicknamed Branka) and her niece Judith, both of whom had escaped to Switzerland. (Both settled in Israel after the war and were parties to the suit in the Yugoslav court.) The first exchange, initiated by Judith, took place on a special Red Cross form which allowed for a message of no more than twenty-five words. It was postmarked in Switzerland dated October 3, 1943, and addressed to Mara under her maiden name, Mara Kuzmanovič. Judith writes:

> Dear Mara. Aunt Branka and I are very well. Grandfather died in Osijek in 1942. Answer on the reverse side how you are.
>
> Kisses to Aunt Roza and yourself.
>
> (signed) Judi

The grandfather referred to was Joseph Herzler, the patriarch of the family who, every Passover, had conducted the Seders which Erich and some forty other relatives used to attend. He was murdered by the Germans in the area of Osijek, near his hometown of Djakovo.

Judith's letter had taken several months to arrive, and on April 8, 1944, Mara replied:

> Aunt Roza, Mara and children are well; happy to receive news of you but still no news from our loved ones. Jovanca married someone else. No news on Bosko.
>
> Write
>
> (signed) Mara

The references are to mutual friends and relatives.

According to the official stamp on this letter, it was only sent out on June 9. About that time Roza wrote a separate letter to her sister Hilda, without space restrictions but also without any assurance that it would reach its destination. However, it did.

My dear sister and all the others,

I have no words to begin this letter. Thanks to the Almighty that you are alive and well. As for me, Mara and the children I can say the same.

But I am alone like a finger. Only my hope and belief in God is what keeps me going. Otherwise I would not have been among the living a long time ago. Since March I know nothing of them. You can imagine what my life is like.

My dear sister, I am glad to be writing to you. I think of you my little Branka all the time. I have a picture in which you are with my youngest son. God, if you are there somewhere have mercy on us all.

Is our old man still living? It is good that you are together....

Write to me more often and don't wait for my answer since it takes a long time. Since the letter came from you, Judita, I feel much relieved. Write, my sister, so I can see your handwriting.

May you remain healthy and blessed and may God look over you and may we all be together and see each other soon, healthy and whole.

I love you very much.

(signed) R

On the day before my trip to Bacina, Irina Subotič, curator at the Belgrade museum, had told me that she had gone several months previously, on her own initiative, to visit the graves of Roza and of Mara's two children. They were badly neglected and the museum, she said, would be glad to help the family rehabilitate them.

Thus, halfway between Bacina and Belgrade we took a detour of several kilometers to visit the town of Smederevska Palanka where Mara had buried her loved ones. The town is less than ten kilometers from where the fateful train crash occurred, halfway between the towns of Velika Plana and Mala Plana. Its cemetery was the closest to the site of the accident. After several inquiries by Fredi, always preceded by a cheerful *dobar-dan* (good day), we were directed to the cemetery at the edge of town.

If the size of a cemetery indicates the age of the metropolis it serves, then Smederevska Palanka must be a very old town. Spread over some twenty hectares, the cemetery contains no less than ten thousand graves.

The caretakers were about to give up their search on our behalf when one of the directors happened by and pointed to the site, which was nearby. There, amid crumbling graves in an older section of the cemetery, close to the entrance, stood two stone slabs with badly worn Stars of David at their apex, etched on a black circular background. They were the only Jewish symbols in a sea of crosses. The stones were separated by a wide space, as if Mara had reserved a plot for herself to be buried next to her children.

On one of the stones, under the Star of David, was the legend "Here Rest Two Brothers" and under it a badly worn photograph of Mara's two sons, followed by the legend:

Miroslav — Miro
Born 24/II 1939
Alexander — Gide
Born 24/VIII 1937
HERZLER
Killed in accident
31/XII 1944

Tombstone erected by
bereaved mother

Next to it, on the gravestone of Erich's mother, was the legend:

Here lies
Roza — Ruza
ŠLOMOVIČ
Born 1890
Killed in accident
31/XII 1944

Tombstone erected by
sister-in-law Mara

I suggested to Fredi, who had been seated on a nearby gravestone, translating the above, that we say the *kaddish,* the Jewish prayer for the dead.

Not having the required skullcaps with us, we each took out a handkerchief and covered our heads. The caretakers stood by silently, a short distance away, as I tried bravely to recite the *kaddish*; but I could only remember a part of it.

So we stood silently with our heads bowed, each with his own thoughts. The panorama of Erich's odyssey seemed to pass across my mind's eye, like a camera panning a distant landscape.

Our last stop for the day was also the last station for Erich, his father Bernard, and his brother Egon: the death camp at Sajmište. Thousands of people daily drive to the new Belgrade built after World War II over one of Belgrade's main bridges over the Sava River shortly before it joins the Danube. Little do they know that just below them, on the opposite river bank, close by but virtually out of sight, stands one of the more horrible death camps of World War II. It was here that the victims were choked to death in sealed trucks, a system which even the Germans complained about as being too horrible, until they devised the more "humane" gas chambers.

Nor is the site noticed by the other thousands of people, Yugoslavs and tourists, who patronize the giant complex of green-tinted, glass-covered office buildings, sports, cultural, and convention centers, built around the five-star Intercontinental Hotel less than five hundred meters away.

The death camp was set up immediately after the German occupation in April-May 1941 as a temporary concentration camp for Jews and other "enemies" in what were then Belgrade's fairgrounds. Its advantages were that it was centrally located, could be easily fenced off, and already contained most of the structures needed to incarcerate the victims except for a barracks or two which were soon added. The Germans put Croatian fascist Ustashis in charge, who were eager to do their bidding.

The place, when we visited, was badly neglected, with some buildings being used as warehouses and others abandoned. In their midst was the exposed metal superstructure of a former tower. Next to it a raised, well-kept lawn supported a simple monument topped by a red star with a memorial plaque telling how forty thousand people had been killed at this site.

I always wondered how Erich — who died six million times — had faced the last moments of his life. When did this young man, basically apolitical, assimilated, and engrossed in a world of aesthetic beauty, realize that his Jewishness had doomed him to another world of hatred, cruelty, and death? What could have passed through his mind as he was shoved into the truck together with his father and brother, the doors slammed shut, all light and air cut off?

Could his short life of twenty-seven years filled with so many accomplishments, and even greater promise, have flashed through his mind's eye in the space of seconds?

Chapter XXIV

JUSTICE SAID BUT NOT DONE

I had photographed the graves of Roza and of Mara's two sons and, upon my return to Belgrade, gave the pictures to David Albahari, Mara's son by her second marriage. Mara had been hospitalized for a month at that time. When I asked David what was wrong with her, he replied: "She's getting old. She is 80 already."

David promised to show her the pictures as soon as she felt better. "We would like to rehabilitate the gravestones and then move the graves to the Jewish cemetery in Belgrade," he told me.

A month later, back in Israel, I received a letter from Fredi with the following note added at the end: "Mara Albahari passed away on Tuesday, March 31. A well attended funeral took place on April 2, 1992, at the Jewish cemetery of Belgrade."

Saying the *kaddish* for her at the graveside was her son, David, who the year before had been elected president of the National Federation of Jewish Communities in Yugoslavia.

At the time of my return to Belgrade, Mara's illness was too severe for me to be able to meet with her; hence, I concentrated on several other key players in the Šlomovič drama. One of them, Bora Neskovič, opened once more the Pandora's box of the missing works, including the *Kolektanea,* that compendium of Yugoslavia's leading men of arts and letters which Erich had begun to organize at the age of eighteen.

As mentioned earlier, Neskovič had come up with a contradictory story as to how the *Kolektanea* had reached his brother's hands and then was supposedly sold by his brother, before his death, to a Swiss antique dealer. He repeated this story and said he did not know where the compendium was today. But at the last minute, on the day of my departure, he admitted that he had a "photostatic copy" of the entire *Kolektanea*.

All subsequent attempts by Fredi Mosič, on my behalf, to look at it or obtain a copy of all or part of it were rebuffed by Neskovič. Could he also have known what happened to fifty or more works missing from Erich's collection at the Belgrade museum?

Mariana Zivkovič, a reporter for Yugoslavia's leading newspaper *Politika*, thought that he did. Having written about the Šlomovič story over the years, she believed that Neskovič, together with other members of the secret police, were responsible in one way or another for the disappearance of these items while the collection was in their control, after it was recovered by Neskovič from Mara's friends.

As for the *Kolektanea*, Mariana Zivkovič believed that it was removed at the same time by the same people and that Neskovič concocted the story of his brother buying it in Switzerland in order to cover his tracks.

One person who would have especially liked to see the compendium was Pavle Vasič, the artist who was first approached by Erich in 1933 to help with it. Vasič, at eighty-five years old, had a sentimental interest: he wanted to see, and perhaps make a copy of, the portrait he had done of Erich at the time for the *Kolektanea*'s cover page.

Of greater interest to him and many others, however, were the compendium's other works of art, as well as its monographs, literary commentary, and other contributions from Yugoslavia's leading men of arts and letters before World War II. Recognizing the great value of this work to Yugoslavia, as well as Erich's other contributions to the country's cultural life in general, one man was lobbying to honor him publicly and perpetuate his memory; he suggested that the Belgrade municipality name a street after him.

Dragan Boskovič was director of cultural affairs for the city of Belgrade when he first made such a proposal to the municipality in the early 1980s. He mobilized a majority in the city council, but the matter was delayed by various political upheavals including the civil war.

"I will keep after them until it is done," Boskovič said, "because Erich Šlomovič deserves to be recognized for his great contribution to Yugoslav culture. After all, he could have taken his collection elsewhere. But he chose to bring it to Yugoslavia and also to build a special center in Belgrade to house it and create a living bridge between Western and Eastern cultures."

Boskovič, a former film distributor, first became interested in the Šlomovič story when he saw *The Donator* at the annual film festival in Pula, Yugoslavia, in August 1989. He was impressed by it and undertook its distribution and promotion on behalf of the producers, Jadran Film. To help with the promotion he made a thorough study of Erich and his background.

"What really got me involved with this story, emotionally," he said, "was my discovery during the course of my research of the real meaning of the Holocaust. I went to one of the earlier residences of the Šlomovič family in Belgrade and sought someone there from the landlord's family who may have remembered them. The owners were a family named Gabbai and as I sought them out, I was told that the particular Gabbai I was looking for had been killed in the Holocaust. I got the same answer for every other member of the family I sought, down to the second and third generation. The entire family of eleven people had been killed in the Holocaust. I couldn't believe it. Until then I had heard about the Holocaust. I had read about it. But I was never touched by it directly. For the first time the extent of the tragedy was brought home tome. Erich and his family were just among the countless victims. This set me off on an intensive search after his roots."

In the process Boskovič found several people who had known Erich, including some lady friends such as the artist Lubika Sokič, who had been a close friend of Jurica Ribar, the son of Dr. Ivan Ribar. Jurica, a top commander in the Partisans, was killed during the war together with his brother. Erich had gone to elementary school with the two brothers.

Before the war Lubika had studied art in Paris, and she remembered seeing Ambroise Vollard on several occasions. Together with Jurica Ribar and other friends, she had visited Erich in his apartment on Dobracina Street and seen his collection. She still remembered it with amazement.

After the war, Lubika mounted a special exhibit of Yugoslav artists killed in the war. Among them were works by Jurica Ribar, who had also been a painter.

People who knew Erich, Boskovič said, all agreed that he had an affair with Liza Krizanič, wife of the well-known cartoonist Pjer Krizanič. A drawing of

Erich by Krizanč is part of the collection. Liza was also the sister of Prof. Sreten Marič who had given Erich a bad name with Kasanin, the director of the Belgrade museum. Liza had apparently visited Erich in Paris on at least two occasions.

Veljko Bulajič, who directed and coscripted *The Donator,* believed that Erich had a serious affair with a Spanish girl in Paris, possibly the one he became engaged to and for whose wedding Erich's parents came to Paris only to find it had been canceled. It was on the basis of this information that Bulajič, as we saw, created a Spanish girlfriend for Erich in his film. After hearing rumors that Erich may have helped Yugoslav volunteers to Spain where they passed through Paris, he made her a sympathizer with the Loyalist cause in Spain's civil war.

According to the Communist Party Museum in Belgrade, where I was the only visitor on a cold Sunday morning, 1,700 Yugoslav volunteers fought in that war of whom three hundred were killed. Most of them passed through Vienna, Geneva (where Tito coordinated their movement), and Paris. The period was 1938-1939, when Erich was most active in Parisian art circles. Considering Erich's apolitical nature, it is unlikely that he was directly involved, except perhaps to help individual Yugoslav volunteers whom he may have met by chance.

The one interview in Belgrade which I approached with the greatest trepidation was with Milan Antonič, the public defender who had been the cog without which the communist wheel of injustice could not have turned during the Herzlers' fifteen-year battle in Yugoslavia; he, more than anyone else, had provided the means to disinherit the Israeli heirs.

I was afraid that if I told him that I was a journalist from Israel he would refuse ipso facto to see me. But not wanting to approach him on false pretenses, I told him the truth and he surprised me with a cordial "Come on over."

Antonič lived in the new section of Belgrade, across the Sava River, on Leninova Street which was an extension of the bridge that touched on the Sajmište fairgrounds where Erich was murdered. In crossing the bridge, the irony of the situation did not escape me: I was passing by the death camp which took Erich's life to see the man who took his fortune.

Antonič lived in one of those ubiquitous high-rise apartment buildings that dotted the communist landscape not only in Yugoslavia but in all of Eastern

Europe. The apartments were small by western standards but more than adequate by local criteria.

A tall, solidly built, gruff man, Antonič greeted me at the door with a barely concealed bravado. We had spoken over the phone in a mutually broken German, and he had invited his son-in-law, who spoke fluent English, to act as interpreter.

I had come well equipped with foreknowledge of the court case, gleaned from Dr. Rozenberger's documents. This included a copy of the letter which Dr. Ivan Ribar had written to Rozenberger before the beginning of the legal process in Yugoslavia, confirming that he had promised Roza Šlomovič state-subsidized compensation for the collection. I had decided to "play dumb" in order to draw Antonič out and hear his version to the end before showing my hand.

He was eighty-one at the time, breathing a bit heavily and obviously slowed down, but conveying a forceful personality and a flash of fire from time to time. His recounting of the Herzlers' legal case followed quite closely the information in my possession.

The basic factor in winning his case, he stressed, was his application of the law on abandoned property, which was passed shortly after the war and allowed no more than one year to file a claim.

"If that's the case," I asked, "why did the courts agree to hear the case in the first place?"

"That was the Zagreb court," he said with a disdainful tone and a flick of his hand. "In Croatia they did what they wanted. That's why we moved the case to Serbia, to Belgrade."

Antonič reviewed the various legal maneuvers by which he got the district court in Varvarin to apply the law on abandoned property. This enabled it to rule that since nobody had filed a claim for the collection within the one year allowed by that law, the collection reverted to the State and there was, in effect, no property to inherit.

"Besides," Antonič added, "Roza wanted to give the collection to the State and that's what happened."

"Against compensation," I added.

"Not so," said Antonič, raising his voice. "We brought a letter from Dr. Ribar in 1962 in which he tells of his meeting with Roza and says nothing of compensation."

I felt it was time to show my cards.

I took out my own Ribar letter, set it firmly on the round coffee table between us, and said: "But here's a letter from Ribar in which he says he promised compensation." I pointed to the passage in the letter and pushed it toward Antonič.

Taken by surprise, he gave it a passing glance, turned red from anger or embarrassment, stuttered a bit, and then discharged a flow of rhetoric toward the interpreter.

"What did he say?" I asked, trying to stop the outpouring before we lost its meaning.

"He says the letter has no legal force. It may have appeared in Rozenberger's petition, but it never appeared in court."

"*Warum* (Why)?" I persisted in German, trying to catch Antonič's eye.

"*Das is nur eine stick papier* (It's just a piece of paper)," he answered showing the letter back at me.

Reverting to English, I turned to Antonič's son-in-law.

"Ask him what was the reason for not accepting it as evidence."

"This was private correspondence between Ribar and the Israeli attorney," Antonič retorted. "It was not addressed to the court as a legal document, the way our letter was presented. Besides, it's a typed letter. Ours was in Ribar's handwriting."

"But it's signed by him in his own hand," I said, pointing to Ribar's signature and pushing the letter back toward Antonič.

He repeated his previous statement in a slightly different version and added: "Besides, when someone gives a gift he doesn't ask for compensation. In any event, my letter from Ribar did not decide the case.[1] The case was decided on another point altogether."

---

1. Antonič had a point here since, as noted in Chapter IV, Rozenberger never submitted Ribar's letter to the court because under the normal rules of evidence, Ribar would have had to appear in court for cross-examination on the letter's contents and neither side invited Ribar to testify. But the underhanded maneuver of the prosecution remains, namely, to try and deny the existence of a promise for compensation and, when that didn't work, to try another tack.

"What was that?"

"The law on abandoned property."

"But don't you think that this law was most unfair and unjust? Considering the confusion after the war, wasn't it virtually impossible to file a legally documented claim within one year after the end of hostilities?"

Antonič didn't answer right away, so I repeated the question in German.

"Yes," he said, as if the word had been pulled out of him like a sick tooth, "it was a cruel and unjust law."

"So?"

"But it was the law and it was my job to uphold the law. Besides... what the hell... around the same time the government passed another law abolishing private property. So what difference did it make?"

That stopped me cold. I recalled the explanation of Irina Subotič, curator at the Belgrade museum, that during most of the years of the communist regime the museum didn't identify the collection because it had belonged to Erich Šlomovič, a private individual.

"Now tell me, Mr. Antonič," I said, looking him in the eye, "when you look back now after more than twenty years, don't you think that in all fairness and justice the Herzlers should have gotten compensation, as the chief of Tito's Bureau declared in his memo to the Belgrade municipality."

"Well, I was asked to reply to that letter. I prepared a brief which told exactly what had transpired in the case. I gave no opinion... just the facts. It covered thirty pages. And you know the result. That ended the case."

"I'm not asking you from the legal standpoint. As Dickens said, 'the law is an ass.' I'm asking you from the standpoint of equity and justice. After all, the family didn't ask for the paintings. They're a national treasure, even though Erich never intended to give them as a gift to the State. But here the State benefited from a Nazi crime. Don't you think that under such circumstances Erich would have wanted the family to get some benefit from his collection?"

By this time Antonič was squirming.

"Well, if fairness and justice are the issue, then the wish of Erich's mother was fulfilled — to give the collection to the 'Yugoslav people.'"

"Only against compensation," I repeated. "But you didn't answer my question, Mr. Antonič."

"What? To give compensation to the family after all? Impossible. All the legal remedies were closed. It would really be up to the president of Yugoslavia to decide."

I looked at Antonič again. To get a direct answer from him, without going through the interpreter, I pointed my finger at him and asked in German: "Mr. Antonič, if *you* were the president what would *you* decide? Would *you* give compensation?"

This time it was not just a tooth that was coming out. It seemed as if he had just swallowed something indigestible and was trying to regurgitate it. He took a deep breath, let out a sigh and, without looking at me directly, uttered one work.

"Yaaah."

Justice, finally, had been said; but it was not done.